The
Love Letters
of
Great Men

Let me not to the marriage of true minds
Admit impediments. Love is not love
Which alters when it alteration finds,
Or bends with the remover to remove:
O no! it is an ever-fixéd mark
That looks on tempests and is never shaken;
It is the star to every wandering bark,
Whose worth's unknown, although his height be taken.
Love's not Time's fool, though rosy lips and cheeks
Within his bending sickle's compass come;
Love alters not with his brief hours and weeks,
But bears it out even to the edge of doom.
If this be error and upon me proved,
I never writ, nor no man ever loved.

William Shakespeare

www.englishrosebooks.co.uk

This English Rose edition first published 18 March, 2011

Cover design by English Rose Publishing®

ISBN: 9781907960055

Letters are among the most significant memorial a person can leave behind them.

Johann Wolfgang von Goethe

Ever has it been that love knows not its own depth until the hour of separation.

Kahlil Gibran

In a man's letters... his soul lies naked, his letters are only the mirror of his breast, whatever passes within him is shown undisguised in its natural process.

Samuel Johnson

Letter writing is the only device for combining solitude with good company.

George Gordon, Lord Byron

The way to love anything is to realise that it may be lost.

G. K. Chesterton

If you love somebody, let them go, for if they return, they were always yours, and if they don't, they never were.

Attributed to Kahlil Gibran

Contents

Introduction

Love expresses itself in many ways. In this collection there are all sorts of letters, containing diverse expressions of love. There are letters of devotion and dedication, letters of loyalty and faithfulness, letters promising continued commitment no matter the distance or conflict, letters of hope in the face of adversity, letters of wooing, flattery and adulation, letters of passion, romance, lust and sauciness, letters of desperation, fear, jealousy, frustration, pining and anticipation, letters of affection, concern and consideration, and letters of sorrow, disappointment, broken-heartedness and loneliness. There are letters from men to their wives, mistresses, lovers, fiancés, objects of affection, crushes, lost loves and first loves. Whatever the tone, the context or style of the writing here displayed, what is true is that these letters are genuinely captivating.

In the past, writing a letter was one of the few ways for a couple to remain in contact when apart. Whether the separation was forced upon them, or chosen, whether brief or long, during courtship or due to obligations, from this division often came an outpouring of emotion. Some authors found that the distance intensified their feelings, leading an intended correspondence to become a letter expressing intense longing and desire. Sometimes writing a letter was preferable to face-to-face contact, because it could be written in private, as the thoughts came to the author's mind. The act of writing allowed feelings to be more easily expressed than if the writer were in his beloved's presence. The increasing rarity and consequent charm of personal mail in modern times perhaps serves to emphasise the emotional importance of the message.

For many of the couples included in this collection, entire volumes have been published about their relationship, and some have love letters running into the hundreds. For some, letters are scant, perhaps even solitary. Today, we have only what history has preserved for us. Some of the love letters of great men have never been published or made public, held in private and only privy to a select few. Some have never been translated from their original language. Some love letters were burned, destroyed, discarded of, and some have merely been lost. After the end of a relationship, returning love letters to the sender or burning them could symbolise the pain and dejection felt. Love letters were also often returned as a matter of honour: they could be compromising or embarrassing later in life. A youthful, perhaps ill-conceived or fanciful romance, might not be what anyone would want to be remembered by. Those immature words, when passion is at its highest, when love is raw and heartfelt, are not the kind of words a man wants everyone to see. Some of the letters of great men have been personally edited: many a section has been scrubbed out, the paper torn or burnt, the offending section removed... Many family members felt it their duty to preserve the honour of a dead relation by burning correspondence which might bring their name into ill-repute. Many of the authors show that they were aware of the risks inherent in parting with personal sentiments. Fear of an affair being uncovered, fear of revealing personal feelings, fear of being seen as weak, or vulnerable, were opinions shared by John Adams, who reserved his emotional outpourings in letters to his wife for fear of showing "weakness and indiscretion".[1] George Washington was less cautious, and found his letters published in the daily news by the enemy (the British). Many knew that their letters would be of interest to the public, many requested that they not be published, but were ignored. Letters, and in turn our communication with others, is never truly private, especially for those in the public eye.

Love letters infectiously render past lives into our modern reality, immersing the reader in the author's home, habits, enjoyments and romances. They show us the human side of men who stand as giants in history, whose actions and legacies have helped to shape the world as we know it. There is a wide scope of authors in this book, ranging in era, nationality and language. There are letters in this book by men who were enemies, who fought against each other, who despised what the other stood for or believed: Oliver Cromwell and King Charles I; Lord Nelson and Napoleon Bonaparte; Robert E. Lee and Abraham Lincoln. We have the love letter of the father, and of their daughter's lover. We have the love letters of the ancestors of great men, and men whose object of affection was the same woman. Robert Schumann's wife wrote that her intentions in publishing the love letters from her husband were "that those who love and honour Schumann as an artist might also learn to know him as a man."[2] As Goethe said: "letters are among the most significant memorial a person can leave behind them." Our interest in reading these letters, is partly in their magnificent language, their eloquent expressions of love, their romantic effluence, but also, it is in their demonstrations of the universal human vulnerability in love. Our capacity for compassion for these men, men who are great for their achievements and accomplishments, leads us to acknowledge that even the very greatest of leaders and minds still want and need to be loved. Feelings of love and the desire to be loved, are universal, irrespective of class, wealth, nationality, age, religion, belief or politics: "only the times change, not men's hearts".[3]

However, the danger in infiltrating the guarded private life of a great man, is that we may discover something unpleasant. Our lascivious nosiness, the intrigue of what their private correspondence might reveal, results in "the ruthless tearing away of the veil which has concealed their happy love life."[4] Happy perhaps in the image which has been presented to the outside world, until that all-concealing veil is pulled away. These letters may alter your feelings towards the men writing them. They may enlighten you on the reality of their lives—on their secret lives—which to the majority of historians, are a mere trifle in the context of their grand actions. They may soften a harsh critic (or not), make you reconsider the facts as you had been taught them (or not), they may leave you with less respect for a man you previously held in high regard, or heighten your respect for him. Reading the

---

[1] John Adams. 20 February, 1779.
[2] Clara Schumann's preface to *Early Letters of Robert Schumann* (1888).
[3] Robert Schumann. 2 January, 1838.
[4] Introduction to *Love Letters of Nathaniel Hawthorne* (1907).

early love letters of Charles Dickens to his first love, who cruelly rejected him, presents us with:

> "important identifications of characters and personal traits of the author which were unknown to his most intimate friends, and new even to the members of his own family... The letters of which it consists—which were written in the strictest confidence and intended for no eyes but those of the one to whom they were addressed—are earnest, sincere, and direct from the heart. They disclose certain life experiences of the author never before imparted to the world; in his own words, "things that I have locked up in my own breast, and that I never thought to bring out any more.""[5]

In their moment of separation, some of these great men show a different nature when alone, without the crowd, without the nobility or the just cause. Naked, stripped bare, they show their vulnerability. In many cases, love has altered the author, from an individual on a solitary mission, to a lovelorn romantic, putting pen, ink or pencil to paper in desperation at being parted from their loved one. Hopelessly devoted, vulnerable, insecure, in need of confirmation, a great leader can be reduced to a pitiful mess upon separation. Here, in their most personal, exposed state, we see the person behind the celebrity. Reading the letters of Nathaniel Hawthorne, whose love for his fiancé, and later his wife, infuses every line, opens our eyes to the man behind the writing, the man whose works many know so well. The introduction to the collected edition of his letters offers this pleasing insight:

> "That anyone can read these letters without a warmer, closer feeling for the "shy, grave Hawthorne" seems impossible... there comes almost a conviction that he wrote them not merely for the woman waiting for the day when pledges should be sanctified, but with the half-wish that all sympathetic spirits might see him and know him as he was. For gaily he speaks of his own bashfulness and reserve; hopefully he passes beyond the drudgery and disappointments of his position in life to the future which allures him; bravely he fights anxiety and care; with quaint humor and lightness of touch he pictures the scenes around that amuse and interest him... a strong affection is breathed in gentleness, a manly tenderness delights in every line.
> And whether toiling with the measurer in the vessel's hold, or chafing with him in the somberness of the custom house, sharing now his relief from distasteful tasks and now his dreams for a happier day, the reader feels the spirit of the past. And above all the shadowy ghostliness of the threescore years seems to come the perfume of the apple blossoms that fell around the Wayside, with the gentle graciousness of a time well known to all, when youth and love and hope are young."[6]

Great men have the ability to incite loyalty, passion and dedication. Thousands followed Napoleon into battle—and also Nelson, Washington and Lincoln.

---

[5] Introduction to *Charles Dickens and Maria Beadnell: Private Correspondence* (1908).
[6] Introduction to *Love Letters of Nathaniel Hawthorne* (1907).

Thousands salivated for the next story by Dickens or Lawrence, for the next play by Schiller, the next composition by Wagner. So, too, their love lives were often filled with extremes of loyalty, passion and dedication. Women threw themselves at these men, fawned over them, adored them, dedicated themselves to them, and even when they were spurned, continued to love them. Love does not always conquer all. Being great denotes superiority, power, strength, knowledge, and with these come responsibility and accountability. Many great men have fallen from grace due to public indiscretions. They are not beyond reproach, and with status, influence and fame their lives become all the more transparent. In the words of Shakespeare, "the truth will out, in the end". There are many indiscretions in these letters, many broken hearts, jilted lovers and abandoned children. Many times an author is writing without the knowledge of their suitor's father or husband, or of their own wives. There is secrecy, deception, promises of a clandestine meeting or a chance encounter. For some, their letters enlighten the reader as to the paramour's 'tricks' or 'lines' for seduction. Poets especially, do not come off well in such a review. However there are also many devoted partners, husbands, fathers, fiancés and lovers. There are many letters of whole-hearted fidelity and constant affection, especially in the face of adversity. Every letter, in fact, is quite different:

> "Passion, tenderness, sweetness, reverence, all the deep tones of love, make beautiful the letters written by various great men... Men of genius and power—kings, commanders, poets, painters—belong not to themselves, but to the world. Greatness destroys privacy; and many a person of note has lived to see described in print the most minute of his little, unsuspected peculiarities. This invasion of the right to be left alone is inevitable."[7]

Throughout history, great men have written noble tomes. Their love letters are no exception. We can find in these correspondences some of the most delectable personal effusions ever written, the most incredible demonstrations of love and affection—not fictional, but real, impassioned, painful and heart-wrenching. With these letters we have the unique ability to spy on the personal lives of men considered 'great', a part of their lives which the authors had no knowledge that we would see, and perhaps which we have no right to. They show us men and women we know from history, in a very different light, perhaps from a new perspective. They come to life through their personal letters, more so than anywhere else. Their humanity, so lacking in the history books, is *all* we are privy to here. There is no great action, no battle won, no literary accomplishment, only deep personal feeling and romantic expression.

---

[7] Introduction to an article entitled "Love Letters of the Great" from *The Scrap Book*, Volume 1, No. 2, April 1906, from which several of the letters in this collection are drawn.

John Adams

John Adams (30 October, 1735–4 July, 1826) was an American statesman, diplomat and political theorist. He came to prominence in the early stages of the American Revolution as a delegate from Massachusetts to the Continental Congress. He played a leading role in persuading Congress to declare American independence, and assisted Thomas Jefferson in drafting the United States Declaration of Independence in 1776. In the first presidential election in 1789, George Washington was elected for the first of his two terms as President, and John Adams became the first Vice President. He served from 21 April, 1789–4 March, 1797 when he was elected the second President of the United States, which he served until 4 March, 1801. Adams was one of the most influential Founding Fathers of the United States.

On 25 October, 1764, Adams married Abigail Smith (11 November, 1744–28 October, 1818), the daughter of Congregational minister Rev. William Smith. As third cousins, Abigail and John had known each other since they were children. In 1762, John accompanied his friend Richard Cranch to the Smith household. Cranch was engaged to Abigail's older sister Mary. John was quickly attracted to Abigail, a petite, shy, 18-year-old brunette. He was surprised to learn that she knew so much about poetry, philosophy and politics, considered unusual for a woman at the time. Although her father approved of the match, her mother did not. At the time, Adams was but a small-town lawyer. Eventually her mother gave in and the couple married in the Smith family home at Weymouth, Massachusetts. Abigail wore a square-necked gown of white challis, John wore a dark blue coat, contrasting light breeches and white stockings, a gold-embroidered satin waistcoat his mother had made for the occasion, and buckle shoes. Rev. Smith performed the nuptials. After the reception, the couple mounted a single horse and rode off to their new home, the small cottage and farm that John had inherited from his father in Braintree, Massachusetts.

Abigail and John's marriage is well documented through their correspondence and other writings. Letters exchanged throughout John's political obligations indicate that his trust in Abigail's knowledge was sincere. He frequently sought the advice of Abigail on many matters, and their letters are filled with intellectual discussions on government and politics. They weathered many long separations as John fought for the independence of America and their correspondence conveys their mutual emotional and intellectual respect. They had six children: Abigail "Nabby"/"Abby" (14 July, 1765–15 August, 1813), future President John Quincy (11 July, 1767–23 February, 1848), Susanna "Suky" (28 December, 1768–4 February, 1770), Charles (29 May, 1770–30 November, 1800), Thomas Boylston (15 September, 1772–13 March, 1832) and Elizabeth (stillborn 11 July, 1777).

Princeton, New Jersey, 28 August, 1774.

I received your kind letter at New York, and it is not easy for you to imagine the pleasure it has given me. I have not found a single opportunity to write since I left Boston, excepting by the post, and I don't choose to write by that conveyance, for fear of foul play. But as we are now within forty-two miles of Philadelphia, I hope there to find some private hand by which I can convey this...

I am anxious for our perplexed, distressed province, I hope they will be directed into the right path. Let me entreat you, my dear, to make yourself as easy and quiet as possible. Resignation to the will of Heaven is our only resource in such dangerous times. Prudence and caution should be our guides. I have the strongest hopes that we shall yet see a clearer sky and better times.

Remember my tender love to little Abby, tell her she must write me a letter and inclose it in the next you send. I am charmed with your amusement with our little Johnny. Tell him I am glad to hear he is so good a boy as to read to his mamma for her entertainment, and to keep himself out of the company of rude children. Tell him I hope to hear a good account of his accidence and nomenclature[8] when I return. Remember me to all inquiring friends, particularly to uncle Quincy, your papa and family, and Dr. Tufts and family. Mr. Thaxter, I hope, is a good companion, in your solitude. Tell him, if he devotes his soul and body to his books, I hope, notwithstanding the darkness of these days, he will not find them unprofitable sacrifices in future. I have received three very obliging letters from Tudor, Trumbull and Hill. They have cheered us in our wanderings and done us much service.

Your account of the rain refreshed me. I hope our husbandry is prudently and industriously man aged. Frugality must be our support. Our expenses in this journey will be very great. Our only recompense will be the consolatory reflection that we toil, spend our time and encounter dangers for the public good, happy indeed if we do any good.

The education of our children is never out of my mind. Train them to virtue. Habituate them to industry, activity and spirit. Make them consider every vice as shameful and unmanly. Fire them with ambition to be useful. Make them disdain to be destitute of any useful or ornamental knowledge or accomplishment. Fix their ambition upon great and solid objects, and their contempt upon little, frivolous and useless ones. It is time, my dear, for you to begin to teach them French. Every decency, grace and honesty should be inculcated upon them.

I have kept a few minutes by way of journal, which shall be your entertainment when I come home; but we have had so many persons and so various characters to converse with, and so many objects to view, that I have not been able to be so particular as I could wish. I am, with the tenderest affection and concern, Your wandering

John Adams

---

[8] accidence: the aspect of grammar that deals with inflections and word order.
nomenclature: the system of principles, procedures and terms related to naming.

Philadelphia, 3 December, 1775.

   My best friend,
   Yours of November 12th is before me. I wish I could write you every day, more than once, for although I have a number of friends and many relations, who are very dear to me, yet all the friendship I have for others is far unequal to that which warms my heart for you. The most agreeable time that I spend here is in writing to you, and conversing with you, when I am alone. But the call of friendship and of private affection must give place to that of duty and honor. Even private friendship and affections require it.
   John Adams

Dedham, 9 January, 1777.

   My Dear,
   The irresistible hospitality of Dr. Sprague and his lady has prevailed upon me and my worthy fellow traveller to put up at his happy seat. We had an agreeable ride to this place, and to-morrow morning, we set off for Providence, or some other route.
   Present my affection in the tenderest manner to my little deserving daughter and my amiable sons. It was cruel parting this morning. My heart was most deeply affected although I had the presence of mind to appear composed. May God Almighty's providence protect you, my dear, and all our little ones. My good genius, my guardian angel, whispers me, that we shall see happier days, and that I shall live to enjoy the felicities of domestic life with her, whom my heart esteems above all earthly blessings.
   John Adams

Passy, 18 December, 1778.

   This moment I had, what shall I say? the pleasure or the pain of your letter of 25th October. As a letter from my dearest friend it gave me a pleasure that it would be in vain to attempt to describe; but the complaints in it gave me more pain than I can express. This is the third letter I have received in this complaining style. The former two I have not answered. I had endeavored to answer them. I have written several answers; but upon a review, they appeared to be such as I could not send. One was angry, another was full of grief, and the third with melancholy, so that I burnt them all. If you write me in this style, I shall leave off writing entirely. It kills me. Can profession of esteem be wanting from me to you? Can protestation of affection be necessary? Can tokens of remembrance be desired? The very idea of this sickens me. Am I not wretched enough in this banishment without this? What course shall I take, to convince you that my heart is warm? You doubt, it seems. Shall I declare it? Shall I swear to it? Would you doubt it the less? and is it possible you should doubt it? I know it is not. If I could once believe it possible, I should not answer for the consequences. But I beg you would never more write to me in such a strain, for it really makes me unhappy. Be assured, that no time nor place can change my heart; but that I think so often and so much of the blessings from which I am separated, as to be too unmindful of those who accompany me; and that I write to you as often as my duty will permit.

I am extremely obliged to the Comte d'Estaing and his officers for their politeness to you, and am very glad you have had an opportunity of seeing so much of the French nation. The accounts from all hands agree, that there was an agreeable intercourse and happy harmony, upon the whole, between the inhabitants and the fleets. The more this nation is known, and the more their language is understood, the more will narrow prejudices wear away. British fleets and armies are very different from theirs. In point of temperance and politeness, there is no comparison.

This is not a correct copy, but you will pardon it, because it is done by a hand as dear to you as to your
John Adams

Passy, 19 February, 1779.

My dearest Friend
I have written three answers to yours of January 4. This is the fourth. The three first I have burned. In one I was melancholy, in another angry, and in the third merry—but either would have given you more pain than pleasure. I have gone through with several others of your letters in the same manner. They are admirably written, but there is such a strain of unhappiness and complaint in them, as has made me very uneasy.—This last goes farther than any other, and contains an expression which alarms me indeed, and convinces me, either that some infernal has whispered in your ear insinuations, or that you have forgotten the unalterable tenderness of my heart.

This letter is an additional motive with me to come home. It is time.—I have written as often as I could. I want to write you every day but I cannot—I have too much to say: but have good reasons for saying nothing. Is it necessary that I should make protestations that I am, with an heart as pure as gold or ether[9], Forever yours.
John Adams

Passy, 20 February, 1779.

In the margin are the dates of all the letters I have received from you. I have written you several times that number. They are almost all lost, I suppose by yours. But you should consider, it is a different thing to have five hundred correspondents and but one. It is a different thing to be under an absolute

---

[9] ether: in myth and legend, the upper regions of the atmosphere; clear sky or heaven.

restraint and under none. It would be an easy thing for me to ruin you and your children by an indiscreet letter, and what is more, it would be easy to throw our country into convulsions. For God's sake never reproach me again with not writing or with writing scrips[10]. Your wounds are too deep. You know not, you feel not the dangers that surround me, nor those that may be brought upon our country. Millions would not tempt me to write you as I used. I have no security that every letter I write you will not be broken open, and copied, and transmitted to Congress and to English newspapers. They would find no treason nor deceit in them, it is true, but they would find weakness and indiscretion, which they would make as ill a use of.

There are spies upon every word I utter, and every syllable I write. Spies planted by the English, spies planted by stockjobbers[11], spies planted by selfish merchants, and spies planted by envious and malicious politicians. I have been all along aware of this, more or less, but more so now than ever. My life has been often in danger, but I never considered my reputation and character so much in danger as now. I can pass for a fool, but I will not pass for a dishonest or a mercenary man. Be upon your guard, therefore. I must be upon mine, and I will.

John Adams

---

[10] scrips: scraps of paper.
[11] stockjobbers: stockbrokers, especially unscrupulous ones (Chiefly British).

Prince Albert

Prince Albert of Saxe-Coburg and Gotha (Francis Albert Augustus Charles Emmanuel, 26 August, 1819–14 December, 1861) was born in the Saxon duchy of Saxe-Coburg-Saalfeld to a family connected to many of Europe's ruling monarchs. At the age of 20 he married his first cousin, Queen Victoria of the United Kingdom of Great Britain and Ireland (Alexandrina Victoria, 24 May, 1819–22 January, 1901). Their uncle, Leopold, King of the Belgians, suggested the match and arranged a meeting in May, 1836. Victoria, who was the heir to the British throne, was well-aware of the various matrimonial plans and critically appraised a parade of eligible princes. She wrote of Albert: he "is extremely handsome; his hair is about the same colour as mine; his eyes are large and blue, and he has a beautiful nose and a very sweet mouth with fine teeth; but the charm of his countenance is his expression, which is most delightful." Although the parties did not undertake a formal engagement, it was widely assumed that the match would take place, though she resisted attempts to be rushed. Victoria came to the throne aged just eighteen on 20 June, 1837, upon the death of her uncle, William IV. Her letters of the time show interest in Albert's education for the role he would have to play. The Queen proposed to him on 15 October, 1839. The Prince wrote afterwards: "The Queen sent for me alone to her room a few days ago, and declared to me, in a genuine outburst of love and affection, that I had gained her whole heart, and would make her intensely happy if I would make her the sacrifice of sharing her life with her, for she said she looked on it as a sacrifice; the only thing that troubled her was, that she did not think she was worthy of me. The joyous openness of manner with which she told me this quite enchanted me, and I was quite carried away by it."

The couple married on 10 February, 1840, at the Chapel Royal, St. James's Palace. At first, Albert felt constrained by his position as consort, which did not confer any power or duties upon him. Over time he adopted many public causes, and took on the responsibilities of running the household, estates and offices. He was heavily involved with the organisation of the Great Exhibition of 1851.

Victoria and Albert had nine children: Victoria (21 November, 1840–5 August, 1901), Albert Edward (9 November, 1841–6 May, 1910), Alice (25 April, 1843–14 December, 1878), Alfred (6 August, 1844–31 July, 1900), Helena (25 May, 1846–9 June, 1923), Louise (18 March, 1848–3 December, 1939), Arthur (1 May, 1850–16 January, 1942), Leopold (7 April, 1853–28 March, 1884) and Beatrice (14 April, 1857–26 October, 1944). All 9 children and 26 of their 42 grandchildren married into royal and noble families across the continent, tying them together and earning Victoria the nickname "the grandmother of Europe." Prince Albert died at the early age of 42, plunging the Queen into a deep mourning which lasted for the rest of her life.

Many of their letters to each other survive. They further reinforce the view that theirs was a loving, devoted marriage. The first letter here presented was written by Albert after their engagement, but before their marriage. The second is from early 1844, when Victoria and Albert were apart for the first time since their marriage, when he returned to Coburg on the death of his father. The Queen found the separation from him hard, and he tried assiduously to encourage her good spirits. The third letter, is from 1849, and another separation, when the Prince travelled to Brocklesby and laid the foundation-stone for the Great Grimsby Docks.

Wiesbaden, 21 November, 1839.

... That I am the object of so much love and devotion often comes over me as something I can hardly realise. My prevailing feeling is—What am I that such happiness should be mine? For excess of happiness it is to me to know that I am so dear to you.

Coburg, 30 November, 1839.

You receive these lines from dear old Coburg, where I have been received with all possible cordiality. All are on the tiptoe of curiosity, anxious to know, and yet not daring to ask, and I am cruel enough to say nothing. This state of uncertainty, however, will not continue long. The next newspaper will probably bring the news of your declaration to the Privy Council, and then there will be a general outburst of joy among the people here. My poor dear grandmama is greatly touched by your letter. She is sadly depressed at the thought of parting from me. She says that since my mother's death she has not wept so much as in these last days; still she hopes, what I am convinced will be the case, that I may find in you, my dear Victoria, all the happiness I could possibly desire. And so I shall, I can truly tell her for her comfort. Hitherto I have been teased and taken up with all sorts of preparations for leaving. But when Stockmar, who is to be here about three, arrives, I shall at once set to work to make a thorough study of the Blackstone, you have so kindly sent me.

Coburg, 7 December, 1839.

So the secret is out, the affair made public, and to all appearance generally received with great satisfaction. This is a good omen for us. Here it has been no easy matter for some days back to keep the secret, and it is well we need do so no longer. That people entertain everywhere so good an opinion of me is not pleasant, for it fills me with uneasiness and apprehension, that when I make my appearance they will be bitterly undeceived not to find me what they expected.

How often are my thoughts with you! The hours I was privileged to pass with you in your dear little room are the radiant points of my life, and I cannot even yet clearly picture to myself that I am to be indeed so happy as to be always near you, always your protector.

28 March, 1844.

My Own Darling
We got over our journey thus far rapidly and well, but the tide was so unmannerly as to be an hour later than the time calculated, so that I cannot sail before three. I have been an hour here, and regret the lost time which I might have spent with you. Poor child! you will, while I write, be getting ready for luncheon, and will find the place vacant where I sat yesterday. In your heart, however, I hope my place will not be vacant.

I at least have you on board with me in spirit. I reiterate my entreaty, 'Bear up!' and don't give way to low spirits, but try to occupy yourself as much as possible. You are even now half a day nearer to seeing me again; by the time you get this letter it will be a whole day; thirteen more and I am again within your arms...

To-morrow Seymour will bring you further news of me.
Your most devoted
Albert.

March, 1849.

Your faithful husband, agreeably to your wishes, reports:
1. That he is still alive.
2. That he has discovered the North Pole from Lincoln Cathedral, but without finding either Captain Ross or Sir John Franklin.
3. That he arrived at Brocklesby and received the address.
4. That he subsequently rode out and got home quite covered with snow and with icicles on his nose.
5. That the messenger is waiting to carry off this letter, which you will have in Windsor by the morning.
6. Last, but not least, that he loves his wife and remains her devoted husband.

Walter Bagehot

Walter Bagehot (3 February, 1826–24 March, 1877) was an English businessman, essayist, and journalist who wrote extensively about literature, government, and economic affairs. He wrote for various periodicals, and in 1855 founded the *National Review* with his friend Richard Holt Hutton. He become editor-in-chief of *The Economist* in 1860, where he remained for seventeen years, until his death. Under his leadership *The Economist* became one of world's leading business and political journals. In 1867, he wrote *The English Constitution*, a book which explores the nature of the constitution of the United Kingdom, specifically the functioning of Parliament and the British monarchy and the contrasts between British and American government. Bagehot also wrote *Physics and Politics* (1872), and *Lombard Street* (1873), which explains the world of finance and banking and focuses particularly on issues in the management of financial crises. Bagehot's observations on finance remain relevant today and are often cited by central bankers, especially in the wake of a financial crisis. Bagehot was once acknowledged as "The Greatest Victorian." Though he was certainly one of 19th-century Britain's most famous intellectuals, his fame has since been somewhat overshadowed by his many more famous contemporaries.

In 1857, Bagehot made the acquaintance of James Wilson, the founder of *The Economist*. Introduced to him as a "young banker in the West of England," Bagehot wanted to write for *The Economist,* and travelled on 24 January, 1857, to Claverton Manor, Wilson's home in Bath to discuss banking and political economy. Of Wilson's six daughters, it was his eldest Elizabeth "Eliza" (16 December, 1832–1921) who caught Bagehot's attention and who he fell in love with. He pursued her during 1857, becoming friendly with the whole family, and a first brother to the other 5 sisters. The proposal took place on 5 November, but the answer was not given until three days later. They married on 21 April, 1858. Though they produced no children, they lived happily until his death.

22 November, 1857.

> *My dearest Eliza,*
> *I fear you will think the answer I wrote yesterday to your most kind and delicious letter, was very superficial, but I wrote it at once while people were talking and bothering me. I have now read yours over and over more times than I should like to admit. I awoke in the middle of the night and immediately lit a candle to read it a few times again. It has given me more pleasure than I ever received from a letter, and infinitely more than I thought it possible I could receive from one. I fancy that it is not now an effort for you to write to me—at*

least it reads as though it was written without effort. Yet it tells me things which with your deep and reserved nature it must have cost you much to put on paper. I wish indeed I could feel worthy of your affection—my reason, if not my imagination, is getting to believe you when you whisper to me that I have it, but as somebody says in Miss Austen, 'I do not at all mind having what is too good for me'; my delight is at times intense. You must not suppose because I tell you of the wild, burning pain which I have felt, and at times, though I am and ought to be much soothed, still feel, that my love for you has ever been mere suffering. Even at the worst there was a wild, delicious excitement which I would not have lost for the world. At first, and before the feeling was very great it was simple pleasure for me to come to Claverton, and the charm of our early intellectual talks was very great, although of late, and particularly since the day in the conservatory, the feeling has been too eager not to have a good deal of pain in it, and the tension of mind has really been very great at times, still the time that I have known and loved you is immensely the happiest I have ever known. My spirits always make me cheerful in a superficial way, but they do not satisfy, and somehow life even before I was engaged to you was sweeter and gentler, and the jars and jangles of action lost their influence, and literature had a new value since you liked my writing, and everything has had a gloss upon it. Though I have come to Claverton the last few times with the notion that the gloss would do—that I should burst out and you would be tranquil and kind and considerate and refuse and I should never see you again—I had a vision of the thing which I keep by me. As it has not happened I am afraid this is egotistical—indeed I know it is—but I am not sure that egotism is bad in letters, and if I write to you I must write about what I feel for you. It is odd how completely our feelings change. No one can tell the effort it was to me to tell you I loved you—why I do not know, but it made me gasp for breath, and now it is absolutely pleasure to me to tell it to you and bore you with it in every form, and I should like to write it in big letters I LOVE YOU all across the page by way of emphasis. I know you will think me very childish and be shaken in your early notion that I am intellectual, but I cannot help it. This is my state of mind...

By incredible researches in an old box I have found the poem I mentioned to you. I wish I had not, for I thought it was better. I have not seen it for several years and it is not so good as I fancied—perhaps not good at all—but I think you may care to read it and you can't read it unless I send it and therefore I do send it. The young lady's name is Orithyia. The Greek legend is that she was carried away by the north wind, but I am not aware that she ever declared her feelings explicitly in any document. By the way, you have. I have just read your letter in that light and I go about murmuring, 'I have made that dignified girl commit herself, I have, I have', and then I vault over the sofa with exultation. Those are the feelings of the person you have connected yourself with. Please don't be offended at my rubbish. Sauciness is my particular line. I am always rude to everybody I respect. I could write to you of the deep and serious feelings which I hope you believe really are in my heart, but my pen jests of itself and always will.

Yours with the fondest and deepest love,
Walter

17 January, 1858.

 I am writing to you on Sunday evening, which is the time I like to write to you best, because I feel the quietest and descend the most into my real self, where my love is strongest and deepest. So you know I always have a fancy at such times that our loves makes us somehow alone together in the world. We seem to have a deep life together apart from all other people on earth, and which we cannot show, explain or impart to them. At least my affection seems to isolate me in the deepest moments from all others, and it makes me speak with my whole heart and soul to you and you only. And perhaps this isolation is one reason why deep love makes one feel—at least in some moments—so religious.

Sullivan Ballou

Sullivan Ballou (28 March, 1829–28 July, 1861) was a lawyer, politician, and Major in the United States Army who served and died in the American Civil War. He practised law in Providence, Rhode Island, and was a member of the Rhode Island House of Representatives from 1853 until 1857. He ran unsuccessfully for state Attorney General in 1861. When war broke out in 1861, Ballou immediately left what appeared to be a promising political career and volunteered for military service. He served as Major in the Second Regiment of the Rhode Island Volunteer Infantry with the Union army. The regiment trained at Camp Clark in Washington, D.C. until mid-July, and was then sent into the field to meet the Confederate army.

Ballou and 93 of his men were mortally wounded in the first battle of Bull Run, also known as the first battle of Manassas. It was the first major land battle of the American Civil War and took place on 21 July, 1861, in Prince William County, Virginia, near the city of Manassas. In an attempt to better direct his men, Ballou took a horse-mounted position in front of his regiment, when a 6-pounder solid shot from Confederate artillery tore off his right leg and simultaneously killed his horse. The badly injured Major was then carried off the field and the remainder of his leg was amputated. Ballou died from his wound a week later and was buried in the nearby Sudley Church. After the battle, the territory was occupied by Confederate forces. According to witness testimony, Ballou's corpse was exhumed, decapitated, and desecrated by Confederate soldiers. His remains were later recovered and reburied in Swan Point Cemetery, Providence, Rhode Island.

Ballou married Sarah Hart Shumway (1836–19 April, 1917) of Poughkeepsie, New York, on 15 October, 1855. They settled in Cumberland, Rhode Island, in what was then the village of Woonsocket. They had two children, Edgar F. (1856–1924) and William B. (1859–1948). After Ballou's death Sarah lived out her life with their sons. She never remarried. She died in 1917 and is buried next to her husband. The gravestone is inscribed: "Come to me, and lead thither my children."

Sullivan Ballou is often best remembered today for the eloquent letter which he wrote to his wife shortly before he fought and was mortally wounded. In the letter, Ballou attempted to crystallise the emotions he was feeling: worry, fear, guilt, sadness and, most importantly, the pull between his love for her and his sense of duty. The letter was never mailed; it was found in Ballou's trunk after he died. It was reclaimed and delivered to Ballou's widow by Governor William Sprague.

Camp Clark, Washington
14th July, 1861.

My very dear Sarah,

The indications are very strong that we shall move in a few days—perhaps tomorrow. Lest I should not be able to write you again, I feel impelled to write lines that may fall under your eye when I shall be no more. Our movement may be one of a few days duration and full of pleasure — and it may be one of severe conflict and death to me. Not my will, but thine O God, be done. If it is necessary that I should fall on the battlefield for my Country, I am ready. I have no misgivings about, or lack of confidence in, the cause in which I am engaged, and my courage does not halt or falter. I know how strongly American Civilization now leans upon the triumph of the Government, and how great a debt we owe to those who went before us through the blood and suffering of the Revolution. And I am willing—perfectly willing—to lay down all my joys in this life, to help maintain this Government, and to pay that debt.

But, my dear wife, when I know that with my own joys I lay down nearly all of yours, and replace them in this life with cares and sorrows—when, after having eaten for long years the bitter fruit of orphanage myself, I must offer it as their only sustenance to my dear little children—is it weak or dishonorable, while the banner of my purpose floats calmly and proudly in the breeze, that my unbounded love for you, my darling wife and children, should struggle in fierce, though useless, contest with my love of Country?

I cannot describe to you my feelings on this calm summer night, when two thousand men are sleeping around me, many of them enjoying the last, perhaps, before that of death—and I, suspicious that Death is creeping behind me with his fatal dart, am communing with God, my Country, and thee.

I have sought most closely and diligently, and often in my heart, for a wrong motive in thus hazarding the happiness of those I loved and I could not find one. A pure love of my Country and of the principles I have often advocated before the people—"the name of honor, that I love more than I fear death" have called upon me, and I have obeyed.

Sarah, my love for you is deathless, it seems to bind me to you with mighty cables that nothing but Omnipotence could break; and yet my love of Country comes over me like a strong wind and bears me irresistibly on with all these chains to the battlefield.

The memories of the blissful moments I have spent with you come creeping over me, and I feel most gratified to God and to you that I have enjoyed them so long. And hard it is for me to give them up and burn to ashes the hopes of future years, when God willing, we might still have lived and loved together and seen our sons grow up to honorable manhood around us. I have, I know, but few and small claims upon Divine Providence, but something whispers to me—perhaps it is the wafted prayer of my little Edgar—that I shall return to my loved ones unharmed. If I do not, my dear Sarah, never forget how much I love you, and when my last breath escapes me on the battlefield, it will whisper your name.

Forgive my many faults, and the many pains I have caused you. How thoughtless and foolish I have oftentimes been! How gladly would I wash out with my tears every little spot upon your happiness, and struggle with all the misfortune of this world, to shield you and my children from harm. But I cannot. I must watch you from the spirit land and hover near you, while you buffet the storms with your precious little freight, and wait with sad patience till we meet to part no more.

But, O Sarah! If the dead can come back to this earth and flit unseen around those they loved, I shall always be near you; in the garish day and in the darkest night—amidst your happiest scenes and gloomiest hours—always, always; and if there be a soft breeze upon your cheek, it shall be my breath; or the cool air fans your throbbing temple, it shall be my spirit passing by.

Sarah, do not mourn me dead; think I am gone and wait for thee, for we shall meet again.

As for my little boys, they will grow as I have done, and never know a father's love and care. Little Willie is too young to remember me long, and my blue-eyed Edgar will keep my frolics with him among the dimmest memories of his childhood. Sarah, I have unlimited confidence in your maternal care and your development of their characters. Tell my two mothers his and hers I call God's blessing upon them. O Sarah, I wait for you there! Come to me, and lead thither my children.

Sullivan

Honoré de Balzac

Honoré de Balzac (20 May, 1799–18 August, 1850) was a famous French novelist and playwright. His magnum opus was a sequence of short stories and novels collectively entitled *La Comédie Humaine* (*The Human Comedy*), which presents a panorama of French life in the years after the fall of Napoleon I in 1815. It also reflects his real-life difficulties, and includes scenes from his own experience. Due to his keen observation of detail and unfiltered representation of society, Balzac is regarded as one of the founders of realism in European literature. He is renowned for his multi-faceted characters, which are complex, morally ambiguous and fully human. His writing influenced many famous authors, novelists and important philosophers. Many of Balzac's works have been made into or inspired films, and they are a continuing source of inspiration for writers, filmmakers, and critics alike.

In February 1832, Balzac received a letter from the city of Odessa, Ukraine—lacking a return address and signed only "L'Étrangère" ("The Foreigner")—expressing sadness at the cynicism and atheism in his work, *La Peau de Chagrin,* and its negative portrayal of women. He responded by purchasing a classified advertisement in the *Gazette de France*, hoping that his secret critic would find it. Thus began a fifteen-year correspondence between Balzac and the Countess Ewelina Hańska, *née* Rzewuska (6 January, 1801–10 April, 1882). Ewelina was wed to a man twenty years older than herself, Wacław Hański, a wealthy Polish landowner living in Kiev. It was a marriage of convenience to preserve her family's fortune. In Balzac, Ewelina found a kindred spirit for her emotional and social desires. Balzac, however, before he had seen her, was raised to a frenzy of excited adoration; the woman became his ideal. In a letter to a friend Balzac called Ewelina "the only woman I have ever loved." They wrote almost daily.

Their correspondence reveals an intriguing balance of passion, propriety and patience. When Ewelina's husband died in 1841, his widow and her admirer finally had the chance to pursue their affections. Balzac visited Ewelina in St. Petersburg in 1843 and impressed himself on her heart. They went on several voyages together (Germany, Belgium, Italy, Ukraine). In 1846 she had a stillborn child. After a series of economic setbacks, health problems, and prohibitions, the couple were finally able to wed. On 14 March, 1850, with Balzac's health in serious decline, they drove from her estate in Wierzchownia to a church in Berdyczów and were married. The ten-hour journey to and from the ceremony took a toll on both husband and wife: her feet were too swollen to walk, and he endured severe heart trouble. In late April the newly married couple set off for Paris, arriving on 20 May, his fifty-first birthday. Five months after his wedding, on 18 August, Balzac died.

6 October, 1833.

Our love will bloom always fairer, fresher, more gracious, because it is a true love, and because genuine love is ever increasing.

It is a beautiful plant growing from year to year in the heart, ever extending its palms and branches, doubling every season its glorious clusters and perfumes; and, my dear life, tell me, repeat to me always, that nothing will bruise its bark or its delicate leaves, that it will grow larger in both our hearts, loved, free, watched over, like a life within our life...

19 June, 1836.

My beloved angel,
I am nearly mad about you, as much as one can be mad: I cannot bring together two ideas that you do not interpose yourself between them. I can no longer think of anything but you. In spite of myself, my imagination carries me to you. I grasp you, I kiss you, I caress you, a thousand of the most amorous caresses take possession of me. As for my heart, there you will always be—very much so. I have a delicious sense of you there. But my God, what is to become of me, if you have deprived me of my reason? This is a monomania which, this morning, terrifies me. I rise up every moment saying to myself, "Come, I am going there!" Then I sit down again, moved by the sense of my obligations. There is a frightful conflict. This is not life. I have never before been like that. You have devoured everything. I feel foolish and happy as soon as I think of you. I whirl round in a delicious dream in which in one instant I live a thousand years. What a horrible situation! Overcome with love, feeling love in every pore, living only for love, and seeing oneself consumed by griefs, and caught in a thousand spiders' threads. O, my darling Eva, you did not know it. I picked up your card. It is there before me, and I talk to you as if you were there. I see you, as I did yesterday, beautiful, astonishingly beautiful. Yesterday, during the whole evening, I said to myself "she is mine!" Ah! The angels are not as happy in Paradise as I was yesterday!

c.1830s.

Oh! how I should have liked to remain half a day kneeling at your feet with my head on your lap, dreaming beautiful dreams, telling you my thoughts with languor, with rapture, sometimes not speaking at all, but pressing my lips to your gown!... O, my well-beloved Eva, the day of my days, the light of my nights, my hope, my adored one, my entirely beloved one, my only darling, when can I see you? Is it an illusion? Have I seen you? Ye gods! how I love your accent, just a shade thick, your mouth of kindness, of voluptuousness—allow me to say it of you, my angel of love. I am working night and day in order to go and see you for a fortnight in December. I shall pass over the Jura covered with snow; but I shall be thinking of the snowy shoulders of my love, my well-beloved. Ah! to breathe in your hair, to hold your hand, to clasp you in my arms—it is from these I get my courage! Some of my friends here are stupefied at the savage will-power I am displaying at this moment. Ah! they do not know my darling, she whose mere image robs grief of its stings. One kiss, my angel of the earth, one kiss tasted slowly, and then good-night!

21 October, 1843.

I leave tomorrow, my seat is reserved, and I am going to finish my letter, because I have to put it in the post myself; my head is like an empty pumpkin, and I am in a state which disquiets me more than I can say. If I am thus in Paris, I shall have to return. I have no feeling for anything, I have no desire to love, I have no longer got the slightest energy, I seem to have no will-power left... I have not smiled since I left you...

Adieu, dear star, a thousand times blessed! There will perhaps come a moment when I shall be able to express to you the thoughts which oppress me. Today I can only say that I love you too much for my repose, because after this August and September, I feel that I can only live near to you, and that your absence is death...

Adieu! I am going to take my letter to the post. A thousand tendernesses to your child a thousand times blessed; my friendly greetings to Lirette, and to you everything that is in my heart, my soul, and my brain... If you knew what emotion seizes me when I throw one of these packets in the box.

My soul flies towards you with these papers; I say to them like a crazy man, a thousand things; like a crazy man I think that they go towards you to repeat them to you; it is impossible for me to understand how these papers impregnates by me will be, in eleven days, in your hands, and why I remain here...

Oh yes, dear star, far and near, count on me like on yourself; neither I nor my devotion will fail you any more than life will fail your body. One can believe, dear fraternal soul, what one says of life at my age; well, believe me that there is no other life for me than yours. My task is done. If misfortune were to happen to you, I would go and bury myself in an obscure corner and ignored by everybody, without seeing anybody in the world; go, this is not an empty word. If happiness for a woman is to know herself unique in a heart, alone, filling it in an indispensable manner, sure to shine in the intelligence of a man as his light, sure to be his blood, to animate each heart-beat, to live in his thought as the substance itself of that thought, and having the certainty that it would be always and always so; well, dear sovereign of my soul, you can call yourself happy, and happy without hunger, for so I shall be for you till death. One can feel satiety for human things, there is none for divine things, and this word alone can explain what you are for me.

Ludwig van Beethoven

Ludwig van Beethoven (c.17 December, 1770–26 March, 1827) was a German composer and pianist. He is considered to have been the most crucial figure in the transitional period between the Classical and Romantic eras in Western classical music, and remains one of the most famous and influential composers of all time. His large body of compositions for piano includes 32 piano sonatas and numerous shorter pieces, including arrangements of some of his other works. Works with piano accompaniment include 10 violin sonatas, 5 cello sonatas, and a sonata for French horn, as well as numerous lieder (songs). He also wrote a significant quantity of chamber music. In addition to 16 string quartets, he wrote five works for string quintet, seven for piano trio, five for string trio, and more than a dozen works for a variety of combinations of wind instruments.

Beethoven's hearing began to deteriorate in the late 1790s, and by 1814 he was almost totally deaf, yet he continued to compose, conduct, and perform. His personal life was troubled by his encroaching deafness, which led him to contemplate suicide. He may have suffered from bipolar disorder and irritability brought on by chronic abdominal pain (beginning in his twenties) that has been attributed to possible lead poisoning. Nevertheless, he had a close and devoted circle of friends all his life, thought to have been attracted by his strength of personality. Toward the end of his life, Beethoven's friends competed in their efforts to help him cope with his incapacities.

Beethoven never married, but did suffer heartbreak. He met Giulietta Guicciardi (1784–1856) in about 1800 and they began a mutual love-relationship. He dedicated to Giulietta his Sonata No. 14, popularly known as the "Moonlight" Sonata. Marriage plans were thwarted by Giulietta's father and perhaps Beethoven's common lineage and in 1803 she married someone else. Beethoven's relationship with Josephine Deym (who he had given piano lessons to before her marriage) notably deepened after the death of her husband in 1804. There is some evidence that Beethoven may have proposed to her, at least informally. While the relationship was apparently reciprocated, she, with some regret, turned him down, and their relationship effectively ended in 1807. She cited her "duty", an apparent reference to the fact that she was born of nobility and he was a commoner. It is also likely that he considered proposing to Therese Malfatti, the dedicatee of *Für Elise* in 1810; his common status may also have interfered with those plans. It has been suggested among historians that Beethoven may possibly have fathered children by his (married) desired romantic partners, but there is no evidence of this.

During 1811–1812 Beethoven became seriously ill, suffering headaches and bad fevers. It is likely that in 1812, in the Bohemian spa town of Teplitz, he wrote the following three love letters. While the identity of the intended recipient is an ongoing subject of debate, the most likely candidate, according to what is known about Beethoven's movements and the contents of the letters, is Antonie Brentano, a married woman with whom he had begun a friendship in 1810. Beethoven travelled to Karlsbad in late July, where he stayed in the same guesthouse as the Brentanos. The letters were never sent, and were found in Beethoven's desk after he died. All three have been included here.

6 July, in the morning.

My angel, my all, my very self.

Only a few words today and at that with pencil (with yours)—Not till tomorrow will my lodgings be definitely determined upon—what a useless waste of time—Why this deep sorrow when necessity speaks—can our love endure except through sacrifices, through not demanding everything from one another; can you change the fact that you are not wholly mine, I not wholly thine—Oh God, look out into the beauties of nature and comfort your heart with that which must be—Love demands everything and that very justly—thus it is to me with you, and to you with me. But you forget so easily that I must live for me and for you; if we were wholly united you would feel the pain of it as little as I.

My journey was a fearful one; I did not reach here until 4 o'clock yesterday morning. Lacking horses the post-coach chose another route, but what an awful one; at the stage before the last I was warned not to travel at night; I was made fearful of a forest, but that only made me the more eager—and I was wrong. The coach must needs break down on the wretched road, a bottomless mud road. Without such postilions as I had with me I should have remained stuck in the road. Esterhazy, travelling the usual road here, had the same fate with eight horses that I had with four—Yet I got some pleasure out of it, as I always do when I successfully overcome difficulties

Now a quick change to things internal from things external. We shall surely see each other soon; moreover, today I cannot share with you the thoughts I have had during these last few days touching my own life—If our hearts were always close together, I would have none of these. My heart is full of so many things to say to you—ah!—there are moments when I feel that speech amounts to nothing at all. Cheer up—remain my true, my only treasure, my all as I am yours. The gods must send us the rest, what for us must and shall be—

Your faithful Ludwig

Evening, Monday, 6 July.

You are suffering, my dearest creature—only now have I learned that letters must be posted very early in the morning on Mondays to Thursdays—the only days on which the mail-coach goes from here to K.[12]—You are suffering—Ah, wherever I am, there you are also—I will arrange it with you and me that I can live with you. What a life!!! thus!!! without you—pursued by the goodness of mankind hither and thither—which I as little want to deserve as I deserve it— Humility of man towards man—it pains me—and when I consider myself in relation to the universe, what am I and what is He—whom we call the greatest— and yet—herein lies the divine in man—I weep when I reflect that you will probably not receive the first report from me until Saturday—Much as you love me—I love you more—But do not ever conceal yourself from me—good night—As I am taking the baths I must go to bed—Oh God—so near! so far! Is not our love truly a heavenly structure, and also as firm as the vault of heaven?

Good morning, on 7 July.

Though still in bed, my thoughts go out to you, my Immortal Beloved, now and then joyfully, then sadly, waiting to learn whether or not fate will hear us—I can live only wholly with you or not at all—Yes, I am resolved to wander so long away from you until I can fly to your arms and say that I am really at home with you, and can send my soul enwrapped in you into the land of spirits—Yes, unhappily it must be so—You will be the more contained since you know my fidelity to you. No one else can ever possess my heart—never—never—Oh God, why must one be parted from one whom one so loves. And yet my life in V. is now a wretched life—Your love makes me at once the happiest and the unhappiest of men—At my age I need a steady, quiet life—can that be so in our connection? My angel, I have just been told that the mailcoach goes every day—therefore I must close at once so that you may receive the letter at once—Be calm, only by a calm consideration of our existence can we achieve our purpose to live together—Be calm—love me—today—yesterday—what tearful longings for you—you—you— my life—my all—farewell. Oh continue to love me—never doubt the most faithful heart of your beloved.
    L.
    Ever thine.
    Ever mine.
    Ever ours.

---

[12] Karlsbad.

Alban Berg

Alban Maria Johannes Berg (9 February, 1885–24 December, 1935) was an Austrian composer, a member of the Second Viennese School and a part of Vienna's cultural elite during the heady *fin de siècle* period. He was largely self-taught musically, taking piano lessons from an aunt, until he met Arnold Schoenberg at age 19. This would prove to be the decisive event in his life, and Schoenberg would remain his teacher for six years. Berg began writing songs, including his *Seven Early Songs*, three of which were his first publicly performed work in a concert that featured the music of Schoenberg's pupils in Vienna that year. The early sonata sketches eventually culminated in Berg's Piano Sonata, Op. 1 (1907–1908); one of the most formidable "first" works ever written. In 1913, two of Berg's *Five Songs on Picture Postcard Texts by Peter Altenberg* were premièred in Vienna, conducted by Schoenberg. The performance caused a riot, and had to be halted. This was a crippling blow to Berg's self-confidence: he effectively withdrew the work. It was not performed in full until 1952, the full score remaining unpublished until 1966. In 1914 Berg began work on his first opera, *Wozzeck*. From 1915 to 1918, he served in the Austrian Army then settled again in Vienna where he taught private pupils. The opera, which Berg completed in 1922, was first performed in excerpts in 1924, bringing Berg his first public success, and in full on 14 December, 1925 in Berlin. Today *Wozzeck* is seen as one of the century's most important works. He completed the orchestration of only the first two acts of his later three-act opera *Lulu*, before he died. The first two acts were successfully premièred in Zürich in 1937.

Berg's only known child was fathered in 1902 by Marie Scheuchl, a servant girl in the Berg family household. Their daughter, Albine, was born on 4 December, 1902. In 1906, Berg met the singer Helene Karoline Nahowski (29 July, 1885–30 August, 1976) who was from a wealthy Austrian family. Helene was the daughter of Franz and Anna Nahowski, but said by some to be in fact the illegitimate daughter of Emperor Franz Joseph I of Austria. Despite the outward hostility of her family, the two were married on 3 May, 1911. Berg began an affair with the married Hanna Fuchs-Robettin in 1925. It was an intensely passionate love affair, and he dedicated his *Lyric Suite* (1926) to her, employing elaborate cyphers in it to document their secret love affair.

To Helene Nahowski

Thursday—Spring, 1909.

There is a delicate scent in my room. I have before me the second of your lovely veils, and when I press it to my face, I can almost feel the sweet warm breath from your mouth. The violets you picked for me yesterday, which nearly withered in my buttonhole, are now blooming anew, and smell soft and fresh. The cushion on the divan and the chair by the window belong to you, Helene, they have become appendages to your presence. Indeed everything in my room is the same: the mirror in front of which you arranged your hair; the window I have seen you looking through so seriously (even in our gayest moments); the last pale rays of sunlight which make your hair gleam gold; the glowing fire in the stove; and then the laurel wreath, and the dear little cover on the bedside table— everything, everything is yours.

And that's no wonder seeing your 'creation.' All my possessions and even thought are somehow a loan or gift from you. Dressing in the morning, for instance, when I get an idea for a theme, a mood, or sometimes even a single chord, at best a whole extended melody—then I always feel it has come flying in from you. It's the same with everything: if I read something out of the ordinary, with difficult parts in it, I imagine myself understanding those parts in it, I imagine myself understanding those parts and penetrating its mysteries only through you, Helene. I mean this reading in the widest sense. If I look at nature with the eyes of a sensitive reader, when I hear music or see paintings or—but why go on with a list of all the things which have come to life in me only through you?

Oh, Helene, how can I live without you!

I am completely yours.

Otto von Bismarck

Otto Eduard Leopold von Bismarck (1 April, 1815–30 July, 1898) was a German-Prussian statesman of the late 19th century, and a dominant figure in world affairs. He was appointed Ministerpräsident, or Prime Minister, of Prussia in 1862 by King Wilhelm I—a position he held until 1890. After the Franco-Prussian War (1870) Bismarck acted immediately to secure the unification of Germany. This was achieved by diplomacy, the reorganisation of the army, and by a new military strategy. He negotiated with representatives of the southern German states, offering special concessions if they agreed to unification. The negotiations succeeded; while the war was in its final phase King Wilhelm of Prussia was proclaimed 'German Emperor' on 18 January, 1871, in the Hall of Mirrors in the Château de Versailles. The new German Empire was a federation: each of its 25 constituent states (kingdoms, grand duchies, duchies, principalities, and free cities) retained some autonomy. Bismarck was raised to the rank of Fürst (Prince) von Bismarck and promoted to lieutenant-general. He was also appointed Imperial Chancellor of the German Empire, but retained his Prussian offices (including those of Prime Minister and Foreign Minister). He designed the German Empire in 1871, becoming its first Chancellor and dominating its affairs until he was removed by Wilhelm II in 1890. He created a new nation with a progressive social policy, a result that went beyond his initial goals as a practitioner of power politics in Prussia. A devout Lutheran who was loyal to his king, he promoted government through a strong, well-trained bureaucracy with a hereditary monarchy at the top. His diplomacy of Realpolitik and powerful rule gained him the nickname "The Iron Chancellor". After his death German nationalists made Bismarck their hero, building hundreds of monuments glorifying this symbol of powerful personal leadership. Historians praised him as a statesman of moderation and balance.

Bismarck married the noblewoman Johanna von Puttkamer (11 April, 1824–27 November, 1894) at Alt-Kolziglow on 28 July, 1847. Their long and happy marriage produced three children, Marie (1847–1926), Herbert (1849–1904) and Wilhelm (1852–1901) and Both of Bismarck's sons served as officers in the Prussian cavalry. Johanna was a shy, retiring and deeply religious woman—although famed for her sharp tongue in later life—and in his public life Bismarck was sometimes accompanied by his sister Malwine ("Malle") von Arnim instead of his wife.

Whilst on holiday alone in Biarritz in the summer of 1862 (prior to becoming Prime Minister of Prussia), Bismarck had a romantic liaison with Kathy Orlov, the twenty-two year old wife of a Russian diplomat—it is not known whether or not their relationship was sexual. Bismarck kept his wife informed of his new friendship by letter, and in a subsequent year Kathy broke off plans to meet Bismarck on holiday again on learning that his wife and family would be accompanying him this time. They continued to write to one another until Kathy's premature death in 1874.

To Johanna von Puttkamer

Schönhausen, 1 February, 1847.

... Snow has fallen very industriously all day long, and the country is white once more, without severe cold. When I arrived it was all free from snow on this side of Brandenburg; the air was warm and the people were ploughing; it was as though I had travelled out of winter into opening spring, and yet within me the short springtime had changed to winter, for the nearer I came to Schönhausen the more oppressive I found the thought of entering upon the old loneliness once more, for who knows how long. Pictures of a wasted past arose in me as though they would banish me from you. I was on the verge of tears, as when, after a school vacation, I caught sight of Berlin's towers from the train. The comparison of my situation with that in which I was on the 10th, when I travelled the same line in the opposite direction; the conviction that my solitude was, strictly speaking, voluntary, and that I could at any time, albeit through a resolve smacking of insubordination and a forty hours' journey, put an end to it, made me see once more that my heart is ungrateful, dismayed, and resentful; for soon I said to myself, in the comfortable fashion of the accepted lover, that even here I am no longer lonely, and I was happy in the consciousness of being loved by you, my angel, and, in return for the gift of your love, of belonging to you, not merely in vassalage, but with my inmost heart. On reaching the village I felt more distinctly than ever before what a beautiful thing it is to have a home— a home with which one is identified by birth, memory, and love. ...

What a different view I take of everything—not merely that which concerns you as well, and because it concerns you, or will concern you also (although I have been bothering myself for two days with the question where your writing-desk shall stand), but my whole view of life is a new one, and I am cheerful and interested even in my work on the dike and police matters. This change, this new life, I owe, next to God, to you, my very dear, my adored Jeanneton—to you who do not heat me occasionally, like an alcohol flame, but work in my heart like warming fire. ...

Farewell, my treasure, my heart. consolation of my eyes.
Your faithful Bismarck.

Berlin, 4 July, 1847.

Juaninina,—Happily, I have left Schönhausen behind me, and do not expect to enter it again without you, my angel. Only some business matters detain me here, which I cannot attend to to-day because it is Sunday; but I confidently anticipate starting for Angermünde to-morrow at four, and accordingly, unless the very improbable event occurs that I am detained outrageously in Kniephof, shall arrive in Schlawe on Thursday. . . . Farewell, my heart. This is probably the last post-marked paper that you will receive from your fiancé (I hate the expression). Our banns were cried to-day for the first time in

Schönhausen. Does that not seem strange to you? But I had learned your given names so badly that I could mention only Johanna Eleonore: the other six you must teach me better. Farewell, my heart. Many salutations to the parents.

Your very faithful B.

Napoleon Bonaparte (15 August, 1769–5 May, 1821) was a military and political leader of France and Emperor of the French as Napoleon I, whose actions shaped European politics in the early 19th century. He rose to prominence under the French First Republic and led successful campaigns against the First and Second Coalitions arrayed against France. In 1799, he staged a *coup d'état* and installed himself as First Consul; five years later the French Senate proclaimed him emperor. In the first decade of the 19th century, the French Empire under Napoleon engaged in a series of conflicts—called the Napoleonic Wars—involving every major European power. After a streak of victories, France secured a dominant position in continental Europe, and Napoleon maintained the French sphere of influence through the formation of extensive alliances and the appointment of friends and family members to rule other European countries as French client states. The French invasion of Russia in 1812 marked a turning point in Napoleon's fortunes. His *Grande Armée* was badly damaged in the campaign and never fully recovered. In 1813, the Sixth Coalition defeated his forces at Leipzig; the following year the Coalition invaded France, forced Napoleon to abdicate and exiled him to the island of Elba. Less than a year later, he escaped Elba and returned to power, but was defeated at the Battle of Waterloo in June 1815. Napoleon spent the last six years of his life in confinement by the British on the island of Saint Helena.

On 21 April, 1795, Napoleon became engaged to Désirée Clary, whose sister, Julie Clary, had married Napoleon's elder brother Joseph. By the end of the year he was romantically attached to Josephine de Beauharnais (*née* Marie Josèphe Rose Tascher de La Pagerie, 23 June, 1763–29 May, 1814), then the mistress of Paul François Jean Nicolas, vicomte de Barras, a politician of the French Revolution. She had two children—Eugène and Hortense—by her first husband, Alexandre de Beauharnais, who had been guillotined in 1794. Josephine and Napoleon were married on 9 March, 1796, after he had broken off his engagement to Désirée. Two days after the wedding, Napoleon left to lead the French army in Italy, and during their separation, sent her many love letters. Many are still intact today, while very few of hers have been found; it is not known whether this is due to their having been lost or to their scarcity. Left behind in Paris, Josephine began an affair in 1796 with a handsome lieutenant, Hippolyte Charles. Napoleon learnt the full extent of her affair while in Egypt, and a letter he wrote to his brother Joseph regarding the subject was intercepted by the British. The letter appeared in the London and Paris presses, much to Napoleon's embarrassment. During the Egyptian campaign of 1798, Napoleon started an affair of his own with Pauline Bellisle Foures, the wife of a junior officer who became known as "Napoleon's Cleopatra." The relationship between Josephine and Napoleon was never the same. His letters became less loving. No subsequent lovers of Josephine are recorded, but Napoleon continued to have sexual affairs with other women, and while his mistresses had children by him, Josephine did not produce an heir. In 1810 they divorced and in March he married the Austrian Marie-Louise, Duchess of Parma (12 December, 1791–17 December, 1847). The couple had one child, Napoleon François Joseph Charles (1811–1832). Napoleon Bonaparte also acknowledged two illegitimate children: Charles Léon (1806–1881) by Eléonore Denuelle de La Plaigne, and Count Alexandre Joseph Colonna-Walewski (1810–1868) by Countess Marie Walewska. He may have had further unacknowledged illegitimate offspring as well, of which there is much speculation.

Napoleon claimed to a friend while in exile on Saint Helena, that "I truly loved my Josephine, but I did not respect her." Despite his numerous affairs, eventual divorce, and remarriage, the Emperor's last words on his death-bed were: "France, the Army, the Head of the Army, Josephine."

Paris, December, 1795.

Seven o'clock in the morning.

I wake filled with thoughts of you. Your portrait and the intoxicating evening which we spent yesterday have left my senses in turmoil. Sweet, incomparable Josephine, what a strange effect you have on my heart! Are you angry? Do I see you looking sad? Are you worried?... My soul aches with sorrow, and there can be no rest for your lover; but is there still more in store for me when, yielding to the profound feelings which overwhelm me, I draw from your lips, from your heart a love which consumes me with fire? Ah! it was last night that I fully realised how false an image of you your portrait gives!

You are leaving at noon; I shall see you in three hours.

Until then, mio dolce amor, a thousand kisses; but give me none in return, for they set my blood on fire.

N. B.

Chanceaux Post House, 14 March, 1796.

... Every moment separates me further from you, my beloved, and every moment I have less energy to exist so far from you. You are the constant object of my thoughts; I exhaust my imagination in thinking of what you are doing. If I see you unhappy, my heart is torn, and my grief grows greater. If you are gay and lively among your friends (male and female), I reproach you with having so soon forgotten the sorrowful separation three days ago; thence you must be fickle, and henceforward stirred by no deep emotions. So you see I am not easy to satisfy; but, my dear, I have quite different sensations when I fear that your health may be affected, or that you have cause to be annoyed; then I regret the haste with which

I was separated from my darling. I feel, in fact, that your natural kindness of heart exists no longer for me, and it is only when I am quite sure you are not vexed that I am satisfied. If I were asked how I slept, I feel that before replying I should have to get a message to tell me that you had had a good night. The ailments, the passions of men influence me only when I imagine they may reach you, my dear. May my good genius, which has always preserved me in the midst of great dangers, surround you, enfold you, while I will face my fate unguarded. Ah! be not gay, but a trifle melancholy; and especially may your soul be free from worries, as your body from illness: you know what our good Ossian says on this subject. Write me, dear, and at full length, and accept the thousand and one kisses of your most devoted and faithful friend.

N. B.

Port Maurice, 3 April, 1796.

I have received all your letters, but none has made me such an impression as the last. How, my beloved, can you write to me like that? Don't you think my position is cruel enough, without adding my sorrows and crushing my spirit? What a style! What feelings you show! They are fire, and they burn my poor heart. My one and only Josephine, apart from you there is no joy; away from you, the world is a desert where I am alone and cannot open my heart. You have taken more than my soul; you are the one thought of my life. When I am tired of the worry of work, when I feel the outcome, when men annoy me, when I am ready to curse being alive, I put my hand on my heart; your portrait hangs there, I look at it, and love brings me perfect happiness, and all is smiling except the time I must spend away from my beloved.

By what art have you captivated all my facilities and concentrated my whole being in you? It is a sweet friend, that will die only when I do. To live for Josephine, that is the history of my life. I try to come near you. Fool! I don't notice that I am going further away. How many countries separate us! How long before you will read these words, this feeble expression of a captive soul where you are queen? Oh, my adorable wife! I don't know what fate has in store for me, but if it keeps me apart from you any longer, it will be unbearable! My courage is not enough for that. Once upon a time I was proud of my courage, and sometimes I would think of the ills destiny might bring me and consider the most terrible horrors without blinking or feeling shaken. But, today the thought that my Josephine might be in trouble, that she may be ill, above this, the cruel, the awful thought that she may love me less blights my soul, stills my blood and makes me sad and depressed, without even the courage of rage and despair. I used often to say men cannot harm one who dies without regret; but, now, to die not loved by you, to die without knowing, would be the torment of Hell, the living image of utter desolation. I feel I am suffocating. My one companion, you whom fate has destined to travel the sorry road of life beside me, the day I lose your heart will be the day Nature loses warmth and life for me. I stop, sweet friend; my soul is sad, my body tired, my spirit oppressed. Men bore me. I ought to hate them: they take me away from my heart...

Don't be frightened. Love me like your eyes; but that is not enough: like yourself, more than yourself, than your thoughts, your life, all of you. Forgive me, dear love, I am raving; Nature is frail when one feels deeply, when one is loved by you.

N. B.

Sincere friendship to Barras, Sucy, Madame Tallien; respects to Madame Chateau-Renard; true love to Eugene, to Hortense.

Goodbye, goodbye! I shall go to bed without you, sleep without you. Let me sleep, I beg you. For several nights I have felt you in my arms; a happy dream, but it is not you.

Carru, 24 April, 1796

To My Sweet Love... I have your letters of the fifth and tenth. There are many days when you don't write. What do you do, then? No, my darling, I am not jealous, but sometimes worried. Come soon; I warn you, if you delay, you will find me ill. Fatigue and your absence are too much.

Your letters are the joy of my days, and my days of happiness are not many. Junot is bringing twenty-two flags to Paris.

You must come back with him, do you understand? Hopeless sorrow, inconsolable misery, sadness without end, if I am so unhappy as to see him return alone. Adorable friend, he will see you, he will breathe in your temple; perhaps you will bestow him the unique and perfect favour of kissing your cheek, and I shall be alone and far, far away. But you are coming, aren't you? You are going to be here beside me, in my arms, on my breast, on my mouth? Take wing and come, come! But travel gently. The road is long, bad, tiring. Suppose you had an accident, or fell ill; suppose fatigue—come gently, my adorable love, but I think of you often.

I have received a letter from Hortense. I will write to her. She is altogether charming. I love her and will soon send her the perfumes she wants.

Read Ossian's poem "Carthon" carefully, and sleep well and happily far from your good friend, but thinking of him.

A kiss on the heart, and one lower down, much lower!

N. B.

Nice, c.May, 1796.

I have not spent a day without loving you; I have not spent a night without embracing you; I have not so much as drunk a single cup of tea without cursing the pride and ambition which force me to remain separated from the moving spirit of my life. In the midst of my duties, whether I am at the head of my army or inspecting the camps, my beloved Josephine stands alone in my heart, occupies my mind, fills my thoughts. If I am moving away from you with the speed of the Rhone torrent, it is only that I may see you again more quickly. If I rise to work in the middle of the night, it is because this may hasten by a matter of days the arrival of my sweet love. Yet in your letter of the 23rd, and 26th Ventose[13], you call me vous. Vous yourself! Ah! wretch, how could you have written this letter? How cold it is. And then there are those four days between the 23rd, and the 26th; what were you doing that you failed to write to your husband?...

Ah, my love, that vous, those four days made me long for my former indifference. Woe to the person responsible! May he as punishment and penalty, experience what my convictions and the evidence (which is in your friend's favour) would make me experience! Hell has no torments great enough! Nor do the Furies have serpents enough! Vous! Vous! Ah! how will things stand in two weeks?...

My spirit is heavy; my heart is fettered and I am terrified by my fantasies... You love me less; but you will get over the loss. One day you will love me no longer; at least tell me; then I shall know how I have come to deserve this misfortune... Farewell, my wife: the torment, joy, hope and moving which draw me close to nature, and with violent impulses as tumultuous as thunder. I ask of you neither eternal love, nor fidelity, but simply... truth, unlimited honesty. The day when you say "I love you less", will mark the end of my love and the last day of my life. If my heart were base enough to love without being loved in return I would tear it to pieces. Josephine! Josephine! Remember what I have sometimes said to you: Nature has endowed me with a virile and decisive character. It has built yours out of lace and gossamer. Have you ceased to love me?

Forgive me, love of my life, my soul is racked by conflicting forces. My heart obsessed by you, is full of fears which prostrate me with misery... I am distressed not to be calling you by name. I shall wait for you to write it. Farewell! Ah! if you love me less you can never have loved me. In that case I shall truly be pitiable.

N. B.

P.S. The war this year has changed beyond recognition. I have had meat, bread and fodder distributed; my armed cavalry will soon be on the march. My soldiers are showing inexpressible confidence in me; you alone are a source of chagrin to me; you alone are the joy and torment of my life. I send a kiss to your children, whom you do not mention. By God! If you did, your letters would be half as long again. Then visitors at ten o'clock in the morning would not have the pleasure of seeing you. Woman!!!

Tortona, Noon, 15 June, 1796.

My life is a perpetual nightmare. A presentiment of ill oppresses me. I see you no longer. I have lost more than life, more than happiness, more than my rest. I am almost without hope. I hasten to send a courier to you. He will stay only four

[13] The sixth month of the calendar adopted by the first French republic. It began 19 February, and ended 20 March.

hours in Paris, and then bring me your reply. Write me ten pages. That alone can console me a little. You are ill, you love me, I have made you unhappy, you are in delicate health, and I do not see you!—that thought overwhelms me. I have done you so much wrong that I know not how to atone for it; I accuse you of staying in Paris, and you were ill there. Forgive me, my dear; the love with which you have inspired me has bereft me of reason. I shall never find it again. It is an ill for which there is no cure. My presentiments are so ominous that I would confine myself to merely seeing you, to pressing you for two hours to my heart and then dying with you. Who looks after you? I expect you have sent for Hortense. I love that sweet child a thousand times more when I think she can console you a little, though for me there is neither consolation nor repose, nor hope until the courier that I have sent comes back; and until, in a long letter, you explain to me what is the nature of your illness, and to what extent it is serious; if it be dangerous, I warn you, I start at once for Paris. My coming shall coincide with your illness. I have always been fortunate, never has my destiny resisted my will, and today I am hurt in what touches me solely. Josephine, how can you remain so long without writing to me; your last laconic letter is dated 22nd May. Moreover, it is a distressing one for me, but I always keep it in my pocket; your portrait and letters are perpetually before my eyes.

I am nothing without you. I scarcely imagine how I existed without knowing you. Ah! Josephine, had you known my heart would you have waited from 18th May to 4th June before starting? Would you have given an ear to perfidious friends who are perhaps desirous of keeping you away from me? I openly avow it to every one, I hate everybody who is near you. I expected you to set out on 24th May, and arrive on 3rd June.

Josephine, if you love me, if you realise how everything depends on your health, take care of yourself. I dare not tell you not to undertake so long a journey, and that, too, in the hot weather. At least, if you are fit to make it, come by short stages; write me at every sleeping-place, and despatch your letters in advance. All my thoughts are concentrated in thy boudoir, in thy bed, on thy heart. Thy illness!—that is what occupies me night and day. Without appetite, without sleep, without care for my friends, for glory, for fatherland, you, you alone, the rest of the world exists no more for me than if it were annihilated. I prize honour since you prize it, I prize victory since it pleases you; without that I should leave everything in order to fling myself at your feet.

Sometimes I tell myself that I alarm myself unnecessarily; that even now she is better, that she is starting, has started, is perhaps already at Lyons. Vain fancies! you are in bed suffering, more beautiful, more interesting, more lovable. You are pale and your eyes are more languishing, but when will you be cured? If one of us ought to be ill it is I more robust, more courageous; I should support illness more easily. Destiny is cruel, it strikes at me through you. What consoles me sometimes is to think that it is in the power of destiny to make you ill; but it is in the power of no one to make me survive you.

In your letter, dear, be sure to tell me that you are convinced that I love you more than it is possible to imagine; that you are persuaded that all my moments are consecrated to you; that to think of any other woman has never entered my *head—they are all in my eyes without grace, wit, or beauty; that you, you alone, such as I see you, such as you are, can please me, and absorb all the faculties of my mind; that you have traversed its whole extent; that my heart has no recess into which you have not seen, no thoughts which are not subordinate to yours; that my strength, my prowess, my spirit are all yours; that my soul is in your body; and that the day on which you change or cease to live will be my death-day; that Nature, that Earth, is beautiful only because you dwell therein. If you do not believe all this, if your soul is not convinced, penetrated by it, you grieve me, you do not love me—there is a magnetic fluid between people who love one another—you know perfectly well that I could not brook a rival, much less offer you one. To tear out his heart and to see him would be for me one and the same thing, and then if I were to carry my hands against your sacred person—no, I should never dare to do it; but I would quit a life in which the most virtuous of women had deceived me. But I am sure and proud of your love; misfortunes are the trials which reveal to each mutually the whole force of our passion. A child as charming as its mamma will soon see the daylight, and will pass many years in your arms. Hapless me! I would be happy with one day. A thousand kisses on your eyes, your lips, your tongue, your heart. Most charming of thy sex, what is thy power over me? I am very sick of thy sickness; I have still a burning fever! Do not keep the courier more than six hours, and let him return at once to bring me the longed-for letter of my Beloved.*

Do you remember my dream, in which I was your boots, your dress, and in which I made you come bodily into my heart? Why has not Nature arranged matters in this way; she has much to do yet.

N. B.

Marmirolo, 17 July, 1796, 9 P.M.

I got your letter, my beloved; it has filled my heart with joy. I am grateful to you for the trouble you have taken to send me news; your health should be better today, I am sure you are cured. I urge you strongly to ride, which cannot fail to do you good. Ever since I left you, I have been sad. I am only happy when by your side. Ceaselessly I recall your kisses, your tears, your enchanting jealousy; and the charms of the incomparable Josephine keep constantly alight a bright and burning flame in my heart and senses. When, free from every worry, from all business, shall I spend all my moments by your side, to have nothing to do but to love you, and to prove it to you? I shall send your horse, but I am hoping that you will soon be able to rejoin me. I thought I loved you some days ago; but, since I saw you, I feel that I love you even a thousand times more. Ever since I have known you, I worship you more every day; which proves how false is the maxim of La Bruyère that "Love comes all at once." Everything in nature has a regular course, and different degrees of growth. Ah! pray let me see some of your faults; be less beautiful, less gracious, less tender, and, especially, less kind; above all never be jealous, never weep; your tears madden me, fire my blood. Be sure that it is no longer possible for me to have a thought except for you, or an idea of which you shall not be the judge.

Have a good rest. Haste to get well. Come and join me, so that, at least, before dying, we could say—"We were happy for so many days!!"

Millions of kisses, and even to Fortuné, in spite of his naughtiness.

N. B.

Verona, 23 November, 1796.

I love you no longer; on the contrary, I detest you. You are a wretch, truly perverse, truly stupid, a real Cinderella.

You never write to me at all, you do not love your husband; you know the pleasure that your letters give him yet you cannot even manage to write him half a dozen lines, dashed off in a moment! What then do you do all day, Madame? What business is so vital that it robs you of the time to write to your faithful lover? What attachment can be stifling and pushing aside the love, the tender and constant love which you promised him? Who can this wonderful new lover be who takes up your every moment, rules your days and prevents you from devoting your attention to your husband? Beware, Josephine; one fine night the doors will be broken down and there I shall be.

In truth, I am worried, my love, to have no news from you; write me a four page letter instantly made up from those delightful words which fill my heart with emotion and joy. I hope to hold you in my arms before long, when I shall lavish upon you a million kisses, burning as the equatorial sun.

N. B.

Tolentino, 19 February, 1797.

... Not a word from you, what on earth have I done? To think only of you, to love only Josephine, to live only for my wife, to enjoy happiness only with my dear one—does this deserve such harsh treatment from her? My dear, I beg you, think often of me, and write me every day.

You are ill, or else you do not love me! Do you think, then, that I have a heart of stone? and do my sufferings concern you so little? You must know me very ill! I cannot believe it! You to whom nature has given intelligence, tenderness, and beauty, you who alone can rule my heart, you who doubtless know only too well the unlimited power you hold over me!

Write to me, think of me, and love me. Yours ever, for life.

N. B.

Rupert Brooke

Rupert Chawner/Chaucer Brooke (3 August, 1887–23 April, 1915) was an English poet known for his idealistic war sonnets written during the First World War (especially *The Soldier*). He was also known for his boyish good looks, which prompted the Irish poet William Butler Yeats to describe him as "the handsomest young man in England".

He attended King's College, Cambridge, where he became a member of the Cambridge Apostles, helped found the Marlowe Society drama club and acted in plays. He made friends among the Bloomsbury group of writers, some of whom admired his talent while others were more impressed by his good looks. Virginia Woolf boasted of once going skinny-dipping with Brooke in a moonlit pool when they were at Cambridge together. Brooke belonged to another literary group known as the Georgian Poets and was one of the most important of the Dymock poets, associated with the Gloucestershire village of Dymock where he spent some time before the war. He also lived in the Old Vicarage, Grantchester.

Brooke's accomplished poetry gained many enthusiasts and followers and he was taken up by Edward Marsh who brought him to the attention of Winston Churchill, then First Lord of the Admiralty. He was commissioned into the Royal Naval Volunteer Reserve as a temporary Sub-Lieutenant shortly after his 27th birthday and took part in the Royal Naval Division's Antwerp expedition in October, 1914. He sailed with the British Mediterranean Expeditionary Force on 28 February, 1915, but developed sepsis from an infected mosquito bite. He died at 4:46 pm on 23 April, 1915, in a French hospital ship moored in a bay off the island of Skyros in the Aegean on his way to battle at Gallipoli. As the expeditionary force had orders to depart immediately, he was buried at 11 pm in an olive grove on Skyros, Greece. The site was chosen by his close friend, William Denis Browne.

As a war poet Brooke came to public attention when the *Times Literary Supplement* quoted two of his five sonnets (*IV: The Dead* and *V: The Soldier*) in full on 11 March, 1915, and subsequently his sonnet *V: The Soldier* was read from the pulpit of St. Paul's on Easter Sunday. Brooke's most famous collection of poetry containing all five sonnets, *1914 and Other Poems* was first published in May, 1915, and in testament to his popularity ran through 11 further impressions that year, and by June, 1918, had reached its 24th impression; a process undoubtedly fuelled through posthumous interest.

Brooke's love life was tumultuous. He was once engaged to Noel Olivier (1892–1969) who he met at a supper party in 1907, prior to a meeting of the Cambridge Fabians which her father had been invited to address. She was fifteen and he was twenty. He was captivated by the shy, intelligent, schoolgirl and began to bombard her with letters. Up to the time of her death, Noel steadfastly refused their publication. Some of Brooke's early poems, such as *The Hill*, were written about and for her. Their secret engagement, which began in 1911, was ill-fated. He shortly became romantically involved with the actress Cathleen Mary Nesbitt, CBE (24 November, 1888–2 August, 1982). He wrote great love sonnets to her, and they were apparently engaged to be married when he died. Brooke suffered from a severe emotional crisis in 1913, resulting in the breakdown of his long relationship with "Ka" Cox (Katherine Laird Cox, 1887–1938). It has been suggested that in 1912 Cox bore their stillborn child. As part of his recuperation, Brooke toured the United States and Canada to write travel diaries for the *Westminster Gazette*. He sailed back across the Pacific, staying some months in the South Seas. Much later it was revealed that he may have fathered a daughter with a Tahitian woman named Taatamata, whilst still writing to Cathleen letters of undying love. Brooke fell heavily in love several times with both men and women, although his bisexuality was edited out of his life by his first literary executor.

To Noel Olivier

2 October, 1911.

I have a thousand images of you in an hour; all different and all coming back to the same... And we love. And we've got the most amazing secrets and understandings. Noel, whom I love, who is so beautiful and wonderful. I think of you eating omlette on the ground. I think of you once against a sky line: and on the hill that Sunday morning.

And that night was wonderfullest of all. The light and the shadow and the quietness and the rain and the wood. And you. You are so beautiful and wonderful that I daren't write to you... And kinder than God.

Your arms and lips and hair and shoulders and voice—you.
Rupert

To Cathleen Nesbitt

Off Gallipoli, 18 March, 1915.

Oh my dear, life is a very good thing. Thank God I met you. Be happy & be good. You have been good to me.

Goodbye, dearest child—
Rupert

Robert Browning

Robert Browning (7 May, 1812–12 December, 1889) was an English poet and playwright whose mastery of dramatic verse, especially dramatic monologues, made him one of the foremost Victorian poets.

In 1845, Browning met Elizabeth Barrett "Ba" (6 March, 1806–29 June, 1861), who though she had been a promising poet in her younger years, lived as a semi-invalid in her father's house in Wimpole Street. Her works had influenced American poets Edgar Allan Poe and Emily Dickinson and her popularity in the United States and Britain was further advanced by her stands against social injustice, including slavery in the United States, and child labour in Britain. Gradually a significant romance developed between Robert and Elizabeth. Six years his elder and an invalid, she could not believe that the vigorous and worldly Browning really loved her as much as he professed to, and her doubts are expressed in the *Sonnets from the Portuguese*, which she wrote over the next two years. Love conquered all, however, and, after a private marriage at St Marylebone Parish Church on 12 September, 1846, Browning imitated his hero Shelley by spiriting his beloved off to Italy, which became their home almost continuously until her death. The marriage was initially secret because Elizabeth's father disapproved of marriage for any of his children. The Brownings lived in Italy, first in Pisa, and then, within a year, finding an apartment in Florence at Casa Guidi (now a museum to their memory). As Elizabeth had inherited some money of her own, the couple were reasonably comfortable in Italy, and their relationship together was content. The Brownings were well respected in Italy and they would be asked for autographs or stopped by people because of their celebrity. Elizabeth grew stronger, and, in 1849, at the age of 43, she gave birth to a son, Robert Wiedeman Barrett Browning (9 March, 1849–8 July, 1912), whom they called Pen. Their son later married but had no legitimate children. It is rumoured that the areas around Florence are peopled with his descendants.

Browning's poetry was known to the cognoscenti from fairly early on in his life, but he remained relatively obscure as a poet till his middle age. (In the middle of the century, Tennyson was much better known). In Florence he worked on the poems that eventually comprised his two-volume *Men and Women*, for which he is now well known; in 1855, however, when these were published, they made little impact. It was only after his wife's death, in 1861, when he returned to England and became part of the London literary scene, that his reputation started to take off. In 1868, after five years work, he completed and published the long blank-verse poem *The Ring and the Book*, and finally achieved really significant recognition. He never remarried.

13 September, 1845.
Saturday Morning.

Now, dearest, I will try and write the little I shall be able, in reply to your letter of last week—and first of all I have to entreat you, now more than ever, to help me and understand from the few words the feelings behind them—(should speak rather more easily, I think—but I dare not run the risk: and I know, after all, you will be just and kind where you can)—I have read your letter again and again. I will tell you—no, not you, but any imaginary other person, who should hear what I am going to avow; I would tell that person most sincerely there is not a particle of fatuity, shall I call it, in that avowal; cannot be, seeing that from the beginning and at this moment I never dreamed of winning your love. I can hardly write this word, so incongruous and impossible does it seem; such a change of our places does it imply—nor, next to that, though long after, would I, if I could, supplant one of any of the affections that I know to have taken root in you—that great and solemn one, for instance. I feel that if I could get myself remade, as if turned to gold, I would not even then desire to become more than the mere setting to that diamond you must always wear. The regard and esteem you now give me, in this letter, and which I press to my heart and bow my head upon, is all I can take and all too embarrassing, using all my gratitude. And yet, with that contented pride in being infinitely your debtor as it is, bound to you for ever as it is; when I read your letter with all the determination to be just to us both; I dare not so far withstand the light I am master of, as to refuse seeing that whatever is recorded as an objection to your disposing of that life of mine I would give you, has reference to some supposed good in that life which your accepting it would destroy (of which fancy I shall speak presently)—I say, wonder as I may at this, I cannot but find it there, surely there. I could no more 'bind you by words,' than you have bound me, as you say—but if I misunderstand you, one assurance to that effect will be but too intelligible to me—but, as it is, I have difficulty in imagining that while one of so many reasons, which I am not obliged to repeat to myself, but which any one easily conceives; while any one of those reasons would impose silence on me for ever (for, as I observed, I love you as you now are, and would not remove one affection that is already part of you)—would you, being able to speak so, only say that you desire not to put 'more sadness than I was born to,' into my life?—that you 'could give me only what it were ungenerous to give'?

Have I your meaning here? In so many words, is it on my account that you bid me 'leave this subject'? I think if it were so, I would for once call my advantages round me. I am not what your generous self-forgetting appreciation would sometimes make me out—but it is not since yesterday, nor ten nor twenty years before, that I began to look into my own life, and study its end, and requirements, what would turn to its good or its loss—and I know, if one may know anything, that to make that life yours and increase it by union with yours, would render me supremely happy, as I said, and say, and feel. My whole suit to you is, in that sense, selfish—not that I am ignorant that your nature would most surely attain happiness in being conscious that it made another happy—but that best, best end of all, would, like the rest, come from yourself, be a reflection of your own gift.

Dearest, I will end here—words, persuasion, arguments, if they were at my service I would not use them—I believe in you, altogether have faith in you—in you. I will not think of insulting by trying to reassure you on one point which certain phrases in your letter might at first glance seem to imply—you do not understand me to be living and labouring and writing (and not writing) in order to be successful in the world's sense? I even convinced the people here what was my true 'honourable position in society,' &c. &c. therefore I shall not have to inform you that I desire to be very rich, very great; but not in reading Law gratis with dear foolish old Basil Montagu, as he ever and anon bothers me to do;— much less—enough of this nonsense.

'Tell me what I have a claim to hear': I can hear it, and be as grateful as I was before and am now—your friendship is my pride and happiness. If you told me your love was bestowed elsewhere, and that it was in my power to serve you there, to serve you there would still be my pride and happiness. I look on and on over the prospect of my love, it is all onwards—and all possible forms of unkindness—I quite laugh to think how they are behind—cannot be encountered in the route we are travelling! I submit to you and will obey you implicitly—obey what I am able to conceive of your least desire, much more of your expressed wish. But it was necessary to make this avowal, among other reasons, for one which the world would recognise too. My whole scheme of life (with its wants, material wants at least, closely cut down) was long ago calculated—and it supposed you, the finding such an one as you, utterly impossible—because in calculating one goes upon chances, not on providence—how could I expect you? So for my own future way in the world I have always refused to care—any one who can live a couple of years and more on bread and potatoes as I did once on a time, and who prefers a blouse and a blue shirt (such as I now write in) to all manner of dress and gentlemanly appointment, and who can, if necessary, groom a horse not so badly, or at all events would rather do it all day long than succeed Mr. Fitzroy Kelly in the Solicitor-Generalship,—such an one need not very much concern himself beyond considering the lilies how they grow. But now I see you near this life, all changes—and at a word, I will do all that ought to be done, that every one used to say could be done, and let 'all my powers find sweet employ' as Dr. Watts sings, in getting whatever is to be got—not very much, surely. I would print these things, get them away, and do this now, and go to you at Pisa with the news—at Pisa where one may live for some £100 a year—while, lo, I seem to remember, I do remember, that Charles Kean offered to give me 500 of those pounds for any play that might suit him—to say nothing of Mr. Colburn saying confidentially that he wanted more than his dinner 'a novel on the subject of Napoleon'! So may one make money, if one does not live in a house in a row, and feel impelled to take the Princess's Theatre for a laudable development and exhibition of one's faculty.

Take the sense of all this, I beseech you, dearest—all you shall say will be best—I am yours—Yes, Yours ever. God bless you for all you have been, and are, and will certainly be to me, come what He shall please!

R.B.

11 January, 1846.
Sunday.

    I have no words for you, my dearest,—I shall never have.
    You are mine, I am yours. Now, here is one sign of what I said... that I must love you more than at first... a little sign, and to be looked narrowly for, or it escapes me, but then the increase it shows can only be little, so very little now— and as the fine French Chemical Analysts bring themselves to appreciate matter in its refined stages by millionths, so—! At first I only thought of being happy in you,—in your happiness: now I most think of you in the dark hours that must come—I shall grow old with you, and die with you—as far as I can look into the night I see the light with me. And surely with that provision of comfort one should turn with fresh joy and renewed sense of security to the sunny middle of the day. I am in the full sunshine now; and after, all seems cared for,—is it too homely an illustration if I say the day's visit is not crossed by uncertainties as to the return through the wild country at nightfall?—Now Keats speaks of 'Beauty, that must die—and Joy whose hand is ever at his lips, bidding farewell!' And who spoke of—looking up into the eyes and asking 'And how long will you love us'?—There is a Beauty that will not die, a Joy that bids no farewell, dear dearest eyes that will love for ever!
    And I—am to love no longer than I can. Well, dear—and when I can no longer—you will not blame me? You will do only as ever, kindly and justly; hardly more. I do not pretend to say I have chosen to put my fancy to such an experiment, and consider how that is to happen, and what measures ought to be taken in the emergency—because in the 'universality of my sympathies' I certainly number a very lively one with my own heart and soul, and cannot amuse myself by such a spectacle as their supposed extinction or paralysis. There is no doubt I should be an object for the deepest commiseration of you or any more fortunate human being. And I hope that because such a calamity does not obtrude itself on me as a thing to be prayed against, it is no less duly implied with all the other visitations from which no humanity can be altogether exempt—just as God bids us ask for the continuance of the 'daily bread'!—'battle, murder and sudden death' lie behind doubtless. I repeat, and perhaps in so doing only give one more example of the instantaneous conversion of that indignation we bestow in another's case, into wonderful lenity when it becomes our own... that I only contemplate the possibility you make me recognise, with pity, and fear... no anger at all; and imprecations of vengeance, for what? Observe, I only speak of cases possible; of sudden impotency of mind; that is possible—there are other ways of 'changing,' 'ceasing to love' &c. which it is safest not to think of nor believe in. A man may never leave his writing desk without seeing safe in one corner of it the folded slip which directs the disposal of his papers in the event of his reason suddenly leaving him—or he may never go out into the street without a card in his pocket to signify his address to those who may have to pick him up in an apoplectic fit—but if he once begins to fear he is growing a glass bottle, and, so, liable to be smashed—do you see? And now, love, dear heart of my heart, my own, only Ba—see no more—see what I am, what God in his constant mercy

ordinarily grants to those who have, as I, received already so much; much, past expression! It is but—if you will so please—at worst, forestalling the one or two years, for my sake; but you will be as sure of me one day as I can be now of myself—and why not now be sure? See, love—a year is gone by—we were in one relation when you wrote at the end of a letter 'Do not say I do not tire you' (by writing)—'I am sure I do.' A year has gone by—Did you tire me then? Now, you tell me what is told; for my sake, sweet, let the few years go by; we are married, and my arms are round you, and my face touches yours, and I am asking you, 'Were you not to me, in that dim beginning of 1846, a joy behind all joys, a life added to and transforming mine, the good I choose from all the possible gifts of God on this earth, for which I seemed to have lived'—which accepting, I thankfully step aside and let the rest get what they can; what, it is very likely, they esteem more—for why should my eye be evil because God's is good; why should I grudge that, giving them, I do believe, infinitely less, he gives them a content in the inferior good and belief in its worth? I should have wished that further concession, that illusion as I believe it, for their sakes—but I cannot undervalue my own treasure and so scant the only tribute of mere gratitude which is in my power to pay. Hear this said now before the few years; and believe in it now for then, dearest!...

How I never say what I sit down to say! How saying the little makes me want to say the more! How the least of little things, once taken up as a thing to be imparted to you, seems to need explanations and commentaries; all is of importance to me—every breath you breathe, every little fact (like this) you are to know!...

And now, my Audience, my crown-bearer, my path-preparer—I am with you again and out of them all—there, here, in my arms, is my proved palpable success! My life, my poetry, gained nothing, oh no!—but this found them, and blessed them. On Tuesday I shall see you, dearest—am much better; well to-day—are you well—or 'scarcely to be called an invalid'? Oh, when I have you, am by you—

Bless you, dearest—And be very sure you have your wish about the length of the week—still Tuesday must come! And with it your own, happy, grateful
R.B.

28 January, 1846.
Wednesday.

Ever dearest—I will say, as you desire, nothing on that subject—but this strictly for myself: you engaged me to consult my own good in the keeping or breaking our engagement; not your good as it might even seem to me; much less seem to another. My only good in this world—that against which all the world goes for nothing—is to spend my life with you, and be yours. You know that when I claim anything, it is really yourself in me—you give me a right and bid me use it, and I, in fact, am most obeying you when I appear most exacting on my own account—so, in that feeling, I dare claim, once for all, and in all possible cases (except that dreadful one of your becoming worse again... in which case I wait till life ends with both of us), I claim your promise's fulfilment—say, at the summer's end: it cannot be for your good that this state of things should continue. We can go to Italy for a year or two and be happy as day and night are long. For me, I adore you. This is all unnecessary, I feel as I write: but you will think of the main fact as ordained, granted by God, will you not, dearest?—so, not to be put in doubt ever again—then, we can go quietly thinking of after matters. Till to-morrow, and ever after, God bless my heart's own, own Ba. All my soul follows you, love—encircles you—and I live in being yours.

12 September, 1846.[14]

You will only expect a few words, what will those be? When the heart is full it may run over, but the real fullness stays within. You asked me yesterday 'if I should repent?' Yes, my own Ba, I could with all the past were to do over again, that in it I might somewhat more, never so little more, conform in the outward homage, to the inward feeling. What I have professed (for I have performed nothing) seems to fall short of what my first love required even, and when I think of this moment's love... I could repent, as I say. Words can never tell you— however, form them, transform them anyway—how perfectly dear you are to me, perfectly dear to my heart and soul. I look back, and in every one point, every word and gesture, every letter, every silence, you have been entirely perfect to me, I would not change one word, one look. My hope and aim are to preserve this love, not to fall from it, for which I trust to God who procured it for me, and doubtless can preserve it.

Enough now, my dearest, dearest, own Ba! You have given me the highest, completest proof of love that ever one human being gave another. I am all gratitude, and all pride (under the proper feeling which ascribes pride to the right source) all pride that my life has been so crowned by you.

God bless you prays your very own R.

---

[14] The morning of their marriage.

Robert Burns

Robert Burns (25 January, 1759–21 July, 1796) was a Scottish poet and lyricist, also known as Rabbie Burns, Scotland's favourite son, the Ploughman Poet, Robden of Solway Firth, the Bard of Ayrshire and in Scotland as simply The Bard. He is widely regarded as the national poet of Scotland, and is celebrated worldwide. He is regarded as a pioneer of the Romantic movement, and after his death he became a great source of inspiration to the founders of both liberalism and socialism. He is the best known of the poets who have written in the Scots language, although much of his writing is also in English and a 'light' Scots dialect, accessible to an audience beyond Scotland. He also wrote in standard English, and in these his political or civil commentary is often at its most blunt.

On 31 July, 1786, his first volume of works, *Poems, Chiefly in the Scottish Dialect*, was published. The success of the work was immediate, and soon he was known across the country. As well as making original compositions, Burns also collected folk songs from across Scotland, often revising or adapting them. His poem (and song) *Auld Lang Syne* is often sung at Hogmanay (New Year's Eve), and *Scots Wha Hae* served for a long time as an unofficial national anthem of the country.

Burns' casual love affairs throughout his life did not endear him to his elders and created for him a reputation for dissoluteness amongst his neighbours. In 1774, at age 15, he wrote a poem called *Handsome Nell* for possibly his first love, Nellie. In 1781 he proposed to Alison Begbie, daughter of a farmer, but she rejected him. His first child, Elizabeth Paton Burns (22 May, 1785–8 January, 1817), was born to his mother's servant, Elizabeth Paton (1760–c.1799). His mother tried to get him to marry her, but he refused. She later married a farm-servant and the child was raised by them. At the same time, Burns was embarking on a relationship with Jean Armour (25 February, 1765–26 March, 1834). She became pregnant with twins, and on 3 September, 1786, Robert and Jean junior were born. Burns signed a paper attesting his marriage to Jean, but her father refused to acknowledge it. To avoid disgrace, her parents sent her to live with her uncle in Paisley. Although Armour's father initially forbade it, they were eventually married formally on 5 August, 1788, after she had given birth to another set of twins, both of whom died within days. Armour bore Burns nine children, but only three survived infancy. Also in 1786, Burns fell in love with Mary Campbell (1763–20/21 October, 1786), who he had seen in church. Their relationship has been the subject of much conjecture. It has been suggested that on 14 May, 1786, they exchanged Bibles and 'plighted their troth' over the Water of Fail in a traditional form of marriage. Soon afterwards Mary left her work and travelled home to her parents. It has been implied that she was pregnant, and died in childbirth that October. Burns dedicated the poems *The Highland Lassie O, Highland Mary* and *To Mary in Heaven* to her. In Edinburgh in 1786 he embarked on a relationship with the separated Agnes "Nancy" McLehose (1758–1841), with whom he exchanged passionate letters under pseudonyms (Burns called himself "Sylvander" and Nancy "Clarinda"). When it became clear that Nancy would not be easily seduced into a physical relationship, Burns moved on to Jenny Clow (1766–1792), Nancy's domestic servant, who bore him a son, Robert Burns Clow in 1788. Another servant, Meg Cameron also bore him a child around the same time and another child, Elizabeth Park Burns, "Betty" (31 March, 1791–13 June, 1873), was born to Helen Anne Park, "Anna" (16 December, 1770–?). His relationship with Nancy concluded in 1791 with a final meeting in Edinburgh before she sailed to Jamaica for what transpired to be a short-lived reconciliation with her estranged husband. Before she left, he sent her the manuscript of *Ae Fond Kiss* as a farewell to her. He eventually went back to Jean, who was tolerant of his behaviour and even raised some of his illegitimate children as her own.

To Agnes McLehose

15 January, 1788.
Tuesday Evening

That you have faults, my Clarinda, I never doubted; but I knew not where they existed, and Saturday night made me more in the dark than ever. O, Clarinda, why will you wound my soul by hinting that last night must have lessened my opinion of you! True; I was "behind the scenes with you", but what did I see? A bosom glowing with honour and benevolence; a mind ennobled by genius, informed and refined by education and reflection, and exalted by native religion, genuine as in the climes of heaven; a heart formed for all the glorious meltings of friendship, love and pity. These I saw—I saw the noblest immortal soul, creation ever shewed me.

I looked long, my dear Clarinda, for your letter; and am vexed that you are complaining. I have not caught you so far wrong as in your idea, that the commerce you have with one friend hurts you, if you cannot tell every tittle of it to another. Why have so injurious a suspicion of a good God, Clarinda, as to think that Friendship and Love, on the sacred, inviolate principles of Truth, Honour and Religion, can be any thing else than an object of His divine approbation?

I have mentioned, in some of my former scrawls, Saturday evening next. Do, allow me to wait on you that evening. Oh my angel! how soon must we part! and when can we meet again! I look forward on the horrid interval with tearful eyes! What have I lost by not knowing you sooner. I fear, I fear my acquaintance with you is too short, to make that lasting impression on your heart I wish I could.
Sylvander

25 January, 1788.

Clarinda, my life, you have wounded my soul.—Can I think of your being unhappy, even tho' it be not described in your pathetic elegance of language, without being miserable? Clarinda, can I bear to be told from you, that "you will not see me tomorrow night-that you wish the hour of parting were come"! Do not let us impose on ourselves by sounds: if in the moment of fond endearment and tender dalliance, I perhaps trespassed against the letter of Decorum's law; I appeal, even to you, whether I ever seemed the very least degree against the spirit of her strictest statute. But why, My Love, talk to me in such strong terms; every word of which cuts me to the very soul? You know, a hint, the slightest signification of your wish, is to me a sacred command. Be reconciled, My Angel, to your God, your self and me; and I pledge you Sylvander's honour, an oath I dare say you will trust without reserve, that you shall never more have reason to complain of his conduct. Now, my Love, do not wound our next meeting with any averted looks or restrained caresses: I have marked the line of conduct, a line I know exactly to your taste, and which I will inviolably keep; but do not you show the least inclination to make boundaries: seeming distrust, where you know you may confide, is a cruel sin against Sensibility.—

"Delicacy, you know it, was which won me to you at once"—take care you do not loosen the dearest most sacred tie that unites us, Clarinda, I would not have stung your soul, I would not have bruised your spirit, as that harsh crucifying, "Take care", did mine; no, not to have gained heaven! Let me again appeal to your dear Self, if Sylvander, even when he seemingly half-transgressed the laws of Decorum, if he did not shew more chastised, trembling, faultering delicacy, than the MANY of the world do in keeping these laws.—

O Love and Sensibility, ye have conspired against My Peace! I love to madness, and I feel to torture! Clarinda, how can I forgive myself, that I ever have touched a single chord in your bosom with pain! would I do it willingly? Would any consideration, any gratification make me do so?

O, did you love like me, you would not, you could not deny or put off a meeting with the Man who adores you; who would die a thousands deaths before he would injure you; and who must soon bid you a long farewell!—

I had proposed bringing my bosom friend, Mr Ainslie, tomorrow evening, at his strong request, to see you; as he only has time to stay with us about ten minutes, for an engagement; but—I shall hear from you: this afternoon, for mercy's sake! for till I hear from you I am wretched.—O Clarinda, the tie that binds me to thee, is entwisted, incorporated with my dearest threads of life!

Sylvander

To ?

c.1788.

Dear Madam,

The passion of love has need to be productive of much delight; as where it takes thorough possession of the man, it almost unfits him for anything else.

The lover who is certain of an equal return of affection, is surely the happiest of men; but he who is a prey to the horrors of anxiety and dreaded disappointment, is a being whose situation is by no means enviable.

Of this, my present experience gives me much proof.

To me, amusement seems impertinent, and business intrusion, while you alone engross every faculty of my mind.

May I request you to drop me a line, to inform me when I may wait upon you?

For pity's sake, do; and let me have it soon.

In the meantime allow me, in all the artless sincerity of truth, to assure you that I truly am, my dearest Madam, your ardent lover, and devoted humble servant.

George Gordon, Lord Byron

George Gordon Byron, 6th Baron Byron, later George Gordon Noel (22 January, 1788–19 April, 1824), commonly known simply as Lord Byron, was a British poet and a leading figure in Romanticism. Amongst Byron's best-known works are the brief poems *She Walks in Beauty*, *When We Two Parted* and *So, We'll Go No More a Roving*, in addition to the narrative poems *Childe Harold's Pilgrimage* and *Don Juan*. He is regarded as one of the greatest British poets and remains widely read and influential.

Byron was celebrated in life for aristocratic excesses including huge debts, numerous love affairs, and self-imposed exile. He was famously described by Lady Caroline Lamb as "mad, bad and dangerous to know". He travelled to fight against the Ottoman Empire in the Greek War of Independence, for which Greeks revere him as a national hero. He died from a fever contracted while in Messolonghi in Greece.

Byron's first loves included Mary Duff and Margaret Parker, his distant cousins, and Mary Chaworth. His love for Mary Chaworth was overwhelming, leading him to refuse to return to school in 1803. Possible homosexual relationships have been suggested in his youth, including with the younger John Edleston, a protégé and close friend who he met at Trinity College, Cambridge in 1806. It is also possible that in 1809 Byron had a son by a maid named Lucy, letters suggest he intended to and did look after her. In 1812, Byron embarked on a well-publicised affair with the married Lady Caroline Lamb (13 November, 1785–26 January, 1828) that shocked the British public. Byron eventually broke off the relationship and moved swiftly on to others (such as Lady Oxford), but Lamb never entirely recovered, pursuing him even after he tired of her. She was emotionally disturbed, and lost so much weight that Byron cruelly commented that he was "haunted by a skeleton". She began to call on him at home, sometimes dressed in disguise as a page boy, at a time when such an act could ruin both of them socially.

Eventually Byron began to court Lady Caroline's cousin Anne Isabella "Annabella" Noel/Milbanke (17 May, 1792–16 May, 1860) who refused his first proposal of marriage but later accepted him. Annabella was a highly moral woman, intelligent and mathematically gifted; she was also an heiress. They married at Seaham Hall, County Durham, on 2 January, 1815. The marriage proved unhappy and he treated her poorly. They had a daughter, Ada Augusta (10 December, 1815–27 November, 1852) but on 16 January, 1816, Lady Byron left him, taking their daughter with her. On 21 April, Byron signed the Deed of Separation. Rumours of marital violence, adultery with actresses, incest with his sister Augusta Leigh, and sodomy were circulated, assisted by a jealous Lady Caroline. Ultimately, Byron resolved to escape the censure of British society by living abroad, he left England later that year. In Venice, he fell in love with

Marianna Segati, in whose house he was lodging, and who was soon replaced by 22-year-old Margarita Cogni; both women were married. In 1817 he had an illegitimate child, Clara Allegra (12 January, 1817–20 April, 1822), with Clara "Claire" Mary Jane Clairmont (27 April, 1798–19 March 1879), the stepsister of writer Mary Shelley. Around 1818 he made the acquaintance of Teresa, Countess Guiccioli (1800–1873), recently married, yet who found love in Byron. They lived in Italy, and spent the remaining years of his life together.

To Lady Caroline Lamb

August, 1812.

> *My dearest Caroline,*
> *If tears, which you saw and know I am not apt to shed—if the agitation in which I parted from you, agitation which you must have perceived through the whole of this most nervous affair, did not commence till the moment of leaving you approached, if all that I have said and done, and am still but too ready to say and do, have not sufficiently proved what my real feelings are and must be ever towards you, my love, I have no other proof to offer.*
> *God knows I wish you happy, and when I quit you, or rather when you from a sense of duty to your husband and mother quit me, you shall acknowledge the truth of what I again promise and vow, that no other in word or deed shall ever hold the place in my affection which is and shall be most sacred to you, till I am nothing.*
> *I never knew till this moment, the madness of—my dearest and most beloved friend—I cannot express myself—this is no time for words—but I shall have a pride, a melancholy pleasure, in suffering what you yourself can hardly conceive—for you do not know me.—I am now about to go out with a heavy heart, because—my appearing this evening will stop any absurd story which the events of today might give rise to—do you think now that I am cold and stern, and artful—will even others think so, will your mother even—that mother to whom we must indeed sacrifice much more, much more on my part, than she shall ever know or can imagine.*
> *"Promises not to love you?" Ah Caroline it is past promising—but I shall attribute all concessions to the proper motive—and never cease to feel all that you have already witnessed—and more than can ever be known but to my own heart—perhaps to yours. May God protect, forgive and bless you—ever and even more than ever.*
> *Yr. most attached*
> *Byron*
> *P.S. These taunts which have driven you to this—my dearest Caroline—were it not for your mother and the kindness of all your connections, is there anything on earth or heaven would have made me so happy as to have made you mine long*

ago? And not less now than then, but more than ever at this time—you know I would with pleasure give up all here and all beyond the grave for you—and in refraining from this—must my motives be misunderstood? I care not who knows this—what use is made of it—it is you and to you only that they owe yourself, I was and am yours, freely and most entirely, to obey, to honour, love—and fly with you when, where, and how you yourself might and may determine.

To Annabella Milbanke

16 November, 1814.

   My Heart—
   We are thus far separated—but after all one mile is as bad as a thousand— which is a great consolation to one who must travel six hundred before he meets you again. If it will give you any satisfaction—I am as comfortless as a pilgrim with peas in his shoes—and as cold as Charity, Chastity or any other Virtue.

To Countess Teresa Guiccioli

25 August, 1819.

   My dearest Teresa,
   I have read this book in your garden;—my love, you were absent, or else I could not have read it. It is a favourite book of yours, and the writer was a friend of mine. You will not understand these English words, and others will not understand them,—which is the reason I have not scrawled them in Italian. But you will recognise the handwriting of him who passionately loved you, and you will divine that, over a book which was yours, he could only think of love.
   In that word, beautiful in all languages, but most so in yours—amor mio—is comprised my existence here and hereafter. I feel I exist here, and I feel I shall exist hereafter,—to what purpose you will decide; my destiny rests with you, and you are a woman, eighteen years of age, and two out of a convent. I love you, and you love me,—at least, you say so, and act as if you did so, which last is a great consolation in all events.
   But I more than love you, and cannot cease to love you. Think of me, sometimes, when the Alps and ocean divide us,—but they never will, unless you wish it.
   Byron

King Charles I of England

Charles I (19 November, 1600–30 January, 1649) was the second son of James VI of Scots and I of England. He was King of England, King of Scotland, and King of Ireland from James' death on 27 March, 1625, until his death in 1649. Charles engaged in a struggle for power with the Parliament of England, attempting to obtain royal revenue whilst Parliament sought to curb his Royal prerogative which he believed was divinely ordained. Many of his English subjects opposed his actions, in particular his interference in the English and Scottish Churches and the levying of taxes without parliamentary consent which grew to be seen as those of a tyrannical absolute monarch.

Religious conflicts permeated Charles' reign. His failure to successfully aid Protestant forces during the Thirty Years' War, coupled with such actions as marrying a Catholic, generated deep mistrust. Charles' later attempts to force religious reforms upon Scotland led to the Bishops' Wars, strengthened the position of the English and Scottish Parliaments and helped precipitate the king's downfall. His last years were marked by the English Civil Wars, in which he fought the forces of the English and Scottish Parliaments, which challenged the King's attempts to overrule and negate Parliamentary authority, whilst simultaneously using his position as head of the English Church to pursue religious policies which generated the antipathy of reformed groups such as the Puritans. Charles was defeated in the First Civil War (1642–45), after which Parliament expected him to accept its demands for a constitutional monarchy. He instead remained defiant by attempting to forge an alliance with Scotland and escaping to the Isle of Wight. This provoked the Second Civil War (1648–49) and a second defeat for Charles, who was subsequently captured, tried, convicted, and executed for high treason. The monarchy was then abolished and a republic called the Commonwealth of England, also referred to as the Cromwellian Interregnum, was declared.

In the early 1620s King James had been seeking marriage between Charles and the Spanish Infanta, Maria Anna of Spain (18 August, 1606–13 May, 1646). Unfortunately this proved generally unpopular, both with the public and James' court and negotiations failed. Charles is believed to have had a daughter, prior to his marriage. Her name was Joanna Brydges, born 1619/20, the daughter of a Miss Brydges. She was provided for by the estate of Mandinam, Carmarthenshire, and was brought up in secrecy at Glamorgan, Wales. While Charles was travelling to Spain to discuss a possible marriage with Maria Anna, he first saw Princess Henrietta Maria (25 November, 1609–10 September, 1669), daughter of Henry IV of France, at a court entertainment in Paris in 1623. They married by proxy on 11 May, 1625, shortly after his accession to the throne. They were then married in person at St. Augustine's Church, Canterbury, Kent, on 13 June, 1625, but her Catholic religion made it impossible for her to be crowned with her husband in an

Anglican service. After an initially difficult period, which was frigid and argumentative, the two formed an extremely close partnership, with Henrietta becoming Charles' closest friend and advisor.

Charles was father to a total of nine legitimate children, two of whom were stillborn and two who would eventually succeed him as King (Charles II and James II). They were: Charles James (stillborn, 13 March, 1629), Charles (29 May, 1630–6 February, 1685), Mary (4 November, 1631–24 December, 1660), James (14 October, 1633–16 September, 1701), Elizabeth (29 December, 1635–8 September, 1650), Anne (17 March, 1637–8 December, 1640), Catherine (stillborn, 29 January, 1639), Henry (8 July, 1640–18 September, 1660) and Henrietta (16 June, 1644–30 June, 1670).

To Henrietta Maria

Oxford, 15/25 February, 1644.

Dear Heart

The expectation of an express from thee (as I find by thine of the 4th of February) is very good news to me, as likewise that thou art now well satisfied with my diligence in writing.

As for our Treaty, there is every day less hopes than other, that it will produce a peace, but I will absolutely promise thee, that if we have one, it shall be such as shall invite thy return, for I avow, that without thy company I can neither have peace nor comfort within my self. The limited days for treating are almost expired, without the least agreement upon any one article, wherefore I have sent for enlargement of days, that the whole treaty may be laid open to the world; and I assure thee, that thou needest not doubt the issue of this Treaty, for my commissioners are so well chosen (though I say it) that they will neither be threatened nor disputed from the grounds I have given them, which, upon my word, is according to the little note, thou so well rememberest, and in this, not only their obedience, but their judgments concur.

I confess, in some respects, thou hast reason to bid me beware of going too soon to London, for indeed, some amongst us had a greater mind that way than was fit, of which persuasion Percy is one of the chief, who is shortly like to see thee; of whom having said this is enough to shew thee how he is to be trusted, or believed by thee, concerning our proceedings here.

In short, there is little or no appearance, but that this summer will be the hottest for war of any that hath been yet; and be confident, that in making peace, I shall ever shew my constancy in adhering to Bishops, and all our friends, and not forget to put a short period to this perpetual parliament: But as thou lovest me, let non persuade thee to slacken thine assistance for him, who is eternally thine, C. R.

Oxford, 9 April, 1645.

Dear Heart
Though it be an uncomfortable thing to write by a slow messenger, yet all occasions of this which is now the only way of conversing with thee are so welcome to me as I shall be loth to lose any; but expect neither news or public business from me by this way of conveyance. Yet, judging thee by myself, even these nothings will not be unwelcome to thee, though I should chide thee—which I could if I would—for thy too sudden taking alarms.

I pray thee consider, since I love thee above all earthly things, and that my contentment is inseparably cojoined with thine, must not all my actions tend to serve and please thee? If thou knew what a life I lead (I speak not in terms of the common distractions), even in point of conversation, which in my mind is the chief joy or vexation of one's life, I dare say thou wouldest pity me. For some are too wise, others too foolish, some too busy, others too reserved, many fantastic...

I confess thy company hath perhaps made me, in this, hard to be pleased, but not less to be pitied by thee, who art the only cure for this disease. The end of all is this, to desire thee to comfort me as often as thou canst with thy letters. And dost not thou think that to know particulars of thy health, and how thou spendest thy time, are pleasing subjects unto me, though hast no other business to write of?

Believe me, sweet heart, thy kindness is as necessary to comfort my heart as thy assistance is for my affairs.
Thine
C. R.

c.1645

Dear Heart
I never knew till now the good of ignorance, for I did not know the danger thou wert in by the storm before I had assurance of thy happy escape, we having had a pleasing false report of thy safe landing at Newcastle, which thine of the 19th of January so far confirmed us in that we were at least not undeceived of that hope till we knew certainly how great a danger thou hast passed, of which I shall not be out of apprehension until I have the happiness of thy company.

For indeed I think it not the least of my misfortunes that for my sake thou hast run so much hazard. But my heart being full of admiration for thee, affection for thee, and impatient passion of gratitude to thee, I cannot but say something, leaving the rest to be read by thee out of thine own noble heart.
C. R.

G. K. Chesterton

Gilbert Keith Chesterton (29 May, 1874–14 June, 1936) was a popular and prolific English writer. He attended the Slade School of Art in order to become an illustrator and also took literature classes at University College London, but left without a degree in 1895. He then worked for the London publisher Redway, and T. Fisher Unwin, where he remained until 1902. Many of his early writings were first published in such publications as *The Speaker*, *Daily News*, *Illustrated London News* and *Eye Witness*. In total he wrote around 80 books, several hundred poems, some 200 short stories, 4000 essays, and several plays. He was a literary and social critic, historian, playwright, novelist, Catholic theologian and apologist, debater, and mystery writer. He was a columnist for the *Daily News*, the *Illustrated London News*, and his own paper, *G. K.'s Weekly*; he also wrote articles for the *Encyclopaedia Britannica*. His best-known character is the priest-detective Father Brown, who appeared only in short stories, while *The Man Who Was Thursday* (1908) is arguably his best-known novel. He was a convinced Christian, and Christian themes and symbolism appear in much of his writing. His prolific and diverse output included philosophy, ontology, poetry, plays, journalism, public lecturing and debating, literary and art criticism, biography, Christian apologetics, and fiction, including fantasy and detective fiction. His writings consistently displayed wit and a sense of humour.

In 1896 he met and fell in love with Frances Alice Blogg (28 June, 1869–12 December, 1938), the daughter of a diamond merchant some time dead. Her mother was initially against the union, seeing Chesterton as a poor journalist with no prospects. However, Frances herself, and the rest of his friends believed he was a genius with a great future and this belief they tried to communicate to Frances's family. Within a few years his works were achieving fame and praise, and they were married at Kensington Parish Church on 28 June, 1901, with the honeymoon being spent on the Norfolk Broads. The long engagement rendered many letters, but unfortunately Frances destroyed many of them. They had no children, but lived happily together for the rest of his life. She was an immense support for him. Chesterton had a tendency to forget where he was supposed to be going and miss the train that was supposed to take him there. It is reported that on several occasions he sent a telegram to his wife from some distant (and incorrect) location, writing such things as "Am at Market Harborough. Where ought I to be?" to which she would reply "Home". Her Christian faith also heavily influenced him. She was a devout Anglican. Gilbert attended church with her but gradually began to examine its doctrines, leading him to convert to Roman Catholicism in 1922. She followed him in 1926.

c.1901.

... I am looking over the sea and endeavouring to reckon up the estate I have to offer you. As far as I can make out my equipment for starting on a journey to fairyland consists of the following items.

1st. A Straw Hat. The oldest part of this admirable relic shows traces of pure Norman work. The vandalism of Cromwell's soldiers has left us little of the original hat-band.

2nd. A Walking Stick, very knobby and heavy: admirably fitted to break the head of any denizen of Suffolk who denies that you are the noblest of ladies, but of no other manifest use.

3rd. A copy of Walt Whitman's poems, once nearly given to Salter, but quite forgotten. It has his name in it still with an affectionate inscription from his sincere friend Gilbert Chesterton. I wonder if he will ever have it.

4th. A number of letters from a young lady, containing everything good and generous and loyal and holy and wise that isn't in Walt Whitman's poems.

5th. An unwieldy sort of a pocket knife, the blades mostly having an edge of a more varied and picturesque outline than is provided by the prosaic cutter. The chief element however is a thing 'to take stones out of a horse's hoof.' What a beautiful sensation of security it gives one to reflect that if one should ever have money enough to buy a horse and should happen to buy one and the horse should happen to have stone in his hoof—that one is ready; one stands prepared, with a defiant smile!

6th. Passing from the last miracle of practical foresight, we come to a box of matches. Every now and then I strike one of these, because fire is beautiful and burns your fingers. Some people think this waste of matches: the same people who object to the building of Cathedrals.

7th. About three pounds in gold and silver, the remains of one of Mr. Unwin's bursts of affection: those explosions of spontaneous love for myself, which, such is the perfect order and harmony of his mind, occur at startlingly exact intervals of time.

8th. A book of Children's Rhymes, in manuscript, called the 'Weather Book' about 3/4 finished, and destined for Mr. Nutt. I have been working at it fairly steadily, which I think jolly creditable under the circumstances. One can't put anything interesting in it. They'll understand those things when they grow up.

9th. A tennis racket—nay, start not. It is a part of the new regime, and the only new and neat-looking thing in the Museum. We'll soon mellow it—like the straw hat. My brother and I are teaching each other lawn tennis.

10th. A soul, hitherto idle and omnivorous but now happy enough to be ashamed of itself.

11th. A body, equally idle and quite equally omnivorous, absorbing tea, coffee, claret, sea-water, and swimming. I think, the sea being a convenient size.

12th. A Heart—mislaid somewhere.

And that is about all the property of which an inventory can be made at present. After all, my tastes are stoically simple. A straw hat, a stick, a box of matches and some of his own poetry. What more does man require?....

The City of Felixstowe, as seen by the local prophet from the neighbouring mountain-peak, does not strike the eye as having anything uncanny about it. At least I imagine that it requires rather careful scrutiny before the eerie curl of a chimney pot, or the elfin wink of a lonely lamp-post brings home to the startled soul that it is really the City of a Fearful Folk. That the inhabitants are not human in the ordinary sense is quite clear, yet it has only just begun to dawn on me after staying a week in the Town of Unreason with its monstrous landscape and grave, unmeaning customs. Do I seem to be raving? Let me give my experiences.

I am bound to admit that I do not think I am good at shopping. I generally succeed in getting rid of money, but other observances, such as bringing away the goods that I've paid for, and knowing what I've bought, often pass over as secondary. But to shop in a town of ordinary tradesmen is one thing: to shop in a town of raving lunatics is another. I set out one morning, happy and hopeful with the intention of buying (a) a tennis racket (b) some tennis balls (c) some tennis shoes (d) a ticket for a tennis ground. I went to the shop pointed out by some villager (probably mad) and went in and said I believed they kept tennis rackets. The young man smiled and assented. I suggested that he might show me some. The young man looked positively alarmed. 'Oh', he said, 'We haven't got any—not got any here.' I asked 'Where?' 'Oh, they're out you know. All round,' he explained wildly, with a graphic gesture in the direction of the sea and the sky. 'All out round. We've left them all round at places.' To this day I don't know what he meant, but I merely asked when they would quit these weird retreats. He said in an hour: in an hour I called again. Were they in now? 'Well not in— not in, just yet,' he said with a sort of feverish confidentialness, as if he wasn't quite well. 'Are they still—all out at places?' I asked with a restrained humour. 'Oh, no!' he said with a burst of reassuring pride. 'They are only out there—out behind, you know.' I hope my face expressed my beaming comprehension of the spot alluded to. Eventually, at a third visit, the rackets were produced. None of them, I was told by my brother, were of any first-class maker, so that was outside the question. The choice was between some good, neat first-hand instruments which suited me, and some seedy-looking second-hand objects with plain deal handles, which would have done at a pinch. I thought that perhaps it would be better to get a good-class racket in London and content myself for the present with economising on one of these second-hand monuments of depression. So I asked the price. '10/6' was the price of the second-hand article. I thought this large for the tool, and wondered if the first-hand rackets were much dearer. What price the first-hand? '7/6' said the Creature, cheery as a bird. I did not faint. I am strong.

I rejected the article which was dearer because it had been hallowed by human possession, and accepted the cheap, new crude racket. Except the newness there was no difference between them whatever. I then asked the smiling Maniac for balls. He brought me a selection of large red globes nearly as big as Dutch cheeses. I said, 'Are these tennis-balls?' He said, 'Oh, did you want tennis-balls?' I said 'Yes—they often came in handy at tennis.' The goblin was quite impervious to satire, and I left him endeavouring to draw my attention to his wares in general, particularly to some zinc baths which he seemed to think should form part of the equipment of a tennis player.

Never before or since have I met a being of that order and degree of creepiness. He was a nightmare of unmeaning idiocy. But some mention ought to be made of the old man at the entrance to the tennis ground who opened his mouth in parables on the subject of the fee for playing there. He seemed to have been wound up to make only one remark, 'It's sixpence.' Under these circumstances the attempt to discover whether the sixpence covered a day's tennis or a week or fifty years was rather baffling. At last I put down the sixpence. This seemed to galvanise him into life. He looked at the clock, which was indicating five past eleven and said, 'It's sixpence an hour—so you'll be all right till two.' I fled screaming.

Since then I have examined the town more carefully and feel the presence of something nameless. There is a claw-curl in the sea-bent trees, an eye-gleam in the dark flints in the wall that is not of this world.

When we set up a house, darling (honeysuckle porch, yew clipt hedge, bees, poetry and eight shillings a week), I think you will have to do the shopping. Particularly at Felixstowe. There was a great and glorious man who said, 'Give us the luxuries of life and we will dispense with the necessities.' That I think would be a splendid motto to write (in letters of brown gold) over the porch of our hypothetical home. There will be a sofa for you, for example, but no chairs, for I prefer the floor. There will be a select store of chocolate-creams... and the rest will be bread and water. We will each retain a suit of evening dress for great occasions, and at other times clothe ourselves in the skins of wild beasts (how pretty you would look) which would fit your taste in furs and be economical.

I have sometimes thought it would be very fine to take an ordinary house, a very poor, commonplace house in West Kensington, say, and make it symbolic. Not artistic—Heaven—O Heaven forbid. My blood boils when I think of the affronts put by knock-kneed pictorial epicures on the strong, honest, ugly, patient shapes of necessary things: the brave old bones of life. There are aesthetic pattering prigs who can look on a saucepan without one tear of joy or sadness: mongrel decadents that can see no dignity in the honourable scars of a kettle. So they concentrate all their house decoration on coloured windows that nobody looks out of, and vases of lilies that everybody wishes out of the way. No: my idea (which is much cheaper) is to make a house really (allegoric) really explain its own essential meaning. Mystical or ancient sayings should be inscribed on every object, the more prosaic the object the better; and the more coarsely and rudely the inscription was traced the better. 'Hast thou sent the Rain upon the Earth?' should be inscribed on the Umbrella-Stand: perhaps on the Umbrella. 'Even the Hairs of your Head are all numbered' would give a tremendous significance to one's hairbrushes: the words about 'living water' would reveal the music and sanctity of the sink: while 'Our God is a consuming Fire' might be written over the kitchen-grate, to assist the mystic musings of the cook—Shall we ever try that experiment, dearest. Perhaps not, for no words would be golden enough for the tools you had to touch: you would be beauty enough for one house...

By all means let us have bad things in our dwelling and make them good things. I shall offer no objection to your having an occasional dragon to dinner, or a penitent Griffin to sleep in the spare bed. The image of you taking a Sunday school of little Devils is pleasing. They will look up, first in savage wonder, then in vague respect; they will see the most glorious and noble lady that ever lived since their prince tempted Eve, with a halo of hair and great heavenly eyes that seem to make the good at the heart of things almost too terribly simple and naked for the sons of flesh: and as they gaze, their tails will drop off, and their wings will sprout: and they will become Angels in six lessons....

I cannot profess to offer any elaborate explanation of your mother's disquiet but I admit it does not wholly surprise me. You see I happen to know one factor in the case, and one only, of which you are wholly ignorant. I know you ... I know one thing which has made me feel strange before your mother—I know the value of what I take away. I feel (in a weird moment) like the Angel of Death... I tell you I have stood before your mother and felt like a thief. I know you are not going to part: neither physically, mentally, morally nor spiritually. But she sees a new element in your life, wholly from outside—is it not natural, given her temperament, that you should find her perturbed? Oh, dearest, dearest Frances, let us always be very gentle to older people. Indeed, darling, it is not they who are the tyrants, but we. They may interrupt our building in the scaffolding stages: we turn their house upside down when it is their final home and rest. Your mother would certainly have worried if you had been engaged to the Archangel Michael (who, indeed, is bearing his disappointment very well): how much more when you are engaged to an aimless, tactless, reckless, unbrushed, strange-hatted, opinionated scarecrow who has suddenly walked into the vacant place. I could have prophesied her unrest: wait and she will calm down all right, dear. God comfort her: I dare not....

One pleasant Saturday afternoon (his friend) Lucian said to him, 'I am going to take you to see the Bloggs.' 'The what?' said the unhappy man. 'The Bloggs,' said the other, darkly. Naturally assuming that it was the name of a public-house he reluctantly followed his friend. He came to a small front-garden; if it was a public-house it was not a businesslike one. They raised the latch—they rang the bell (if the bell was not in the close time just then). No flower in the pots winked. No brick grinned. No sign in Heaven or earth warned him. The birds sang on in the trees. He went in.

The first time he spent an evening at the Bloggs there was no one there. That is to say there was a worn but fiery little lady in a grey dress who didn't approve of 'catastrophic solutions of social problems.' That, he understood, was Mrs. Blogg. There was a long, blonde, smiling young person who seemed to think him quite off his head and who was addressed as Ethel. There were two people whose meaning and status he couldn't imagine, one of whom had a big nose and the other hadn't.... Lastly, there was a Juno-like creature in a tremendous hat who eyed him all the time half wildly, like a shying horse, because he said he was quite happy....

But the second time he went there he was plumped down on a sofa beside a being of whom he had a vague impression that brown hair grew at intervals all down her like a caterpillar. Once in the course of conversation she looked straight at him and he said to himself as plainly as if he had read it in a book: 'If I had anything to do with this girl I should go on my knees to her: if I spoke with her she would never deceive me: if I depended on her she would never deny me: if I loved her she would never play with me: if I trusted her she would never go back on me: if I remembered her she would never forget me. I may never see her again. Goodbye.' It was all said in a flash: but it was all said....

Two years, as they say in the playbills, is supposed to elapse. And here is the subject of this memoir sitting on a balcony above the sea. The time, evening. He is thinking of the whole bewildering record of which the foregoing is a brief outline: he sees how far he has gone wrong and how idle and wasteful and wicked he has often been: how miserably unfitted he is for what he is called upon to be. Let him now declare it and hereafter for ever hold his peace.

But there are four lamps of thanksgiving always before him. The first is for his creation out of the same earth with such a woman as you. The second is that he has not, with all his faults, 'gone after strange women.' You cannot think how a man's self restraint is rewarded in this. The third is that he has tried to love everything alive: a dim preparation for loving you. And the fourth is—but no words can express that. Here ends my previous existence. Take it: it led me to you.

Lord Randolph Churchill

Lord Randolph Henry Spencer Churchill MP (13 February, 1849–24 January, 1895) was a British statesman. He was the third son of the 7th Duke of Marlborough and his wife Lady Frances Anne Emily Vane, daughter of the 3rd Marquess of Londonderry. He went to Eton College, and matriculated at Merton College, Oxford. He had a liking for sport, but was also an avid reader, and obtained a second-class degree in jurisprudence and modern history in 1870. In 1874 he was elected to Parliament as Conservative member for Woodstock, Oxfordshire. His maiden speech, delivered in his first session, prompted compliments from Harcourt and Disraeli, who wrote to the Queen of Churchill's "energy and natural flow". It was not until 1878 that he came to public notice as the exponent of a species of independent Conservatism. In the new parliament of 1880 he speedily began to play a more notable role and made himself known as the audacious opponent of the Liberal administration and the unsparing critic of the Conservative front bench. By 1885 he had formulated the policy of progressive Conservatism which was known as "Tory Democracy". He declared that the Conservatives ought to adopt, rather than oppose, popular reforms, and to challenge the claims of the Liberals to pose as champions of the masses. His views were largely accepted by the official Conservative leaders in the treatment of the Gladstonian Franchise Bill of 1884. After the general election of 1886 he became Chancellor of the Exchequer and Leader of the House of Commons. His management of the House was on the whole successful, and was marked by tact, discretion and temper. But he had never really reconciled himself with some of his colleagues, and there was a good deal of friction in his relations with them, which ended with his sudden resignation on 20 December, 1886.

Churchill married on 15 April, 1874, at the British Embassy in Paris, Jeanette "Jennie" Jerome (9 January, 1854–9 June, 1921), an American from New York, by whom he had two sons, future Prime Minister Winston Leonard Spencer Churchill (30 November, 1874–24 January, 1965) and John Strange Churchill (4 February, 1880–23 February, 1947). Long considered one of the most beautiful women of the time, Jennie was a strong personality, well-respected and influential in the highest British social and political circles. She was thought to be intelligent, witty, and quick to laughter. It was said that Queen Alexandra especially enjoyed her company, despite the fact that Jennie had been involved in an affair with her husband, Edward VII. Lady Randolph had numerous lovers during her marriage. After Lord Randolph's death she married George Cornwallis-West in 1900, and then in 1918 Montague Phippen Porch.

August, 1873.

I cannot keep myself from writing any longer to you dearest, although I have not had any answer to either of my two letters. I suppose your mother does not allow you to write to me. Perhaps you have not got either of my letters... I am so dreadfully afraid that perhaps you may think I am forgetting you. I can assure you dearest Jeannette you have not been out of my thoughts hardly for one minute since I left you Monday. I have written to my father everything, how much I love you how much I long and pray and how much I would sacrifice if it were necessary to be married to you and to live ever after with you... I shall not get an answer till Monday and whichever way it lies I shall go to Cowes soon after and tell your mother everything. I am afraid she does not like me very much from what I have heard... I would do anything she wished if she only would not oppose us.

Dearest if you are as fond of me as I am of you... nothing human could keep us long apart. This last week has seemed an eternity to me; Oh, I would give my soul for another of those days we had together not long ago... Oh if I could only get one line from you to reassure me, but I dare not ask you to do anything that your mother would disapprove of or has perhaps forbidden you to do... Sometimes I doubt so, I cannot help it, whether you really like me as you said at Cowes you did. If you do I cannot fear for the future tho' difficulties may lie in our way only to be surmounted by patience.

Goodbye dearest Jeannette. My first and only love...
Believe me ever to be
Yrs devotedly and lovingly,
Randolf S. Churchill

Samuel Taylor Coleridge

Samuel Taylor Coleridge (21 October, 1772–25 July, 1834) was an English poet, Romantic, literary critic and philosopher who, with his friend William Wordsworth, was a founder of the Romantic Movement in England, a member of the Lake Poets and co-author of a collected volume of poetry entitled *Lyrical Ballads* (1798). He is probably best known for his poems *The Rime of the Ancient Mariner* and *Kubla Khan*, as well as for his major prose work *Biographia Literaria* (1817). His critical work, especially on Shakespeare, was highly influential, and he helped introduce German idealist philosophy to English-speaking culture. He coined many familiar words and phrases, including the celebrated 'suspension of disbelief'. He was a major influence, via Emerson, on American transcendentalism.

Throughout his adult life, Coleridge suffered from crippling bouts of anxiety and depression; it has been speculated that he suffered from bipolar disorder, a mental disorder which was unknown during his life. Coleridge chose to treat these episodes with opium, becoming an addict in the process.

Around 1788, Coleridge visited the home of a school friend, Tom Evans. It was there that he met Mary Evans (1770–1843), the oldest of Tom's three sisters, and Coleridge became infatuated with her. Evans became Coleridge's first love, in a letter he wrote "whom for five years I loved-almost to madness". Although he felt passionately about her, she did not feel the same way. He tried to get over her by becoming engaged to Sarah Fricker (10 September, 1770–24 September, 1845), but again, in 1794 his feelings for Mary drove him to contact her again and he sent her a long, impassioned letter. She rejected him, and in October 1795, married Fryer Todd.

From 1791-1794, Coleridge attended Jesus College, Cambridge. In 1793 he was rumoured to have had a bout with severe depression, and he never received a degree. At the university, he was introduced to political and theological ideas then considered radical, including those of the poet Robert Southey. In trying to decide if he truly loved Sarah, Coleridge wrote in a letter to Southey "I certainly love her. I think of her incessantly and with unspeakable tenderness." They married in St Mary Redcliffe, Bristol, on 4 October, 1795. They had four children: David Hartley (19 September, 1796–6 January, 1849), Berkeley (14 May, 1798–10 February, 1799), Derwent (14 September, 1800–28 March, 1883) and Sara (23 December, 1802–3 May, 1852), but eventually, the marriage proved unhappy and they separated in 1808. At the end of 1799 Coleridge fell in love with Sara Hutchinson, the sister of Wordsworth's future wife, Mary, to whom he devoted his work "Dejection: An Ode" (1802) and the ballad-poem "Love".

To Mary Evans

December, 1794.

    Too long has my heart been the torture house of suspense. After infinite struggles of irresolution, I will at last dare to request of you, Mary, that you will communicate to me whether or no you are engaged to Mr.—. I conjure you not to consider this request as presumptuous indelicacy. Upon mine honour, I have made it with no other design or expectation than that of arming my fortitude by total hopelessness. Read this letter with benevolence — and consign it to oblivion. For four years I have endeavoured to smother a very ardent attachment; in what degree I have succeeded you must know better than I can. With quick perceptions of moral beauty, it was impossible for me not to admire in you your sensibility regulated by judgment, your gaiety proceeding from a cheerful heart acting on the stores of a strong understanding. At first I voluntarily invited the recollection of these qualities into my mind. I made them the perpetual object of my reveries, yet I entertained no one sentiment beyond that of the immediate pleasure annexed to the thinking of you. At length it became a habit. I awoke from the delusion, and found that I had unwittingly harboured a passion which I felt neither the power nor the courage to subdue. My associations were irrevocably formed, and your image was blended with every idea. I thought of you incessantly; yet that spirit (if spirit there be that condescends to record the lonely beatings of my heart), that spirit knows that I thought of you with the purity of a brother. Happy were I, had it been with no more than a brother's ardour!

    The man of dependent fortunes, while he fosters an attachment, commits an act of suicide on his happiness. I possessed no establishment. My views were very distant; I saw that you regarded me merely with the kindness of a sister. What expectations could I form? I formed no expectations. I was ever resolving to subdue the disquieting passion; still some inexplicable suggestion palsied my efforts, and I clung with desperate fondness to this phantom of love, its mysterious attractions and hopeless prospects. It was a faint and rayless hope! Yet it soothed my solitude with many a delightful day-dream. It was a faint and rayless hope! Yet I nursed it in my bosom with an agony of affection, even as a mother her sickly infant. But these are the poisoned luxuries of a diseased fancy. Indulge, Mary, this my first, my last request, and restore me to reality, however gloomy. Sad and full of heaviness will the intelligence be; my heart will die within me. I shall, however, receive it with steadier resignation from yourself, than were it announced to me (haply on your marriage day!) by a stranger. Indulge my request; I will not disturb your peace by even a look of discontent, still less will I offend your ear by the whine of selfish sensibility. In a few months I shall enter at the Temple and there seek forgetful calmness, where only it can be found, in incessant and useful activity.

    Were you not possessed of a mind and of a heart above the usual lot of women, I should not have written you sentiments that would be unintelligible to three fourths of your sex. But our feelings are congenial, though our attachment is doomed not to be reciprocal. You will not deem so meanly of me as to believe that I shall regard Mr.— with the jaundiced eye of disappointed passion. God forbid! He whom you honour with your affections becomes sacred to me. I shall love him for your sake; the time may perhaps come when I shall be philosopher enough not to envy him for his own.

S. T. Coleridge.

24 December, 1794.

I have this moment received your letter, Mary Evans. Its firmness does honour to your understanding, its gentleness to your humanity. You condescend to accuse yourself—most unjustly! You have been altogether blameless. In my wildest day-dream of vanity, I never supposed that you entertained for me any other than a common friendship.

To love you, habit has made unalterable. This passion, however, divested as it now is of all shadow of hope, will lose its disquieting power. Far distant from you I shall journey through the vale of men in calmness. He cannot long be wretched, who dares be actively virtuous.

I have burnt your letters—forget mine; and that I have pained you, forgive me!

May God infinitely love you!

S. T. Coleridge.

To his wife, Sarah

Hamburg, 19 September, 1798.

Over what place does the moon hang to your eye, my dearest Sara? To me it hangs over the left bank of the Elbe, and a long trembling road of moonlight reaches from thence up to the stern of our vessel, and there it ends...

I can do little more than give you notice of my safety and my faithful affection to you...

Good-night, my dear, dear Sara! Every night when I go to bed, and every morning when I rise, I will think with yearning love of you and of my blessed babies! Once more, my dear Sara! Good-night... Kiss my Hartley and Bercoo baby brodder (kiss them for their dear father, whose heart will never be absent from them many hours together). My dear Sara! I think of you with affection and a desire to be home, and in the full and noblest sense of the word, and after the antique principles of Religion, unsophisticated by Philosophy, will be, I trust, your husband faithful unto death,

S. T. Coleridge.

Ratzeburg, 26 November, 1798.

Another and another and yet another post day; and still Chester greets me with, "No letters from England!" A knell, that strikes out regularly four times a week. How is this, my Love? Why do you not write to me? Do you think to shorten my absence by making it insupportable to me? Or perhaps you anticipate that if I received a letter I should idly turn away from my German to dream of you, of you and my beloved babies! Oh, yes! I should indeed dream of you for hours and hours; of you, and of beloved Poole, and of the infant that sucks at your breast, and of my dear, dear Hartley. You would be present, you would be with me in the air that I breathe; and I should cease to see you only when the tears rolled out of my eyes, and this naked, undomestic room became again visible. But oh, with what leaping and exhilarated faculties should I return to the objects and realities of my mission. But now nay, I cannot describe to you the gloominess of thought, the burthen and sickness of heart, which I experience every post day. Through the whole remaining day I am incapable of everything but anxious imaginations, of sore and fretful feelings. The Hamburg newspapers arrive here four times a week; and almost every newspaper commences with, "Schreiben aus London"—They write from London. This day's, with "schreiben aus London, vom November 13". But I am certain that you have written more than once; and I stumble about in dark and idle conjectures, how and by what means it can have happened that I have not received your letters. I recommence my journal, but with feelings that approach to disgust for in very truth I have nothing interesting to relate.

Bei dem Radermacher Gohring, in der Bergstrasse, Göttingen
12 March, 1799. Sunday Night.

My Dearest Love,—It has been a frightfully long time since we have heard from each other. I have not written, simply because my letters could have gone no further than Cuxhaven, and would have stayed there to the no small hazard of their being lost. Even now the mouth of the Elbe is so much choked with ice that the English Pacquets cannot set off. Why need I say how anxious this long interval of silence has made me! I have thought and thought of you, and pictured you and the little ones so often and so often that my imagination is tired down, flat and powerless, and I languish after home for hours together in vacancy, my feelings almost wholly unqualified by thoughts. I have at times experienced such an extinction of light in my mind—I have been so forsaken by all the forms and colourings of existence, as if the organs of life had been dried up; as if only simply Being remained, blind and stagnant. After I have recovered from this strange state and reflected upon it, I have thought of a man who should lose his companion in a desert of sand, where his weary Halloos drop down in the air without an echo. I am deeply convinced that if I were to remain a few years among objects for whom I had no affection I should wholly lose the powers of intellect. Love is the vital air of my genius, and I have not seen one human being in Germany whom I can conceive it possible for me to love, no, not one; in my mind they are an unlovely race, these Germans...

We are quite well. Chester will write soon to his family; in the mean time he sends duty, love, and remembrance to all to whom they are due. I have drunk no wine or fermented liquor for more than three months, in consequence of which I am apt to be wakeful; but then I never feel any oppression after dinner, and my spirits are much more equable, blessings which I esteem inestimable! My dear Hartley—my Berkeley—how intensely do I long for you! My Sara, O my dear Sara! To Poole, God bless him! To dear Mrs. Poole and Ward, kindest love, and to all love and remembrance.

S. T. Coleridge.

William Congreve

William Congreve (24 January, 1670–19 January, 1729) was an English playwright and poet. He wrote some of the most popular English plays of the Restoration period of the late 17th century. Educated at Trinity College, Dublin, he met Jonathan Swift, who would be his friend for the remainder of his life. Upon graduation, he matriculated in the Middle Temple in London to study law, but felt himself pulled toward literature, drama, and the fashionable life. Artistically, he became a disciple of John Dryden. By the age of thirty, he had written four comedies—*The Old Bachelor* (1693), *The Double Dealer* (1693), *Love for Love* (premiered 30 April, 1695) and his masterpiece *The Way of the World* (premiered 1700)—and one tragedy, *The Mourning Bride* (1697). Other works include poems, translations, and two opera librettos. Congreve shaped the English comedy of manners with his brilliant comic dialogue, satirical portrayal of fashionable society, uproarious bawdiness, and ironic scrutiny of the affectations of his age.

Unfortunately, his career ended almost as soon as it began. After writing five plays, he produced no more as public tastes turned against the sort of high-brow sexual comedy of manners in which he specialised. A member of the Whig Kit-Kat Club, Congreve's career shifted to the political sector, where he held various minor political positions despite his stance as a Whig among Tories.

Congreve never married; in his own era and through subsequent generations, he was famous for his relationships with prominent actresses and noblewomen, including the actress Anne Bracegirdle (c.1671–12 September, 1748), for whom he wrote major parts in all his plays, and Henrietta Godolphin, 2nd Duchess of Marlborough (19 July, 1681–24 October, 1733), whom he had probably met around 1703 and with whom he allegedly had a daughter, Mary (1723–1764). In the 1690s he had a prominent relationship with Arabella Hunt (1662–26 December, 1705). In 1680 she had married "James Howard" however the marriage was later annulled in 1682 due to James actually being a woman called Amy Gomeldon. Arabella was a vocalist and lutenist, celebrated for her beauty and talents. Princess Anne had lessons from her, and Mary II found her some employment in the royal household in order to enjoy her singing. She was admired and respected by the best wits of the time; Blow and Purcell wrote difficult music for her; John Hughes, the poet, was her friend. Congreve wrote a long irregular ode on "Mrs. Arabella Hunt singing" (1693) and after her death penned an epigram under a portrait of her sitting on a bank singing.

To Arabella Hunt

c.1690.

Dear Madam,

Not believe that I love you? You cannot pretend to be so incredulous. If you do not believe my tongue, consult my eyes, consult your own. You will find by yours that they have charms; by mine that I have a heart which feels them.

Recall to mind what happened last night. That at least was a love's kiss. Its eagerness, its fierceness, its warmth, expressed the God its parent. But oh! its sweetness, and its melting softness expressed him more. With trembling in my limbs, and fevers in my soul I ravish'd it. Convulsions, pantings, murmurings shew'd the mighty disorder within me: the mighty disorder increased by it. For those dear lips shot through my heart, and thro' my bleeding vitals, delicious poison, and an avoidless but yet a charming ruin.

What cannot a day produce? The night before I thought myself a happy man, in want of nothing, and in fairest expectation of fortune; approved of by men of wit, and applauded by others. Pleased, nay charmed with my friends, my then dearest friends, sensible of every delicate pleasure, and in their turn possessing all.

But Love, almighty Love, seems in a moment to have removed me to a prodigious distance from every object but you alone. In the midst of crowds I remain in solitude. Nothing but you can lay hold of my mind, and that can lay hold of nothing but you. I appear transported to some foreign desert with you (oh, that I were really thus transported!), where, abundantly supplied with everything, in thee, I might live out an age of uninterrupted ecstasy.

The scene of the world's great stage seems suddenly and sadly chang'd. Unlovely objects are all around me, excepting thee; the charms of all the world appear to be translated to thee. Thus in this sad but oh, too pleasing state! my soul can fix upon nothing but thee; thee it contemplates, admires, adores, nay depends on, trusts on you alone.

If you and hope forsake it, despair and endless misery attend it.

John Constable

John Constable (11 June, 1776–31 March, 1837) was an English Romantic painter. Born in Suffolk, he is known principally for his landscape paintings of Dedham Vale, the area surrounding his home—now known as "Constable Country"—which he invested with an intensity of affection. "I should paint my own places best", he wrote to his friend John Fisher in 1821, "painting is but another word for feeling". His most famous paintings include *Dedham Vale* of 1802, *The Hay Wain* of 1821 and *Salisbury Cathedral from the Bishop's Grounds* of 1823. Although his paintings are now among the most popular and valuable in British art, he was never financially successful and did not become a member of the establishment until he was elected to the Royal Academy at the age of 52. He sold more paintings in France than in his native England. He also delivered public lectures on the history of landscape painting, which were attended by distinguished audiences.

From 1809 onwards, his childhood friendship with Maria Bicknell (1788–November 1828) developed into a deep, mutual love. The match was opposed by Maria's grandfather, Dr. Rhudde, rector of East Bergholt, who considered the Constables his social inferiors and threatened Maria with disinheritance. Maria's father, Charles Bicknell, a solicitor, was reluctant to see Maria throw away this inheritance, and Maria herself pointed out that a penniless marriage would detract from any chances John had of making a career in painting. Constable's parents, while approving the match, held out no prospect of supporting the marriage until Constable was financially secure; but they died in quick succession, and Constable inherited a fifth share in the family business.

John and Maria were thus finally able to marry, and did so on 2 October, 1816, at St Martin-in-the-Fields. The wedding was followed by a honeymoon tour of the south coast, where the sea at Weymouth and Brighton stimulated Constable to develop new techniques of brilliant colour and vivacious brushwork. At the same time, a greater emotional range began to register in his art.

Their first child, John Charles, was born on 4 December, 1817, with a total of seven being born in eleven years: Maria Louisa in 1819, Charles Golding in 1821, Isabel in 1822, Emily in 1825, Alfred Abram in 1826 and Lionel Bricknell in 1828. "His fondness for children," a friend wrote, "exceeded, indeed, that of any man I ever knew". After the birth of their seventh child in January 1828, Maria fell ill and died of tuberculosis that November at the age of forty-one. Intensely saddened, Constable wrote to his brother Golding, "hourly do I feel the loss of my departed Angel—God only knows how my children will be brought up... the face of the World is totally changed to me". He cared for his seven children alone for the rest of his life.

East Bergholt.

27 February, 1816.

I received your letter my ever dearest Maria, this morning. You know my anxious disposition too well not to be aware how much I feel at this time. At the distance we are from each other every fear will obtrude itself on my mind. Let me hope that you are not really worse than your kindness, your affection, for me makes you say... I think... that no more molestation will arise to the recovery of your health, which I pray for beyond every other blessing under heaven.

Let us... think only of the blessings that providence may yet have in store for us and that we may yet possess. I am happy in love—an affection exceeding a thousand times my deserts, which has continued so many years, and is yet undiminished... Never will I marry in this world if I marry not you. Truly can I say that for the seven years since I avowed my love for you, I have... foregone all company, and the society of all females (except my own relations) for your sake.

I am still ready to make my sacrifice for you... I will submit to any thing you may command me—but cease to respect, to love and adore you I never can or will. I must still think that we should have married long ago—we should have had many troubles—but we have yet had no joys, and we could not have starved... Your friends have never been without a hope of parting us and see what that has cost us both—but no more.

Believe me, my beloved and ever dearest Maria, most faithfully yours
John

Oliver Cromwell

Oliver Cromwell (25 April, 1599–3 September, 1658) was an English military and political leader. He was elected Member of Parliament for Cambridge in 1640. When the English Civil War broke out in 1642 he entered it on the side of the "Roundheads" or Parliamentarians and became a key military leader. Nicknamed "Old Ironsides", he was quickly promoted from leading a single cavalry troop to command of the entire army. He was one of the commanders of the New Model Army which defeated the royalists in the English Civil War. In 1649 he was one of the signatories of Charles I's death warrant, leading to his execution, and was a member of the Rump Parliament (1649–1653), which selected him to take command of the English campaign in Ireland during 1649–50 and in Scotland between 1650 and 1651. Cromwell dominated the short-lived Commonwealth of England, and conquered Ireland and Scotland. On 20 April, 1653, he dismissed the Rump Parliament by force, setting up a short-lived nominated assembly known as the Barebones Parliament, before being made Lord Protector of England, Wales, Scotland and Ireland on 16 December, 1653 which he remained until his death in 1658. He is thought to have died from malaria, and was buried in Westminster Abbey. After the Royalists returned to power, they had his corpse dug up, hung in chains, and beheaded. Cromwell has been one of the most controversial figures in the history of the British Isles—considered a regicidal dictator by some historians; but as a hero of liberty by others

On 22 August, 1620, at St Giles-without-Cripplegate, London, Cromwell married Elizabeth Bourchier (1598–November 1665). The marriage to Elizabeth was very advantageous for Cromwell, as her father brought him into contact with the wealthy merchant community of London. This family association would later guarantee him much support from the influential families of the local puritan gentry. At the time of his marriage, however, Cromwell had not yet become a puritan zealot. Elizabeth is sometimes referred to as the Lady Protectress or Protectress Joan. The Royalists accused her of every manner of vice, among which drunkenness and adultery were the most prominent. As the charges, however, appear to have been without foundation, the libels fell probably harmless.

Oliver and Elizabeth had nine children: Robert (1621–1639), Oliver (1622–1644), Bridget (1624–1681), Richard (1626–1712), Henry (1628–1674), Elizabeth (1629–1658), James (born and died 1632), Mary (1637–1713) and Frances (1638–1720). Their marriage was happy, and they were devoted to one another. This can be attested by the solicitous love letters Cromwell wrote to Elizabeth while away on his military campaigns.

Dunbar, 4 December, 1650.

For my beloved wife Elizabeth Cromwell, at the Cockpit:

My Dearest,
I have not leisure to write much, but I could chide thee that in many of thy letters thou writest to me, that I should not be unmindful of thee and thy little ones. Truly, if I love thee not too well, I think I err not on the other hand much. Thou art dearer to me than any creature; let that suffice.

The Lord hath showed us an exceeding mercy: who can tell how great it is. My weak faith hath been upheld. I have been in my inward man marvellously supported; though I assure thee, I grow an old man, and feel infirmities of age marvellously stealing upon me. Would my corruptions did as fast decrease. Pray on my behalf in the latter respect. The particulars of our late success Harry Vane or Gil. Pickering will impart to thee. My love to all dear friends. I rest thine,
Oliver Cromwell

Edinburgh, 3 May, 1651.

My Dearest,
I could not satisfy myself to omit this post, although I have not much to write; yet indeed I love to write to my dear, who is very much in my heart. It joys me to hear thy soul prospereth; the Lord increase His favours to thee more and more. The great good thy soul can wish is, That the Lord lift upon thee the light of His countenance, which is better than life. The Lord bless all thy good counsel and example to all those about thee, and hear all thy prayers, and accept thee always.

I am glad to hear thy son and daughter are with thee. I hope thou wilt have some good opportunity of good advice to him. Present my duty to my Mother, my love to all the family. Still pray for
Thine,
O. Cromwell

Pierre Curie

Pierre Curie (15 May, 1859–19 April, 1906) was a French physicist, a pioneer in crystallography, magnetism, piezoelectricity and radioactivity, and a Nobel laureate. Born in Paris, he attended the Sorbonne, where he became an assistant teacher in 1878. By 1880 he and his older brother, Jacques, had earned notice for their work demonstrating the electrical potential generated from quartz crystals when pressure was applied, a phenomenon called piezoelectricity. He then went on to do important work in magnetism, including the discovery that there is a critical temperature at which the magnetic properties of a substance disappear (called the Curie point or Curie temperature).

On 25 July, 1895, he married Marie Skłodowska (7 November, 1867–4 July, 1934), a Polish-born French physicist and chemist. They had met in Paris two years earlier when she was studying at the Sorbonne. He was an instructor at the School of Physics and Chemistry, the École Supérieure de Physique et de Chimie Industrielles (ESPCI). Skłodowska had begun her scientific career in Paris with an investigation of the magnetic properties of various steels; it was their mutual interest in magnetism that drew them together. Her departure for the summer to Warsaw only enhanced their mutual feelings for each other. She still was labouring under the illusion that she would be able to return to Poland and work in her chosen field of study. When she was denied a place at Kraków University merely because she was a woman, however, she returned to Paris. After their marriage the two physicists hardly ever left their laboratory. They shared two hobbies, long bicycle trips and journeys abroad, which brought them even closer.

Pierre and his wife worked together in isolating polonium and radium. They were the first to use the term "radioactivity", and were pioneers in its study. Their work, including Marie's celebrated doctoral work, made use of a sensitive piezoelectric electrometer constructed by Pierre and his brother Jacques. In 1903 Pierre, Marie and Henri Becquerel received the Nobel Prize in Physics "in recognition of the extraordinary services they have rendered by their joint researches on the radiation phenomena".

Pierre and Marie had two daughters: Irène (12 September, 1897–17 March 1956) who also became a noted scientist and Nobel prize winner, and Ève Denise (6 December, 1904–22 October, 2007). Pierre died in Paris on 19 April, 1906. He tried to run across the street while it was raining, but he slipped, and then was hit and run over by a horse drawn vehicle.

To Marie Sklodowska

10 August, 1894.

Nothing could have given me greater pleasure than to get news of you. The prospect of remaining two months without hearing about you had been extremely disagreeable to me: that is to say, your little note was more than welcome.

I hope you are laying up a stock of good air and that you will come back to us in October. As for me, I think I shall not go anywhere; I shall stay in the country, where I spend the whole day in front of my open window or in the garden.

We have promised each other—haven't we?—to be at least great friends. If you will only not change your mind! For there are no promises that are binding; such things cannot be ordered at will. It would be a fine thing, just the same, in which I hardly dare believe, to pass our lives near each other, hypnotized by our dreams: your patriotic dream, our humanitarian dream, and our scientific dream. Of all those dreams the last is, I believe, the only legitimate one. I mean by that that we are powerless to change the social order and, even if we were not, we should not know what to do; in taking action, no matter in what direction, we should never be sure of not doing more harm than good, by retarding some inevitable evolution. From the scientific point of view, on the contrary, we may hope to do something; the ground is solider here, and any discovery that we may make, however small, will remain acquired knowledge.

See how it works out: it is agreed that we shall be great friends, but if you leave France in a year it would be an altogether too Platonic friendship, that of two creatures who would never see each other again. Wouldn't it be better for you to stay with me? I know that this question angers you, and that you don't want to speak of it again—and then, too, I feel so thoroughly unworthy of you from every point of view.

I thought of asking your permission to meet you by chance in Fribourg. But you are staying there, unless I am mistaken, only one day, and on that day you will of course belong to our friends the Kovalskis.

Believe me your very devoted

Pierre Curie

I should be happy if you would write to me and give me the assurance that you intend to come back in October. If you write direct to Sceaux the letters would get to me quicker: Pierre Curie, 13 Rue des Sablons, Sceaux (Seine).

Charles Darwin

Charles Robert Darwin FRS (12 February, 1809–19 April, 1882) was an English naturalist. He established that all species of life have descended over time from common ancestry, and proposed the scientific theory that this branching pattern of evolution resulted from a process that he called natural selection. He published his theory with compelling evidence for evolution in his 1859 book *On the Origin of Species*. The scientific community and much of the general public came to accept evolution as a fact in his lifetime. However, it was not until the emergence of the modern evolutionary synthesis from the 1930s to the 1950s that a broad consensus developed that natural selection was the basic mechanism of evolution. In modified form, Darwin's scientific discovery is the unifying theory of the life sciences, explaining the diversity of life.

In 1837 Darwin fell in love with his charming, intelligent, and cultured cousin Emma Wedgwood (2 May, 1808–7 October 1896). He visited her regularly, but was undecided on whether to propose. His fascinating diary contains an entry for July 1838 with columns headed "Marry" and "Not Marry". Advantages for marrying included "constant companion (and friend in old age)... better than a dog anyhow", against disadvantages such as "less money for books... fatness & idleness... terrible loss of time." Not marrying included propositions such as "conversation of clever men at clubs" and "not forced to visit relatives." In conclusion he decided "only picture to yourself a nice soft wife on a sofa with good fire, and books and music perhaps—compare this vision with the dingy reality of Grt. Marlboro St... Marry—Marry—Marry." He visited Emma on 29 July. He did not get around to proposing, but against his father's advice he mentioned his ideas on transmutation. On 11 November, he returned and this time proposed, once more telling her his ideas. She accepted, and showed how she valued his openness in sharing their differences, also expressing her strong Unitarian beliefs and concerns that his honest doubts might separate them in the afterlife. While he was house-hunting in London, bouts of illness, which affected him throughout his life, continued and Emma wrote urging him to get some rest. He found what they called "Macaw Cottage" (because of its gaudy interiors) in Gower Street, then moved his "museum" in over Christmas. On 24 January, 1839, Darwin was elected a Fellow of the Royal Society and on 29 January Darwin and Emma Wedgwood were married at Maer Hall, Staffordshire, in an Anglican ceremony arranged to suit the Unitarians, then immediately caught the train to London and their new home. The Darwins had ten children: two died in infancy, and their daughter Annie's death at the age of ten had a devastating effect. Charles was a devoted father and uncommonly attentive to his children. Whenever they fell ill, he feared that they might have inherited weaknesses from inbreeding due to the close family ties he shared with his wife and cousin. He examined this topic in his writings, contrasting it with the advantages of crossing amongst many organisms. Despite his fears, most of the surviving children and many of their descendants went on to have distinguished careers. George, Francis and Horace became Fellows of the Royal Society, distinguished as astronomer, botanist and civil engineer, respectively. His son Leonard went on to be a soldier, politician, economist and eugenicist.

To Emma Wedgwood

Sunday Night. Athenaeum
20th January, 1839.

... I cannot tell you how much I enjoyed my Maer visit,—I felt in anticipation my future tranquil life: how I do hope you may be as happy as I know I shall be: but it frightens me, as often as I think of what a family you have been one of. I was thinking this morning how it came, that I, who am fond of talking and am scarcely ever out of spirits, should so entirely rest my notions of happiness on quietness, and a good deal of solitude: but I believe the explanation is very simple and I mention it because it will give you hopes, that I shall gradually grow less of a brute, it is that during the five years of my voyage (and indeed I may add these two last) which from the active manner in which they have been passed, may be said to be the commencement of my real life, the whole of my pleasure was derived from what passed in my mind, while admiring views by myself, travelling across the wild deserts or glorious forests or pacing the deck of the poor little "Beagle" at night. Excuse this much egotism,—I give it you because I think you will humanize me, and soon teach me there is greater happiness than building theories and accumulating facts in silence and solitude. My own dearest Emma, I earnestly pray, you may never regret the great, and I will add very good, deed, you are to perform on the Tuesday: my own dear future wife, God bless you...

The Lyells called on me to-day after church; as Lyell was so full of geology he was obliged to disgorge,—and I dine there on Tuesday for an especial confidence. I was quite ashamed of myself to-day, for we talked for half an hour, unsophisticated geology, with poor Mrs. Lyell sitting by, a monument of patience. I want practice in ill-treatment of the female sex,—I did not observe Lyell had any compunction; I hope to harden my conscience in time: few husbands seem to find it difficult to effect this. Since my return I have taken several looks, as you will readily believe, into the drawing-room; I suppose my taste for harmonious colours is already deteriorated, for I declare the room begins to look less ugly. I take so much pleasure in the house, I declare I am just like a great overgrown child with a new toy; but then, not like a real child, I long to have a co-partner and possessor.

Charles Dickens

Charles John Huffam Dickens (7 February, 1812–9 June, 1870) was the most popular English novelist of the Victorian era, and remains popular today, responsible for some of English literature's most iconic characters. Many of his novels, with their recurrent concern for social reform, first appeared in magazines in serialised form, a popular format at the time. Unlike other authors who completed entire novels before serialisation, Dickens often created the episodes as they were being serialised. The practice lent his stories a particular rhythm, punctuated by cliffhangers to keep the public looking forward to the next installment. The continuing popularity of his novels and short stories is such that they have never gone out of print. Amongst his most popular works are: *Oliver Twist* (1838), *A Christmas Carol* (1843), *David Copperfield* (1850), *Bleak House* (1853), *Little Dorrit* (1857), *Great Expectations* (1861) and *Our Mutual Friend* (1865).

In 1830, Dickens met his first love, Maria Beadnell (1810-1886). Maria's parents disapproved of the courtship and effectively ended the relationship by sending her to school in Paris. His love for her lasted for many years however, and he was heartbroken at the rejection. On 2 April, 1836, he married Catherine Thomson Hogarth (19 May, 1815–22 November, 1879) the daughter of George Hogarth, music critic for the *Morning Chronicle* where Dickens was a young journalist. After a brief honeymoon in Chalk, Kent, they set up home in Bloomsbury. They had ten children. Dickens' younger brother Frederick and Catherine's 17-year-old sister Mary moved in with them. Dickens became very attached to Mary, and she died in his arms after a brief illness in 1837. Later, Georgina Hogarth, another sister of Catherine's, joined the Dickens household, to care for the young family. She remained with them as housekeeper, organiser, adviser and friend. Dickens later claimed that his children were more attached to her than to their own mother.

In 1857, Dickens hired professional actresses for the play *The Frozen Deep*, which he and his protégé Wilkie Collins had written. With one of these, Ellen Lawless Ternan (3 March, 1839–25 April, 1914), Dickens formed a bond which was to last the rest of his life. He separated from his wife, Catherine, in May 1858—after Catherine accidentally received a bracelet meant for Ellen. Divorce was still unthinkable for someone as famous as he was and rumours of Dickens' affairs were numerous, all of which he strenuously denied.

In early September, 1860, in a field behind his home, Dickens made a great bonfire of nearly his entire correspondence. Only those letters on business matters were spared. Since Ellen burned all of his letters as well, the dimensions of the affair between the two were unknown until the publication of *Dickens and Daughter*, a book about Dickens's relationship with his daughter Kate, in 1939.

Kate alleged that her father and Ellen had a son who died in infancy, though no contemporary evidence exists.

To Maria Beadnell

c.May, 1833.

18 Bentinck Street.
Sunday Morning.

... And now to the object of my present note. I have considered and reconsidered the matter, and I have come to the unqualified determination that I will allow no feeling of pride, no haughty dislike to making a conciliation to prevent my expressing it without reserve. I will advert to nothing that has passed; I will not again seek to excuse any part I have acted or to justify it by any course you have ever pursued; I will revert to nothing that has ever passed between us,— I will only openly and at once say that there is nothing I have more at heart, nothing I more sincerely and earnestly desire, than to be reconciled to you.—It would be useless for me to repeat here what I have so often said before; it would be equally useless to look forward and state my hopes for the future—all that any one can do to raise himself by his own exertions and unceasing assiduity I have done, and will do. I have no guide by which to ascertain your present feelings and I have, God knows, no means of influencing them in my favour. I never have loved and I never can love any human creature breathing but yourself. We have had many differences, and we have lately been entirely separated. Absence, however, has not altered my feelings in the slightest degree, and the Love I now tender you is as pure and as lasting as at any period of our former correspondence. I have now done all I can to remove our most unfortunate and to me most unhappy misunderstanding. The matter now of course rests solely with you, and you will decide as your own feelings and wishes direct you. I could say much for myself and I could entreat a favourable consideration on my own behalf but I purposely abstain from doing so because it would be only a repetition of an oft told tale and because I am sure that nothing I could say would have the effect of influencing your decision in any degree whatever. Need I say that to me it is a matter of vital import and the most intense anxiety?—I fear that the numerous claims which must necessarily be made on your time and attention next week will prevent your answering this note within anything like the time which my impatience would name. Let me entreat you to consider your determination well whatever it be and let me implore you to communicate it to me as early as possible.—As I am anxious to convey this note into the City in time to get it delivered today I will at once conclude by begging you to believe me,
    Yours sincerely, Charles Dickens

Denis Diderot

Denis Diderot (5 October, 1713–31 July, 1784) was a French philosopher, art critic, and writer. In 1732 he earned a master of arts degree in philosophy. He abandoned the idea of entering the clergy and decided instead to study law. His study of law was short-lived however and in 1734 Diderot decided instead to become a writer. Because of his refusal to enter one of the learned professions, he was disowned by his father, and for the next ten years he lived a rather bohemian existence. In 1742 he befriended Jean-Jacques Rousseau.

Diderot was a prominent figure during the Enlightenment and is best-known for serving as co-founder and chief editor of and contributor to the *Encyclopédie*. Diderot also contributed to literature, notably with *Jacques le Fataliste et son Maître* (*Jacques the Fatalist and his Master,* 1765–1780), which emulated Laurence Sterne in challenging conventions regarding novels and their structure and content, while also examining philosophical ideas about free will. Diderot is also known as the author of the dialogue, *Le Neveu de Rameau* (*Rameau's Nephew,* 1761–1772), upon which many articles and sermons about consumer desire have been based. His articles included many topics of the Enlightenment.

In 1743 Diderot further alienated his father by secretly marrying Antoinette Champion, a devout Roman Catholic. The match was considered inappropriate due to Champion's low social status, poor education, fatherless status, lack of a dowry, and she being four years his senior. They had been in love, however, since meeting in 1741. The marriage produced one surviving child, a girl. Her name was Angélique, after both Diderot's dead mother and sister, born 1753.

Diderot had affairs with the writer Madame Madeleine Puisieux and with Louise Henriette "Sophie" Volland (c.1716–22 February 1784). His letters to Sophie contain some of the most vivid of all the insights that we have of the daily life of the philosophic circle of Paris during this time period. Their relationship lasted from about 1755 until her death in 1784. A few months later, he joined her.

To Sophie Volland

July, 1759.

I cannot leave this place without saying a few words to you. So, my pet, you expect a good deal from me. Your happiness, your life, even, depend, you say, upon my ever loving you!

Never fear, my dear Sophie, that will endure, and you shall live and be happy. I have never committed a crime yet, and am not going to begin. I am wholly yours—you are everything to me; we will sustain each other in all the ills of life it may please fate to inflict upon us; you will soothe my troubles; I will comfort you in yours. Would that I could always see you as you have been lately! As for myself, you must confess that I am just as I was on the first day you saw me. This is no merit of my own, but I owe it in justice to myself to tell you so. It is one effect of good qualities to be felt more vividly from day to day. Be assured of my constancy to yours, and of my appreciation of them. Never was a passion more justified by reason than mine. Is it not true, my dear Sophie, that you are very amiable? Examine yourself—see how worthy you are of being loved; and know that I love you very much. That is the unvarying standard of my feelings.

Good night, my dear Sophie. I am as happy as a man can be in knowing that I am loved by the best of women.

17 October, 1759.

Sentiment and life are eternal. Someone who lives has always lived and will continue to live forever. The only difference I know between death and life is that now you live as a single entity (mass) and that later, after dissolution, twenty years from now, you will live in scattered distinct molecules...

Those who love each other during their life and who insist on being buried side by side are perhaps not as crazy as you might think. Perhaps their ashes touch, blend, and join together. What do I know? Perhaps they have kept a residue of warmth and life that gives them pleasure deep in the cold urn that encloses them...

Oh, my Sophie, then I could keep the hope of touching you, feeling you, loving you, seeking for you, joining with you and becoming one with you when we are no more!...

Let me keep this fantasy; it's sweet; it guarantees me eternity in you and with you.

Au Grandval, 20 October, 1759.

You are well! You think of me! You love me. You will always love me. I believe you: now I am happy. I live again. I can talk, work, play, walk—do anything you wish. I must have made myself very disagreeable the last two or three days. No! my love; your very presence would not have delighted me more than your first letter did.

How impatiently I waited for it! I am sure my hands trembled when opening it. My countenance changed; my voice altered; and unless he were a fool, he who handed it to me would have said "That man receives news from his father or mother, or someone else he loves". I was just at that moment about to send you a letter expressing my great uneasiness. While you are amusing yourself, you forget how much my heart suffers...

Adieu, my dearest love. My affection for you is ardent and sincere. I would love you even more than I do, if I knew how.

Paul Laurence Dunbar

Paul Laurence Dunbar (27 June, 1872–9 February, 1906) was a seminal African American poet of the late 19th and early 20th centuries. Dunbar was born in Dayton, Ohio to parents who had escaped from slavery in Kentucky; his father was a veteran of the American Civil War, having served in the 55th Massachusetts Infantry Regiment and the 5th Massachusetts Colored Cavalry Regiment. His parents instilled in him a love of learning and history. He was the only African-American student during the years he attended Dayton's Central High School, and he participated actively as a student. During high school, he was both the editor of the school newspaper and class president, as well as the president of the school literary society. Dunbar had also started the first African-American newspaper in Dayton.

His first collection of poetry, *Oak and Ivy*, was published in 1893 and attracted the attention of James Whitcomb Riley, the popular "Hoosier Poet". Both Riley and Dunbar wrote poems in both standard English and dialect. His second book, *Majors and Minors* (1895) brought him national fame and the patronage of William Dean Howells, the novelist and critic and editor of *Harper's Weekly*. After Howells' praise, his first two books were combined as *Lyrics of Lowly Life* and Dunbar started on a career of international literary fame. He wrote a dozen books of poetry, four books of short stories, five novels, and a play. He also wrote lyrics for a musical and many essays which were published widely in the leading journals of the day

Dunbar married the poet and author, Alice Ruth Moore (19 July, 1875–18 September, 1935) on 6 March, 1898, in New York. A graduate of Straight University (now Dillard University) in New Orleans, her most famous works include a short story entitled "Violets" and the collection *Violets and Other Tales* (1895). She and Dunbar began a correspondence after he saw her picture accompanying one of her poems. She and her husband also wrote books of poetry as companion pieces. In 1900, Dunbar was diagnosed with tuberculosis and moved to Colorado with his wife on the advice of his doctors. Dunbar and his wife separated in 1902, but they never divorced. He was reported to have been disturbed by her lesbian affairs. She remarried twice.

Low's Exchange, 3 Northumberland Ave., Trafalgar Square
7 March, 1897.

    Alice, My Darling,
    Someday, when I can hold you in my arms and punctuate every sentence with a kiss and an embrace I may be able to tell you how happy your letter has made

me. *Happy and yet unhappy from the very strength of my longing to be with you, a longing not to be satisfied it seems to so distant a day.*

You love me, Alice, you say; ah yes but could you know the intensity with which I worship you, you would realize that your strongest feelings are weak beside. You gave me no time to think or to resist had I willed to do so! You took my heart captive, at once I yielded bravely, weak coward that I am, without a struggle. And how glad I am of my full surrender. I would rather be your captive than another woman's king. You have made life a new thing to me—a precious and sacred trust.

Will I love you tenderly and faithfully? Darling, darling, can you ask! You who are my heart, my all, my life, I will love you as no man has ever loved before. Already I am living for you and working for you and through the gray days and the long nights I am longing and yearning for you;—for the sound of your voice, the touch of your hand, the magic of your presence, the thrill of your kiss.

You did wrong to kiss me? Oh sweet heart of mine, does the flower that turns its golden face up to the amorous kisses of the sun do wrong? Does the crystal wave that wrinkles at the touch of the moving wind do wrong? Does the cloud that clasps the mountain close to its dewy breast do wrong? Do any of the eternal forces of nature do wrong? If so then you have done a wrong. But darling you could not have helped it. This love of ours was predestined. I had thought that I loved you before, and I had. I loved Alice Ruth Moore the writer of "Violets," but how I love Alice Ruth Moore, the woman,—and my queen. "All the current of my being runs to thee."

I am writing wildly my dear I know, but I am not stopping to think. My head has retired and it is my heart and my pen for it.

For your sake I will be true and pure. You will help me to be this for you are always in my thoughts. Last night I started out upon a rather new undertaking, or rather, phase of action, I took your letter with me and read it as I drove down town. "It will give me heart," I said. It did and I have never had before such a brilliant success. It was at a dinner of the Savage Club; artists, literateurs, scientists and actors, where every man could do some thing. I was an honored guest and held a unique position as the representative of a whole race. I took my turn with the rest, and,—dear is this egotism?—was received with wonderful enthusiasm.

You were with me all the time! You do not leave my thoughts. Alice, Alice, how I love you! Tell me over and over again that you love me. It will hearten me for the larger task that I have set myself here. I am so afraid that you may grow to care less for me. May God forbid! But if you do, let me know at once. I love you so that I am mindful only of your happiness. This is why I shall not complain about your being in New York although I do not like it. It is a dangerous place. But I know, darling that you will do me no injustice, and yourself no dishonor, so I am content. Go often to Miss Brown's but do not entirely usurp my place in the heart of that queen of women. Love me, dear, and tell me so. Write to me often and believe me ever.

Your Devoted Lover, Paul

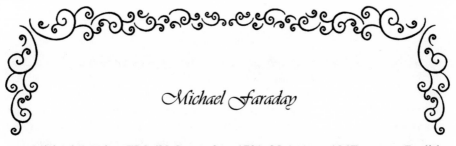

Michael Faraday

Michael Faraday, FRS (22 September, 1791–25 August, 1867) was an English chemist and physicist (or natural philosopher, in the terminology of the time) who contributed to the fields of electromagnetism and electrochemistry. Faraday studied the magnetic field around a conductor carrying a DC electric current. While conducting these studies, he established the basis for the electromagnetic field concept in physics, subsequently enlarged upon by James Maxwell. He similarly discovered electromagnetic induction, diamagnetism, and laws of electrolysis. He established that magnetism could affect rays of light and that there was an underlying relationship between the two phenomena. His inventions of electromagnetic rotary devices formed the foundation of electric motor technology, and it was largely due to his efforts that electricity became viable for use in technology. As a chemist, Faraday discovered benzene, investigated the clathrate hydrate of chlorine, invented an early form of the Bunsen burner and the system of oxidation numbers, and popularised terminology such as anode, cathode, electrode, and ion. He was the first and foremost Fullerian Professor of Chemistry at the Royal Institution of Great Britain, a position to which he was appointed for life.

Although Faraday received little formal education and knew little of higher mathematics, such as calculus, he was one of the most influential scientists in history. Historians of science refer to him as the best experimentalist in the history of science. The SI unit of capacitance, the farad, is named after him, as is the Faraday constant, the charge on a mole of electrons.

Faraday was highly religious; he was a member of the Sandemanian Church, a Christian sect founded in 1730 that demanded total faith and commitment. Through the church he met Sarah Barnard (7 January, 1800–6 January, 1879). They married on 12 June, 1821. Little is known of their relationship, they were rarely separated and so no correspondence exists after their marriage. They had no children.

Royal Institution, Thursday evening
December, 1820.

My Dear Sarah,

It is astonishing how much the state of the body influences the powers of the mind.

I have been thinking all the morning of the very delightful and interesting letter I would send you this evening, and now I am so tired, and yet have so much to do, that my thoughts are quite giddy, and run round your image without any power of themselves to stop and admire it.

I want to say a thousand kind and, believe me, heartfelt things to you, but am not master of words fit for the purpose; and still, as I ponder and think on you, chlorides, trials, oil, Davy, steel, miscellanea, mercury, and fifty other professional fancies swim before and drive me further and further into the quandary of stupidness.

From your affectionate

Michael

George Farquhar

George Farquhar (1677–29 April, 1707) was an Irish dramatist. His first comedy, *Love and a Bottle*, was premiered in London in 1698. It was said to have been well received by the audience and so Farquhar decided to devote himself to playwriting. He also at this point received a commission in the regiment of the Earl of Orrery, so his time for the next few years was divided between the vocations of soldier and dramatist.

In 1700, Farquhar's *The Constant Couple* was acted at Drury Lane and proved a great success, helped considerably by his friend Wilks' portrayal of the character of Sir Henry Wildair. The playwright followed up with a sequel, *Sir Harry Wildair*, the following year, and in 1702 wrote both *The Inconstant, or the Way to Win Him* and *The Twin Rivals*. Also in 1702, Farquhar published *Love and Business*, a collection that included letters, verse, and *A Discourse Upon Comedy*. He was engaged in recruiting for the army for the next three years, writing little except *The Stage Coach*, an adaptation of a French play, in collaboration with Peter Motteux. He drew on his recruiting experience for his next comedy, *The Recruiting Officer* (1706). However, Farquhar had to sell his army commission to pay debts. This, and his last play, *The Beaux' Stratagem* (1707), written while he was seriously ill, are his best, and those for which he is especially noted for his contributions to late Restoration comedy.

In 1699 Farquhar discovered Anne Oldfield (1683–23 October, 1730), then a beautiful sixteen-year-old. He heard her reading aloud at her aunt's tavern. Impressed, he brought her to the notice of another dramatist, and this led to her theatrical career, during which she was the first performer of major female roles in Farquhar's last comedies. According to some, Farquhar fell violently in love with her, but there is no evidence of a relationship.

In 1703, Farquhar married Margaret Pemell, "a widow with three children, ten years his senior," who reportedly tricked him into the marriage by pretending to have a great fortune. His 18th century biographer records that "though he found himself deceived, his circumstances embarrassed, and his family increasing, he never upbraided her for the cheat, but behaved to her with all the delicacy and tenderness of an indulgent husband." They had two children, both daughters; Anne Marguerite and Mary.

To Anne Oldfield

Sunday, after Sermon, 1699.

I came, I saw, and was conquered; never had man more to say, yet can I say nothing; where others go to save their souls, there have I lost mine; but I hope that Divinity which has the justest title to its service has received it; but I will endeavour to suspend these raptures for a moment, and talk calmly.

Nothing on earth, madam, can charm beyond your wit but your beauty: after this not to love you would proclaim me a fool; and to say I did when I thought otherwise would pronounce me a knave; if anybody called me either I should resent it; and if you but think me either I shall break my heart.

You have already, madam, seen enough of me to create a liking or an aversion; your sense is above your sex, then let your proceeding be so likewise, and tell me plainly what I have to hope for. Were I to consult my merits my humility would chide any shadow of hope; but after a sight of such a face whose whole composition is a smile of good nature, why should I be so unjust as to suspect you of cruelty. Let me either live in London and be happy or retire again to my desert to check my vanity that drew me thence; but let me beg you to receive my sentence from your own mouth, that I may hear you speak and see you look at the same time; then let me be unfortunate if I can.

If you are not the lady in mourning that sat upon my right hand at church, you may go to the devil, for I'm sure you're a witch.

Friday Night, eleven o'clock, 1699.

If you find no more rest from your thoughts in bed than I do, I could wish you, madam, to be always there, for there I am most in love. I went to the play this evening and the music roused my soul to such a pitch of passion that I was almost mad with melancholy. I flew thence to Spring Garden where with envious eyes I saw every man pick up his mate, whilst I alone walked like solitary Adam before the creation of Eve, but the place was no paradise to me, nothing I found entertaining but the nightingale which methought in sweet notes like your own pronounced the name of my dear Penelope—as the fool thinketh the bell clinketh. From hence I retired to the tavern where methought the shining glass represented your fair person, and the sparkling wine within it looked like your lovely wit and spirit. I met my dear mistress in everything, and I propose presently to see her in a lively dream, since the last thing I do is to kiss her dear letter, clasp her charming ideal in my arms, and so fall asleep—

My morning songs, my evening prayers,
My daily musings, nightly cares.

Adieu!

Gustave Flaubert

Gustave Flaubert (12 December, 1821–8 May, 1880) was a French writer who is counted among the greatest Western novelists, known especially for his scrupulous devotion to his art and style. His first finished work was *November*, a novella, which was completed in 1842. In September 1849, he completed the first version of a novel, *The Temptation of Saint Anthony*, but it was after this, in 1850, that he began work on his masterpiece, *Madame Bovary*. The novel, which took five years to write, was serialised in the *Revue de Paris* in 1856. The story of a doctor's wife who has adulterous affairs and lives beyond her means in order to escape the banalities and emptiness of provincial life, it was instantly attacked for obscenity by public prosecutors, resulting in a trial in January 1857 that made the story notorious. After the acquittal, on 7 February, 1857, the complete book was published and became a bestseller. It now stands virtually unchallenged not only as a seminal work of Realism, but as one of the most influential novels ever written.

From 1846 to 1854, Flaubert had a relationship with the poet Louise *née* Revoil Colet (15 August, 1810–9 March, 1876). They supposedly met at a sculptor's studio in Paris, where she was posing and Flaubert fell madly in love with her. She was already married to Hippolyte Colet, an academic musician, though their marriage came about partly so that she could escape provincial life and live in Paris. Her affair with Flaubert was well-known, and their large correspondence remains available today. The relationship turned sour, however, and they broke up. Louise is said to be the inspiration for Madame Bovary, of which she was well aware, and furious about. Later she became the lover of Alfred de Musset, and Abel Villemain. After her husband died, Colet supported herself and her daughter with her own writing.

Flaubert did have other love affairs, but they were never central to his life and he never married. Juliet Herbert, the governess of his niece, was a lover in the mid-1850s possibly to the end of his life, but their correspondence was burnt and only speculation on their relationship exists. He visited prostitutes and was very open about his sexual activities with prostitutes of both sexes in his writings on his travels. Eventually, he lost interest in romance and sought platonic companionship, particularly with other writers. He had a close friendship and correspondence with the author George Sand (the pseudonym used by Amantine Aurore Lucile Dupin, 1 July, 1804–8 June, 1876), which began in 1863 and lasted for the rest of his life.

To Louise Colet

6 August, 1846

I am shattered, numb, as though after a long orgy. I miss you terribly. There is an immense void in my heart. Formerly I was calm, proud of my serenity. I worked keenly and steadily from morning to night. Now I cannot read, or think, or write. Your love has made me sad. I can see you are suffering, I foresee I will make you suffer. Both for your sake and for my own I wish we had never met, and yet the thought of you is never absent from my mind. In it I find an exquisite sweetness. Ah! How much better it would have been to stop short after our first ride together!...

Separated, destined to see one another but rarely, it is frightful! What a prospect! And yet what is to be done? I cannot conceive how I managed to leave you. But that is how I am; there you see my wretched character. If you were not to love me, I should die, but you do love me, and I am writing you to stop. I am disgusted by my own stupidity. But in whatever direction I look I see unhappiness! I wish I might have come into your life like a cool brook to refresh its thirst, not as a devastating torrent. At the thought of me your flesh would have thrilled, your heart smiled. Never curse me! Ah, I shall love you well before loving you no longer. I shall always bless you—your image will remain for me suffused with poetry and tenderness, as was last night's sky in the milky vapours of its silvery mist. This month I will come to see you, I will be with you one big whole day...

You are certainly the only woman that I have loved. You are the only woman that I have ventured to wish to please. Thank you, thank you for that! But will you understand me to the end? Will you be able to bear the burden of my spleen, my manias, my whims, my prostrations and my wild reversals? You tell me, for example, to write you every day, and if I don't you will reproach me. But the very idea that you want a letter every morning will prevent me from writing it. Let me love you in my own way, in the way my nature demands, with what you call my originality. Force me to do nothing, and I will do everything. Understand me, do not reproach me. If I thought you frivolous and stupid like other women, I would placate you with words, promises, vows. That would cost me nothing. But I prefer to express less, not more, than the true feelings of my heart...

Tomorrow I expect your poems, and in a few days your volumes. Farewell, think of me, yes, kiss your arm for me. Every evening now I read some of your poems. I keep looking for traces of yourself in them, sometimes I find them.

Adieu, adieu, I lay my head on your breasts and look up to you, as to a madonna.

11 P.M.
Adieu, I seal my letter. This is the hour when, alone amidst everything that sleeps, I open the drawer that holds my treasures. I look at your slippers, your handkerchief, your hair, your portrait, I reread your letters and breathe their

musky perfume. If you could know what I am feeling at this moment! My heart expands in the night, suffused with a dew of love!

A thousand kisses, a thousand everywhere—everywhere.

8 August, 1846.

The sky is clear, the moon is shining. I hear sailors singing as they raise anchor, preparing to leave with the oncoming tide. No clouds, no wind. The river is white under the moon, black in the shadows. Moths are playing around my candles, and the scent of the night comes to me through my open windows. And you, are you asleep? Or at your window? Are you thinking of the one who thinks of you? Are you dreaming? What is the colour of your dream? A week ago we were taking our beautiful drive in the Bois de Boulogne. What an abyss since that day! For others, those charming hours doubtless went by like those that preceded them and those that followed; but for us it was a radiant moment whose glow will always brighten our hearts. It was beautiful in its joy and tenderness, was it not, poor soul? If I were rich I would buy that carriage and put it in my stable and never use it again. Yes, I will come back, and soon, for I think of you always; I keep dreaming of your face, of your shoulders, your white neck, your smile, of your voice that is like a love-cry, at once impassioned, violent, and sweet. I told you, I think, that it was above all your voice that I loved.

This morning I waited a whole hour on the quay for the postman: he was late today. How many heartbeats that red-collared fool must be the cause of, all unknowing! Thank you for your good letter. But do not love me so much, do not love me so much. You hurt me! Let me love you. Don't you know that to love excessively brings bad luck to both? It's like over-fondled children: they die young. Life is not made for that. Happiness is a monstrosity; they who seek it are punished...

Before I knew you, I was calm; I had become so. I was entering a vigorous period of moral health. My youth is over. My nervous illness, which lasted two years, was its conclusion, its close, its logical result. To have had what I had, something very serious must have happened earlier inside my brain pan. Then everything became itself again. I had experienced a clear vision of things—and of myself, which is rarer. I was living soundly, according to my particular system, devised for my particular case. I had arrived at an understanding of everything within myself, I had sorted it all, classified it all, with the result that I was more at peace than at any period of my existence, whereas everyone imagined the opposite—that now I was to be pitied. Then you came along, and with the touch of a fingertip stirred everything up again. The old dregs were set boiling once more; the lake of my heart began to churn. But the tempest is for the ocean; ponds, when they are disturbed, produce nothing but unhealthy smells. I must love you to tell you this. Forget me if you can, tear your soul from your body with your two hands and trample on it, to obliterate the traces I left there.

Come, don't be angry. No, I embrace you, I kiss you. I feel crazy. Were you here, I'd bite you; I long to—I, whom women jeer at for my coldness—I, charitably supposed to be incapable of sex, so little have I indulged in it. Yes, I feel within me now the cravings of wild beasts, the instincts of a love that is carnivorous, capable of tearing flesh to pieces. Is this love? Perhaps it is the opposite. Perhaps in my case it's the heart that is impotent.

My deplorable mania for analysis exhausts me. I doubt everything, even my doubt. You thought me young, and I am old. I have often spoke with old people about the pleasures of this earth, and I have always been astonished by the brightness that comes into their lackluster eyes; just as they could never get over their amazement at my way of life, and kept saying "At your age! At your age! You! You!" Take away my nervous exaltation, my fantasy of mind, the emotion of the moment, and I have little left. That's what I am underneath. I was not made to enjoy life! You must not take these words in a down-to-earth sense, but rather grasp their metaphysical intensity. I keep telling myself that I'll bring misfortune, that were it not for me your life would have continued undisturbed, that the day will come when we shall part (and I protest in advance). Then the nausea of life rises to my lips, and I feel immeasurable self-disgust and a wholly Christian tenderness for you.

At other times—yesterday, for example, when I had sealed my letter—the thought of you sings, smiles, shines, and dances like a joyous fire that gives out a thousand colours and penetrating warmth. I keep remembering the graceful, charming, provocative movement of your mouth when you speak—that rosy, moist mouth that calls forth kisses and sucks them irresistibly in. What a good idea I had, to take your slippers. If you knew how I keep looking at them! The bloodstains are fading: is that their fault? We shall do the same: one year, two years, six, what does it matter? Everything measurable passes, everything that can be counted has an end. Only three things are infinite: the sky in its stars, the sea in its drops of water, and the heart in its tears. Only in that capacity is the heart large; everything else about it is small. Am I lying? Think, try to be calm. One or two shreds of happiness fill it to overflowing, whereas it has room for all the miseries of mankind.

You speak of work, yes you must work, love art. Of all lies, art is the least untrue. Try to love it with a love that is exclusive, ardent, devoted. It will not fail you. Only the idea is eternal and necessary. There are no more artists as they once existed, artists whose loves and minds were the blind instruments of the appetite for the beautiful, God's organs by means of which he demonstrated to himself his own existence. For them the world did not exist, no one has ever known anything of their sufferings, each night they lay down in sadness, and they look at human life with wonder, as we contemplate ant hills.

You judge me from the woman's point of view: am I supposed to complain of your judgment? You love me so much that you delude yourself about me, you find in me talent, intelligence, style. In me! In me! You'll make me vain, and I was proud of not being so! See, you have already lost something as a result of meeting me. Your critical sense is forsaking you, and you imagine this person who loves you is a great man. Would that I were, to make you proud of me! (It is I who am proud of you. I keep telling myself "But she loves me! Is it possible? She!") Yes, I wish that I could write beautiful things, great things, and that you would weep with admiration of them. I think of you at a performance of a play by me, in a box, listening, hearing the applause. But I fear the contrary—that you will weary of constantly raising me to your level. When I was a child I dreamed of fame like everyone else, no more nor less; in me good sense sprouted late, but it is firmly planted. So it is very doubtful that the public will ever have occasion to read a single line written by me; if this happens it will not be before ten years at least.

I don't know what led me to read you something, forgive that weakness. I could not resist the temptation to make you think highly of me. But I was sure of success, wasn't I? What puerility on my part! It was a sweet idea you had, that we should write a book together, it moved me, but I do not want to publish anything. That is a stand I have taken, a vow I made to myself at a solemn period in my life. I work with absolute disinterestedness and without ulterior motive or concern. I am not a nightingale, but a shrill warbler, hiding deep in the woods lest I be heard by anyone except myself. If I make an appearance, one day, it will be in full armour, but I shall never have the assurance. Already my imagination is fading, my zest is not what it was. I am bored by my own sentences, and if I keep those that I have written it is because I like to surround myself with memories, just as I never sell my old clothes. I go and look at them sometimes in the attic where I keep them, and dream of the time when they were new and of everything I did when I was wearing them.

By the way—so we'll christen the blue dress together. I'll arrive some evening about six. We'll have all night and the next day. We'll set the night ablaze! I'll be your desire, you'll be mine, and we'll gorge ourselves on each other to see whether we can be satiated. Never! No, never! Your heart is an inexhaustible spring, you let me drink deep, it floods me, penetrates me, I drown. Oh! The beauty of your face, all pale and quivering under my kisses! But how cold I was! I did nothing but look at you, I was surprised, charmed. If I had you here now... Come, I'll take another look at your slippers. They are something I'll never give up, I think I love them as much as I do you. Whoever made them, little suspected how my hands would tremble when I touch them. I breathe their perfume, they smell of verbena[15]—and of you in a way that makes my heart smell.

Adieu, my life, adieu my love, a thousand kisses everywhere. Phidias has only to write, and I will come. Next winter there will no longer be any way for us to see each other, but write and I will come to Paris for at least three weeks. Adieu, I kiss you on the place where I will kiss you, where I wanted to, I put my mouth there, I cover you with a thousand kisses. Oh! Give me some, give me some.

15 August, 1846.

How beautiful they are, the poems you send me! Their rhythm is as gentle as the caresses of your voice when you murmur my name among your other endearments. Forgive me if I think them the best you've done. It wasn't pride I felt when I saw they had been written for me, no. It was love, tenderness. Yours

---

[15] A flower.

are the seductions of a siren, fatal even to the most callous. Yes, my beautiful one, you've enwrapped me in your charm, infused me with your very self. Oh! If I have perhaps seemed cold to you, if my sarcasms are harsh and hurt you, I will cover you with love when next I see you, with caresses, with ecstasy. I want to gorge you with all the joys of the flesh, so that you faint and die. I want you to be amazed by me, and to confess to yourself that you had never even dreamed of such transports. I am the one who has been happy, now I want you to be the same. When you are old, I want you to recall those few hours. I want your dry bones to quiver with joy when you think of them. Not yet having received Phidias' letter (I await it with impatience and annoyance) I cannot be with you Sunday evening. And even if I could, we wouldn't have the night together. Besides, you'll be entertaining friends. I'd have to dress, and so should need luggage. I want to come without anything, without bundles or bags, to be freer, unencumbered...

Do you think I don't find it sweet to be able to say to myself "She is mine, mine!"? On Sunday two weeks will have passed since you knelt on the floor and gazed at me with sweetly eager eyes, I was looking at your forehead, thinking of all that lay behind it, staring at your face, with infinite wonder at the lightness and thickness of your hair.

I wouldn't like you to see me now, I am frighteningly ugly. I have an enormous boil on my right cheek, which has half closed one of my eyes and swollen the entire upper part of my face. I must look ridiculous. If you saw me thus, love might draw back, for it is alarmed at the grotesque. But don't worry, I'll be all right when we meet, just as I was, the way you love me.

Tell me whether you use the verbena. Do you put it on your handkerchiefs? Put some on your shift. But no—don't use perfume, the best perfume is yourself, your own natural fragrance. Perhaps I shall have a letter tomorrow.

Adieu, I bite your lip, is the little red spot still there?

Adieu, a thousand kisses. Perhaps on Monday I will taste the sweetness of yours again.

Yours, body and soul.

21 August, 1853.

Have you really not noticed, then, that here of all places, in this private, personal solitude that surrounds me, I have turned to you? All the memories of my youth speak to me as I walk, just as the sea shells crunch under my feet on the beach. The crash of every wave awakens far-distant reverberations within me.

I hear the rumble of bygone days, and in my mind the whole endless series of old passions surge forward like the billows. I remember my spasms, my sorrows, gusts of desire that whistled like wind in the rigging, and vast vague longings that swirled in the dark like a flock of wild gulls in a storm cloud.

On whom should I lean, if not on you? My weary mind turns for refreshment to the thought of you as a dusty traveller might sink onto a soft and grassy bank.

To George Sand

12 November, 1866.

Monday night

You are sad, poor friend and dear master; it was you of whom I thought on learning of Duveyrier's death. Since you loved him, I am sorry for you. That loss is added to others. How we keep these dead souls in our hearts. Each one of us carries within himself his necropolis.

I am entirely UNDONE since your departure; it seems to me as if I had not seen you for ten years. My one subject of conversation with my mother is you, everyone here loves you. Under what star were you born, pray, to unite in your person such diverse qualities, so numerous and so rare?

I don't know what sort of feeling I have for you, but I have a particular tenderness for you, and one I have never felt for anyone, up to now. We understood each other, didn't we, that was good.

I especially missed you last evening at ten o'clock. There was a fire at my wood-seller's. The sky was rose colour and the Seine the colour of gooseberry syrup. I worked at the engine for three hours and I came home as worn out as the Turk with the giraffe.

A newspaper in Rouen, le *Nouvelliste*, told of your visit to Rouen, so that Saturday after leaving you I met several bourgeois indignant at me for not exhibiting you. The best thing was said to me by a former sub-prefect: "Ah! if we had known that she was here... we would have... we would have..." he hunted five minutes for the word; "we would have smiled for her." That would have been very little, would it not?

To "love you more" is hard for me—but I embrace you tenderly. Your letter of this morning, so melancholy, reached the BOTTOM of my heart. We separated at the moment when many things were on the point of coming to our lips. All the doors between us two are not yet open. You inspire me with a great respect and I do not dare to question you.

Sigmund Freud

Sigmund Freud (born Sigismund Schlomo Freud, 6 May, 1856–23 September, 1939), was an Austrian neurologist who founded the psychoanalytic school of psychiatry. Freud is best known for his theories of the unconscious mind and the defence mechanism of repression, and for creating the clinical practice of psychoanalysis for treating psychopathology through dialogue between a patient, technically referred to as an "analysand", and a psychoanalyst. Freud redefined sexual desire as the primary motivational energy of human life, developed therapeutic techniques such as the use of free association, created the theory of transference in the therapeutic relationship, and interpreted dreams as sources of insight into unconscious desires. He was an early neurological researcher into cerebral palsy, and a prolific essayist, drawing on psychoanalysis to contribute to the history, interpretation and critique of culture.

Freud began his study of medicine at the University of Vienna. He took nine years to complete his studies, due to his interest in neurophysiological research. He developed his first topology of the psyche in *The Interpretation of Dreams* (1899) in which he proposed that the unconscious exists and described a method for gaining access to it. Interest in his theories began to grow, and a circle of supporters developed in the following period. However, Freud often clashed with those supporters who critiqued his theories, the most famous being Carl Jung, who had originally supported Freud's ideas. Part of the disagreement between the two was in Jung's interest and commitment to religion, which Freud saw as unscientific.

Freud married Martha Bernays (26 July, 1861–2 November, 1951) on 14 September, 1886, in Hamburg. They had met in April 1882, and got engaged the same year. Sigmund and Martha's love letters sent during the engagement years, emphasise their devotion and continued love. They had six children: Mathilde (1887–1978), Jean-Martin (1889–1967), Oliver (1891–1969), Ernst (1892–1970), Sophie (1893–1920) and Anna (1895–1982).

Vienna
19 June, 1882.

My precious, most beloved girl,

I knew it was only after you had gone that I would realise the full extent of my happiness and, alas! the degree of my loss as well. I still cannot grasp it, and if that elegant little box and that sweet picture were not lying in front of me, I would think it was all a beguiling dream and be afraid to wake up. Yet friends tell me it's true, and I myself can remember details more charming, more mysteriously enchanting than any dream phantasy could create. It must be true. Martha is mine, the sweet girl of whom everyone speaks with admiration, who despite all my resistance captivated my heart at our first meeting, the girl I feared to court and who came toward me with high-minded confidence, who strengthened the faith in my own value and gave me new hope and energy to work when I needed it most.

When you return, darling girl, I shall have conquered the shyness and awkwardness which have hitherto inhibited me in your presence.

Vienna, Sunday, 3 P.M.
9 September, 1883.

My sweetheart

Don't you ever again say that you are cold and cannot find the right words; you write such unspeakably sweet, such movingly tender letters that I could answer them only with a long kiss, holding you lovingly in my arms. I hope one day it will be nothing but a pleasant memory when I tell you how I have yearned for you and I will never quite believe it when I really have you with me. I daren't think much about it for fear that my patience to bear it till then would melt away...

20 June, 1885.

Princess, my little Princess,

Oh, how wonderful it will be! I am coming with money and staying a long time and bringing something beautiful for you and then go on to Paris and become a great scholar and then come back to Vienna with a huge, enormous halo, and then we will soon get married, and I will cure all the incurable nervous cases and through you I shall be healthy and I will go on kissing you till you are strong and gay and happy—and "if they haven't died, they are still alive today."

Johann Wolfgang von Goethe

Johann Wolfgang von Goethe (28 August, 1749–22 March, 1832) was a German writer and polymath. Goethe is considered the supreme genius of modern German literature, his works spanning the fields of poetry, drama, literature, philosophy, and science. His first major work, the epistolary novel *The Sorrows of Young Werther* (1774) made Goethe one of the first international literary celebrities. Featuring a hero driven to suicide by despair, the eponymous hero of his second novel the Bildungsroman *Wilhelm Meister's Apprenticeship (*1795–96), undergoes a journey of self-realisation. His *Faust* (1808-1832), a tragic play in two parts has been called the greatest long poem of modern European literature.

Goethe's love affairs were many, passionate and torrid and many feature in his works. In 1765, while a student at Leipzig University, he fell in love with Anna Katharina Schönkopf, the daughter of a wine-merchant at whose house he dined. In 1770 it was Friederike Brion, the daughter of an Alsatian village pastor in Sesenheim. Later that same year it was Charlotte "Lotte" Buff, who he met at a ball, but his unrequited love only served to inspire his first novel. In 1775 he became engaged to Lili Schönemann, the daughter of a wealthy Frankfort banker, but the romance faded.

Around 1774, Goethe began a close relationship with Charlotte von Stein (25 December, 1742–6 January, 1827), the wife of a Weimar official, who was older, married and already a mother of seven. Their intimate bond and deep friendship lasted for twelve years. During this time she had a strong influence on his life and work. In 1786 the relationship ended with his sudden departure to Italy without even telling her he wanted to go. Not until after 1800 did their relationship begin to normalise and even then it never became as close as before.

In July, 1788, Goethe met Johanna Christiana Sophie Vulpius "Christiane" (1 June, 1765–6 June, 1816). She soon became his lover and they lived together in Weimar. They had five children together, but only one, their first, survived to adulthood: Julius August Walter (25 December, 1789–28 October, 1830). On 13 October, 1806, Napoleon's army invaded and occupied Goethe's house. The next day, Goethe legitimised his eighteen year relationship with Christiane by marrying her in a quiet marriage service at the court chapel.

In 1822, having recovered from a near fatal illness, Goethe fell in love with Ulrike von Levetzow (4 February, 1804–13 November, 1899). She was 18 and he was 72. He was so carried away with her wit and beauty that he thought for a time of marrying her. Their last meeting in Carlsbad on 5 September, 1823, inspired him to the famous *Marienbad Elegy* which he considered one of his finest works.

To Charlotte von Stein

17 June, 1784.

My letters will have shown you how lovely I am. I don't dine at Court, I see few people, and take my walks alone, and at every beautiful spot I wish you were there.

I can't help loving you more than is good for me; I shall feel all the happier when I see you again. I am always conscious of my nearness to you, your presence never leaves me. In you I have a measure for every woman, for everyone; in your love a measure for all that is to be. Not in the sense that the rest of the world seems obscure to me, on the contrary, your love makes it clear; I see quite clearly what men are like and what they plan, wish, do and enjoy; I don't grudge them what they have, and comparing is a secret joy to me, possessing as I do such an imperishable treasure.

You in your household must feel as I often do in my affairs; we often don't notice objects simply because we don't choose to look at them, but things acquire an interest as soon as we see clearly the way they are related to each other. For we always like to join in, and the good man takes pleasure in arranging, putting in order and furthering the right and its peaceful rule...

Adieu, you whom I love a thousand times.

Nathaniel Hawthorne

Nathaniel Hawthorne (4 July, 1804–19 May, 1864) was an American novelist and short story writer. He was born in the city of Salem, Massachusetts. His ancestors include John Hathorne, a judge during the Salem Witch Trials. He entered Bowdoin College in 1821, was elected to Phi Beta Kappa in 1824, and graduated in 1825. Hawthorne anonymously published his first work, a novel entitled *Fanshawe*, in 1828. He published several short stories in various periodicals which he collected in 1837 as *Twice-Told Tales*. His most famous work, *The Scarlet Letter*, was not published until 1850. It has been said that the work represents the height of Hawthorne's literary genius. It remains relevant for its philosophical and psychological depth, and continues to be read as a classic tale on a universal theme. His other major works followed in quick succession, including: *The House of the Seven Gables* (1851), *The Blithedale Romance* (1852) and *Tanglewood Tales* (1853).

Much of Hawthorne's writing centres on New England, many works featuring moral allegories with a Puritan inspiration. His fiction works are considered part of the Romantic movement and, more specifically, dark romanticism. His themes often centre on the inherent evil and sin of humanity, and his works often have moral messages and deep psychological complexity. His published works include novels, short stories, and a biography of his friend Franklin Pierce.

In 1837, after public flirtations with local women Mary Silsbee and Elizabeth Peabody, Hawthorne began pursuing the latter's sister, illustrator and transcendentalist Sophia Amelia Peabody (21 September, 1809–26 February, 1871). They were engaged by 1839. Seeking a possible home for himself and Sophia, he joined the transcendentalist Utopian community at Brook Farm in 1841, not because he agreed with the experiment but because it helped him save money to marry Sophia. He left later that year. Hawthorne married Sophia Peabody on 9 July, 1842, at a ceremony in the Peabody parlour on West Street in Boston. The couple moved to The Old Manse in Concord, Massachusetts, later moving to Salem, the Berkshires, then to The Wayside in Concord. The Hawthornes enjoyed a long marriage, often taking walks in the park. Of his wife, whom he referred to as his "Dove", Hawthorne wrote that she "is, in the strictest sense, my sole companion; and I need no other—there is no vacancy in my mind, any more than in my heart... Thank God that I suffice for her boundless heart!" Sophia greatly admired and supported her husband's work. Nathaniel and Sophia Hawthorne had three children: Una (3 March, 1844–10 September 1877), Julian (22 June, 1846–21 July, 1934) and Rose (20 May, 1851–9 July, 1926).

Custom House, 8 August, 1839.

Your letter, my beloved wife, was duly received into your husband's heart yesterday. I found it impossible to keep it all day long, with unbroken seal, in my pocket; and so I opened and read it on board of a salt vessel, where I was at work, amid all sorts of bustle, and gabble of Irishmen, and other incommodities. Nevertheless its effect was very blessed, even as if I had gazed upward from the deck of the vessel, and beheld my wife's sweet face looking down upon me from a sun-brightened cloud. Dearest, if your dove-wings will not carry you so far, I beseech you to alight upon such a cloud sometimes, and let it bear you to me. True it is, that I never look heavenward without thinking of you, and I doubt whether it would much surprise me to catch a glimpse of you among those upper regions. Then would all that is spiritual within me so yearn towards you, that I should leave my earthly incumbrances behind, and float upward and embrace you in the heavenly sunshine. Yet methinks I shall be more content to spend a lifetime of earthly and heavenly happiness intermixed. So human am I, my beloved, that I would not give up the hope of loving and cherishing you by a fireside of our own, not for any unimaginable bliss of higher spheres. Your influence shall purify me and fit me for a better world—but it shall be by means of our happiness here below.

Was such a rhapsody as the foregoing ever written in the Custom House before?...

Oh, how happy you make me by calling me your husband—by subscribing yourself my wife. I kiss that word when I meet it in your letters; and I repeat over and over to myself, "she is my wife—I am her husband." Dearest, I could almost think that the institution of marriage was ordained, first of all, for you and me, and for you and me alone; it seems so fresh and new—so unlike anything that the people around us enjoy or are acquainted with. Nobody ever had a wife but me— nobody a husband, save my Dove. Would that the husband were worthier of his wife; but she loves him and her wise and prophetic heart could never do so if he were utterly unworthy.

Boston, 5 December, 1839—5 P.M.

Dearest wife,

I do wish that you would evince the power of your spirit over its outward manifestations, in some other way than by raising an inflammation over your eye. Do, belovedest, work another miracle forthwith, and cause this mountain—for I fancy it as of really mountainous bulk—cause it to be cast into the sea, or anywhere else; so that both eyes may greet your husband, when he comes home. Otherwise, I know not but my eyes will have an inflammation too;—they certainly smarted in a very unwonted manner, last evening. "The naughty swelling!" as my Dove (or Sophie Hawthorne) said of the swollen cheek that afflicted me last summer. Will kisses have any efficacy? No; I am afraid not, for if they were medicinal, my Dove's eyelids have been so imbued with them that no ill would have come there. Nevertheless, though not a preventive, a kiss may chance to be a remedy. Can Sophie Hawthorne be prevailed upon to let me try it?

I went to see my wife's (and of course my own) sister Mary, on Tuesday evening. She appeared very well; and we had a great deal of good talk, wherein my Dove was not utterly forgotten (now will Sophie Hawthorne, thinking the Dove slighted, pout her lip at that expression)—well then, my Dove was directly or indirectly concerned in all my thoughts, and most of my words. Mrs. Park was not there, being gone, I believe, to some lecture. Mary and your husband talked with the utmost hopefulness and faith of my Dove's future health and well-being. Dearest, you are well (all but the naughty swelling) and you always will be well. I love Mary because she loves you so much;—our affections meet in you, and so we become kindred. But everybody loves my Dove—everybody that knows her—and those that know her not love her also, though unconsciously, whenever they image to themselves something sweeter, and tenderer, and nobler, than they can meet with on earth. It is the likeness of my Dove that has haunted the dreams of poets, ever since the world began. Happy me, to whom that dream has become the reality of all realities—whose bosom has been warmed, and is forever warmed, with the close embrace of her who has flitted shadowlike away from all other mortals! Dearest, I wish your husband had the gift of making rhymes; for methinks there is poetry in his head and heart, since he has been in love with you. You are a Poem, my Dove. Of what sort, then?

Epic?—Mercy on me,—no! A sonnet?—no; for that is too labored and artificial. My Dove is a sort of sweet, simple, gay, pathetic ballad, which Nature is singing, sometimes with tears, sometimes with smiles, and sometimes with intermingled smiles and tears.

I was invited to dine at Mr. Bancroft's yesterday with Miss Margaret Fuller; but Providence had given me some business to do: for which I was very thankful. When my Dove and Sophie Hawthorne can go with me I shall not be afraid to accept invitations to meet literary lions and lionesses, because then I shall put the above-said redoubtable little personage in the front of the battle. What do you think, Dearest, of the expediency of my making a caucus speech? A great many people are very desirous of listening to your husband's eloquence; and that is considered the best method of making my debut. Now, probably, will Sophie Hawthorne utterly refuse to be kissed, unless I give up all notion of speechifying at a caucus. Silly little Sophie! I would not do it, even if thou thyself besought it of me.

Belovedest, I wish, before declining your ticket to Mr. Emerson's lectures, that I had asked whether you wished me to attend them; for if you do, I should have more pleasure in going, than if the wish were originally my own.

Dearest wife, nobody can come within the circle of my loneliness, save you;—you are my only companion in the world:—at least, when I compare other intercourse with our intimate communion, it seems as other people were the world's width asunder. And yet I love all the world better for my Dove's sake.

Good bye, belovedest. Drive away that "naughty swelling."
YOUR OWNEST HUSBAND.

Boston, 1 January, 1840. 6 o'clock P.M.

Belovedest wife,
... Belovedest, I have not yet wished you a Happy New Year! And yet I have—
many, many of them; as many, mine own wife, as we can enjoy together—and
when we can no more enjoy them together, we shall no longer think of Happy
New Years on earth, but look longingly for the New Year's Day of eternity. What
a year the last has been! Dearest, you make the same exclamation; but my heart
originates it too. It has been the year of years—the year in which the flower of
our life has bloomed out—the flower of our life and of our love, which we are to
wear in our bosoms forever. Oh, how I love you, belovedest wife!—and how I
thank God that He has made me capable to know and love you! Sometimes I feel,
deep, deep down in my heart, how dearest above all things you are to me; and
those are blissful moments. It is such a happiness to be conscious, at last, of
something real. All my life hitherto, I have been walking in a dream, among
shadows which could not be pressed to my bosom; but now, even in this dream of
time, there is something that takes me out of it, and causes me to be a dreamer no
more. Do you not feel, dearest, that we live above time and apart from time, even
while we seem to be in the midst of time? Our affection diffuses eternity round
about us...
Oh, belovedest, I want you. You have given me a new feeling, blessedest
wife—a sense, that strong as I may have deemed myself, I am insufficient for my
own support; and that there is a tender little Dove, without whose help I cannot
get through this weary world at all. God bless you, ownest wife.
YOUR OWNEST HUSBAND.

Boston, 31 March, 1840.—Evening.

Best Wife, it is scarcely dark yet; but thy husband has just lighted his lamps,
and sits down to talk to thee. Would that he could hear an answer in thine own
sweet voice; for his spirit needs to be cheered by that dearest of all harmonies,
after a long, listless, weary day. Just at this moment, it does seem as if life could
not go on without it. What is to be done?
Dearest, if Elizabeth Howe is to be with you on Saturday, it would be quite a
calamity to thee and thy household, for me to come at the same time. Now will
Sophie Hawthorne complain, and the Dove's eyes be suffused, at my supposing
that their husband's visit could be a calamity at any time. Well, at least, we
should be obliged to give up many hours of happiness, and it would not even be
certain that I could have the privilege of seeing mine own wife in private, at all.
Wherefore, considering these things, I have resolved, and do hereby make it a
decree of fate, that my present widowhood shall continue one week longer. And
my sweetest Dove—yes, and naughtiest Sophie Hawthorne too—will both concur
in the fitness of this resolution, and will help me to execute it with what of
resignation is attainable by mortal man, by writing me a letter full of strength and
comfort. And I, infinitely dear wife, will write to thee again; so that, though my

earthly part will not be with thee on Saturday, yet thou shalt have my heart and soul in a letter. Will not this be right, and for the best? "Yes, dearest husband," saith my meekest little Dove; and Sophie Hawthorne cannot gainsay her.

Mine unspeakably ownest, dost thou love me a million of times as much as thou didst a week ago?

As for me, my heart grows deeper and wider every moment, and still thou fillest it in all its depths and boundlessness. Wilt thou never be satisfied with making me love thee? To what use canst thou put so much love as thou continually receivest from me? Dost thou hoard it up, as misers do their treasure?

THINE OWN BLESSEDEST HUSBAND.

Custom-House, 6 April, 1840. 5 P.M.

... Hearts never do understand the mystery of separation—that is the business of the head. My sweetest, dearest, purest, holiest, noblest, faithfullest wife, dost thou know what a loving husband thou hast? Dost thou love him most immensely?—beyond conception, and dost thou feel, as he does, that every new throb of love is worth all other happiness in the world?

Dearest, my soul drank thy letter this forenoon, and has been conscious of it ever since, in the midst of business and noise and all sorts of wearisome babble. How dreamlike it makes all my external life, this continual thought and deepest, inmostest musing upon thee! I live only within myself; for thou art always there. Thou makest me a disembodied spirit; and with the eye of a spirit, I look on all worldly things and this it is that separates thy husband from those who seem to be his fellows—therefore is he "among them, but not of them." Thou art transfused into his heart, and spread all round about it; and it is only once in a while that he himself is even imperfectly conscious of what a miracle has been wrought upon him...

Never did I know what love was before—I did not even know it when I began this letter. Ah, but I ought not to say that; it would make me sad to believe that I had not always loved thee. Farewell, now, dearest. Be quiet, my Dove; lest my heart be made to flutter by the fluttering of thy wings.

Salem, 5 July, 1848.

Unspeakably Belovedest,
—Thy letter has just been handed to me. It was most comfortable to me, because it gives such a picture of thy life with the children. I could see the whole family of my heart before my eyes, and could hear you all talking together...

The other night, I dreamt that I was at Newton, in a room with thee and with several other people and thou tookst occasion to announce that thou hadst now ceased to be my wife, and hadst taken another husband. Thou madest this intelligence known with such perfect composure and sang-froid,—not particularly addressing me, but the company generally,—that it benumbed my thoughts and feelings, so that I had nothing to say. But, hereupon, some woman who was there present, informed the company that, in this state of affairs, having ceased to be thy husband, I had become hers, and, turning to me, very coolly inquired whether she or I should write to inform my mother of the new arrangement! How the children were to be divided, I know not. I only know that my heart suddenly broke loose, and I began to expostulate with thee in an infinite agony, in the midst of which I awoke. But the sense of unspeakable injury and outrage hung about me for a long time, and even yet it has not quite departed. Thou shouldst not behave so when thou comest to me in dreams.

Oh, Phoebe, I want thee much. Thou art the only person in the world that ever was necessary to me. Other people have occasionally been more or less agreeable; but I think I was always more at ease alone than in anybody's company, till I knew thee. And now I am only myself when thou art within my reach. Thou art an unspeakably beloved woman. How couldst thou inflict such frozen agony upon me in that dream?

If I write any more, it would only be to express more lovings and longings; and as they are impossible to express, I may as well close.

THY HUSBAND.

William Hazlitt

William Hazlitt (10 April, 1778–18 September, 1830) was an English writer, remembered for his humanistic essays and literary criticism, and as a grammarian and philosopher. He is considered to be one of the great critics and essayists of the English language, placed in the company of Samuel Johnson and George Orwell. He was also an accomplished painter, journalist and lecturer. His first book, *An Essay on the Principles of Human Action* (1805), began his career as an essayist, leading to his masterpiece, *The Spirit of the Age* (1825). Other books include *Characters of Shakespeare's Plays* (1817), *The Round Table* (1817), *Political Essays* (1819), *Table-Talk* (1822), *Liber Amoris* (1823) and *The Life of Napoleon Bonaparte* (four volumes, 1828–1830). During his lifetime he befriended many well-known people of the 19th-century, including Charles and Mary Lamb, Stendhal, Samuel Taylor Coleridge and William Wordsworth.

In Hazlitt's youth he was tormented by sexual desires, and sought the company of prostitutes and 'loose women' of lower social and economic strata. In 1808, he married Sarah Stoddart (c.1775–unknown), a friend of Mary Lamb's. At first the union seemed to work well enough. Sarah was an unconventional woman who was accepted by one as unconventional in his ways as Hazlitt, and would in turn tolerate his eccentricities. They made an agreeable social foursome with the Lambs, who visited them when they set up a household in Winterslow, a village a few miles from Salisbury, Wiltshire. The couple had three sons over the next few years, but only one who survived infancy: William (26 September, 1811–23 February, 1893).

After a few years Hazlitt grew resigned to the lack of love between him and Sarah. He had been visiting prostitutes and displayed more idealised amorous inclinations toward a number of women. In 1819 he was unable to pay the rent and the family were evicted. That was the last straw for his wife, who took their son and broke with Hazlitt for good. In August, 1820, he rented rooms from a tailor named Micaiah Walker. Immediately, Hazlitt became infatuated with Walker's 19-year-old daughter Sarah, though she was more than 22 years his junior. Sarah Walker was, as some of Hazlitt's friends could see, a fairly ordinary girl who had aspirations to better herself. When another lodger named Tomkins came along, she entered into a romantic entanglement with him as well, leading each of her suitors to believe he was the sole object of her affection. Hazlitt discovered the truth about Tomkins, and from then on his jealousy and suspicions of Sarah Walker's real character afforded him little rest. He dreamed of marrying her, but that would require a divorce from his wife. The divorce was finalised in Scotland on 17 July, 1822, and Hazlitt returned to London to see his beloved—only to find her cold and resistant. It was over, though Hazlitt could not for some time persuade himself to believe so.

In 1823, Hazlitt met Isabella *née* Shaw Bridgwater, who married him in March or April 1824. Little is known about this Scottish-born widow of a planter in the West Indies, or about her interaction with Hazlitt, but the union afforded the two of them the opportunity to travel. First, they toured parts of Scotland, then, later in 1824, began a European tour lasting over a year.

To Sarah Walker

February, 1822.

You will scold me for this, and ask me if this is keeping my promise to mind my work. One half of it was to think of Sarah; and besides, I do not neglect my work either, I assure you. I regularly do ten pages a day, which mounts up to thirty guineas' worth a week, so that you see I should grow rich at this rate, if I could keep on so; and I could keep on so, if I had you with me to encourage me with your sweet smiles, and share my lot. The Berwick smacks sail twice a week, and the wind sits fair. When I think of the thousand endearing caresses that have passed between us, I do not wonder at the strong attachment that draws me to you; but I am sorry for my own want of power to please. I hear the wind sigh through the lattice, and keep repeating over and over to myself two lines of Lord Byron's Tragedy—

So shalt thou find me ever at thy side
Here and hereafter, if the last may be.

—applying them to thee, my love, and thinking whether I shall ever see thee again. Perhaps not—for some years at least—till both thou and I are old—and then, when all else have forsaken thee, I will creep to thee, and die in thine arms.

You once made me believe I was not hated by her I loved; and for that sensation, so delicious was it, though but a mockery and a dream, I owe you more than I can ever pay. I thought to have dried up my tears for ever, the day I left you; but as I write this, they stream again. If they did not, I think my heart would burst. I walk out here of an afternoon, and hear the notes of the thrush, that come up from a sheltered valley below, welcome in the spring; but they do not melt my heart as they used; it is grown cold and dead. As you say, it will one day be colder. Forgive what I have written above; I did not intend it; but you were once my little all, and I cannot bear the thought of having lost you for ever, I fear through my own fault. Has anyone called? Do not send any letters that come. I should like you and your mother (if agreeable) to go and see Mr. Kean in Othello, and Miss Stephens in Love in a Village. If you will, I will write to Mr. T—, to send you tickets. Has Mr. P— called? I think I must send to him for the picture to kiss and talk to. Kiss me, my best beloved. Ah! if you can never be mine, still let me be your proud and happy slave.

H.

Prince Henry, Duke of Cumberland and Strathearn

Prince Henry, Duke of Cumberland and Strathearn (born Henry Frederick, 7 November, 1745–18 September, 1790) was the sixth child of Frederick, Prince of Wales (son of George II) and Princess Augusta of Saxe-Gotha. He was a younger brother of George III. In 1768, at the fairly late age of 22, the Duke entered the Royal Navy as a midshipman and was sent to Corsica in HMS Venus. However, he returned in September when the ship was recalled following the French invasion of the Corsican Republic. He was promoted to Rear-Admiral the following year and Vice-Admiral in 1770. In 1775, the Duke established the Cumberland Fleet, which would later become the Royal Thames Yacht Club. He was promoted Admiral in 1778, though was forbidden from assuming any command.

On 4 March, 1767, the Duke of Cumberland allegedly married Olive Wilmot (later Mrs Payne), a commoner, in a secret ceremony. There reportedly was one child, Olivia Wilmot (3 April, 1772–21 November, 1834), from this relationship, though the Duke's paternity was never proven, and Olivia was accused of forging the evidence. A landscape painter and novelist, Olivia Wilmot later, controversially, assumed the style of Princess Olivia of Cumberland.

Henrietta Vernon, Lady Grosvenor (c.1740–2 January, 1828) was his lover for some time in the late 1760s. In 1769, the Duke of Cumberland was sued by Lord Grosvenor for "criminal conversation" (that is, adultery), after his wife and the Duke were discovered *in flagrante delicto* (caught in the act). Lord Grosvenor was awarded damages, but was also known to be guilty of adultery himself, so he could not sue for divorce. The couple separated and he settled an annual allowance on his estranged wife.

The Duke's marriage to the commoner Anne Horton (or Houghton) *née* Luttrell (24 January, 1742–28 December, 1808) on 2 October, 1771, caused a rift with King George III, the Duke's brother, and was the catalyst for the Royal Marriages Act of 1772, which forbids any descendant of George II to marry without the monarch's permission. There were no children from this marriage.

To Lady Grosvenor

My dear little Angel,

I wrote my last letter to you yesterday at eleven o'clock just when we sailed. I dined at two o'clock and as for the afternoon I had some music. I have my own servant a-board that plays... and so got to bed about 10—I then prayed for you my dearest love kissed your dearest little hair and lay down and dreamt of you had you on the dear little couch ten thousand times in my arms kissing you and telling you how much I loved and adored you and you seemed pleased but alas when I woke I found it all dillusion nobody by me but myself at sea...

When I shall return to you that instant Oh my love mad and happy beyond myself to tell you how I love you and have thought of you ever since I have been separated from you... I hope you are well I am sure I need not tell you I have had nothing in my thoughts but your dearself and long for the time to come back again to you I will all the while take care of myself because you desire my dear little friend does the angel of my heart pray do you take care of your dearself for the sake of your faithful servant who lives but to love you to adore you, and to bless the moment that has made you generous enough to own it to him I hope my dear nay I will dare to say you never will have reason to repent it...

Indeed my dear angel I need not tell you I know you read the reason too well that made me do so it was to write to you for God knows I wrote to no one else nor shall I at any other but to the King God bless you most amiable and dearest little creature living...

God bless you till I shall again have an opportunity of sending to you, I shall write to you a letter a day as many days as you miss herein of me when I do they shall all come Friday 16th June God bless I shant forget you God knows you have told me so before I have your heart and it lies warm at my breast I hope mine feels as easy to you thou joy of my life adieu.

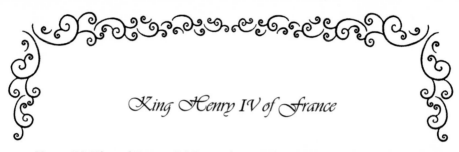

King Henry IV of France

Henry IV, King of France (13 December, 1553–14 May, 1610) was born Henri de Bourbon, the son of Queen Jeanne III and King Antoine of Navarre. Henry was nicknamed Henri le Grand (Henry the Great), and in France is also called le bon roi Henri (the good king Henry) or le vert galant (the green/young gallant), a reference to both his dashing character and his attractiveness to women. As a Huguenot, Henry was involved in the Wars of Religion before ascending the throne in 1589. Before his coronation as King of France at Chartres, he changed his faith from Calvinism to Catholicism and enacted the Edict of Nantes, which guaranteed religious liberties to the Protestants, thereby effectively ending the civil war. One of the most popular French kings, both during and after his reign, Henry showed great care for the welfare of his subjects and displayed an unusual religious tolerance for the time. He brought a high degree of unity to a country divided by religious differences. King of Navarre from 1572 and King of France from 1589, he was a skilled negotiator and a brilliant soldier in the field.

It had been arranged before his mother's death (in 1572), that Henry would marry Marguerite de Valois (14 May, 1553–27 March, 1615), daughter of Henry II and Catherine de' Medici. The wedding took place in Paris on 19 August, 1572, on the parvis of Notre Dame Cathedral. On 24 August, the Saint Bartholomew's Day Massacre began in Paris and several thousand Protestants who had come to Paris for Henry's wedding were killed, as well as thousands more throughout the country in the days that followed. Henry narrowly escaped death thanks to the help of his wife and was forced to convert to Catholicism. He was made to live at the court of France, but escaped in early 1576; on 5 February of that year, he renounced Catholicism at Tours and rejoined the Protestant forces in the military conflict.

In 1591 Henry gained a mistress, the great love of his life, Gabrielle d'Estrées (c.1573–10 April, 1599). Although he was still married, Henry and Gabrielle were openly affectionate with each other in public. Fiercely loyal, Gabrielle accompanied Henry during his campaigns. Even when heavily pregnant, she insisted on living inside his tent near the battlefield, making sure his clothing was clean and that he ate well after a battle, handling the day to day correspondence while he fought. As she was an intelligent and practical woman, Henry confided his secrets to her and followed her advice. When the two were apart, they wrote each other frequent letters.

In 1594, their first child was born, a son, César de Bourbon (3 June, 1594–22 October, 1665). On 4 January, 1595, Henry IV officially recognised and legitimised his son in a text validated by the Parlement de Paris. In that text, he also recognised Gabrielle d'Estrées as the mother of his son; in other words, he officially ratified Gabrielle's position as his mistress. He later recognised and legitimised two more children he had with Gabrielle: Catherine-Henriette de Bourbon, a daughter born in 1596, and Alexandre de Bourbon, a son born in 1598.

After applying to Pope Clement VIII for an annulment of his marriage and authority to remarry, in March of 1599 Henry gave his mistress his coronation ring. On 9 April, Gabrielle suffered an attack of eclampsia and gave birth to a stillborn son. King Henry was at the Château de Fontainebleau when news arrived of her illness. The next day, 10 April, 1599, while Henry was on his way to her, she died. The King was grief-stricken. He wore black in mourning, something no previous French monarch had done before, and he gave her the funeral of a Queen. However, still without a legitimate heir, he married Marie de Médici (26 April, 1575–3 July, 1642) in 1600. They had six children in ten years, before he was assassinated in Paris on 14 May, 1610, by a Catholic fanatic.

To Gabrielle d'Estrées from the battle field before Dreux

16 June, 1593.

I have waited patiently for one whole day without news of you; I have been counting the time and that's what it must be. But a second day—I can see no reason for it, unless my servants have grown lazy or been captured by the enemy, for I dare not put the blame on you, my beautiful angel: I am too confident of your affection—which is certainly due to me, for my love was never greater, nor my desire more urgent; that is why I repeat this refrain in all my letters: come, come, come, my dear love.

Honour with your presence the man who, if only he were free, would go a thousand miles to throw himself at your feet and never move from there. As for what is happening here, we have drained the water from the moat, but our cannons are not going to be in place until Friday when, God willing, I will dine in town.

The day after you reach Mantes, my sister will arrive at Anet, where I will have the pleasure of seeing you every day. I am sending you a bouquet of orange blossom that I have just received. I kiss the hands of the Vicomtess[16] if she is there, and of my good friend,[17] and as for you, my dear love, I kiss your feet a million times.

---

[16] Gabrielle's sister, Françoise.
[17] His sister, Catherine of Bourbon.

King Henry VIII of England

Henry VIII (28 June, 1491–28 January, 1547) was King of England from 21 April, 1509, until his death. He was Lord of Ireland (later King of Ireland) and claimant to the Kingdom of France. He was the second monarch of the House of Tudor, succeeding his father, Henry VII.

Henry was an attractive and charismatic man in his prime, educated and accomplished. He was an author and a composer. He ruled with absolute power. His desire to provide England with a male heir—which stemmed partly from personal vanity and partly because he believed a daughter would be unable to consolidate the Tudor Dynasty and the fragile peace that existed following the Wars of the Roses—led to the two things that Henry is best remembered for today: his six wives, and the English Reformation that made England a mostly Protestant nation. In later life he became morbidly obese and his health suffered; his public image is frequently depicted as one of a lustful, egotistical, harsh and insecure King.

Catherine of Aragon (16 December, 1485–7 January, 1536) was Henry's first wife, previously the wife of his brother Arthur who died a few months into the marriage. They wed on 11 June, 1509. She had several pregnancies, but suffered miscarriages, premature births, stillborns and a son who died at 52 days old. Their only surviving child, the future Mary I, was born on 18 February, 1516. During their marriage Henry took several mistresses. One, Elizabeth Blount (c.1500–c.1539), bore him a son, Henry FitzRoy (15 June, 1519–23 July, 1536). FitzRoy was the only illegitimate offspring whom Henry acknowledged.

Anne Boleyn (19 April, 1501–19 May, 1536) had initially resisted the King's attempts to seduce her in 1526, refusing to become his mistress, as her sister, Mary Boleyn, had done. At the time a Roman Catholic, Henry sought the Pope's approval for an annulment of his marriage to Catherine on the grounds that the marriage was invalid. Despite the Pope's refusal, Henry separated from Catherine in 1531 and on 23 May, 1533, the marriage was ruled null and void. This led to a break from the Roman Catholic Church and the later establishment of the Church of England. Henry and Anne were married in secret in early 1533 and on 28 May, 1533, she and the King were pronounced legally married. On 7 September, 1533, she gave birth to the future Elizabeth I. To Henry's displeasure, however, she failed to produce a male heir, and had several miscarriages. By March, 1536, Henry was courting Jane Seymour (10 October, 1508–24 October, 1537). By April he had Anne investigated for high treason. On 2 May, she was arrested and sent to the Tower of London, where she was tried and found guilty on 15 May. She was beheaded four days later. Henry and Jane married on 30 May, 1536. She gave him his only male heir, the future Edward VI, born 12 October, 1537. She died of postnatal complications less than two weeks later.

Anne of Cleves (15 September, 1515–16 July, 1557) became Henry's fourth wife, for only six months in 1540, from 6 January to 9 July. The marriage was annulled, and allegedly unconsummated.

Catherine Howard (c.1521–13 February, 1542) was Henry's fifth wife. They were married on 28 July, 1540. She however conducted an indiscreet affair with a courtier, which Henry was informed of on 1 November, 1541. She was imprisoned and beheaded in 1542.

Catherine Parr (11 November, 1512–7 September, 1548), was the sixth and last wife of Henry VIII. They married 12 July, 1543, and she remained with him until his death.

To Anne Boleyn

c.1527

My mistress and friend, my heart and I surrender ourselves into your hands, beseeching you to hold us commended to your favour, and that by absence your affection to us may not be lessened: for it were a great pity to increase our pain, of which absence produces enough and more than I could ever have thought could be felt, reminding us of a point in astronomy which is this: the longer the days are, the more distant is the sun, and nevertheless the hotter; so is it with our love, for by absence we are kept a distance from one another, and yet it retains its fervour, at least on my side; I hope the like on yours, assuring you that on my part the pain of absence is already too great for me; and when I think of the increase of that which I am forced to suffer, it would be almost intolerable, but for the firm hope I have of your unchangeable affection for me: and to remind you of this sometimes, and seeing that I cannot be personally present with you, I now send you the nearest thing I can to that, namely, my picture set in a bracelet, with the whole of the device, which you already know, wishing myself in their place, if it should please you. This is from the hand of your loyal servant and friend,
H. R.

c.1528

In debating with myself the contents of your letters I have been put to a great agony; not knowing how to understand them, whether to my disadvantage as shown in some places, or to my advantage as in others.

I beseech you now with all my heart definitely to let me know your whole mind as to the love between us; for necessity compels me to plague you for a reply, having been for more than a year now struck by the dart of love, and being uncertain either of failure or of finding a place in your heart and affection, which point has certainly kept me for some time from naming you my mistress, since if you only love me with an ordinary love the name is not appropriate to you, seeing that it stands for an uncommon position very remote from the ordinary; but if it pleases you to do the duty of a true, loyal mistress and friend, and to give yourself body and heart to me, who have been, and will be, your very loyal servant (if your rigour does not forbid me), I promise you that not only the name will be due to you, but also to take you as my sole mistress, casting off all others than yourself out of mind and affection, and to serve you only; begging you to make me a complete reply to this my rude letter as to how far and in what I can trust; and if it does not please you to reply in writing, to let me know of some place where I can have it by word of mouth, the which place I will seek out with all my heart. No more for fear of wearying you.

Written by the hand of him who would willingly remain yours,
H. R.

Victor Hugo

Victor-Marie Hugo (26 February, 1802–22 May, 1885) was a French poet, playwright, novelist, essayist, visual artist, statesman, human rights activist and exponent of the Romantic movement in France. Though a committed royalist when he was young, Hugo's views changed as the decades passed; he became a passionate supporter of republicanism, and his work touches upon most of the political and social issues and artistic trends of his time. In France, Hugo's literary fame comes first from his poetry but also rests upon his novels and his dramatic achievements. Among many volumes of poetry, *Les Contemplations* (1841–1855) and *La Légende des Siècles* (*The Legend of the Ages*, 1855–1876) stand particularly high in critical esteem, and Hugo is sometimes identified as the greatest French poet. Outside France, his best-known works are the novels *Notre-Dame de Paris* (also known in English as *The Hunchback of Notre-Dame*, 1831) and *Les Misérables* (1862).

Young Victor fell in love and against his mother's wishes, became secretly engaged to his childhood friend Adèle Foucher (1803–1868). They married in 1822, only after his mother's death in 1821. They had their first child Léopold in 1823, but the boy died in infancy. Hugo's other children were Léopoldine (28 August, 1824–4 September, 1843), Charles (4 November, 1826–13 March, 1871), François-Victor (28 October, 1828–26 December, 1873) and Adèle (24 August, 1830–21 April, 1915). All but one died before him.

His wife conducted an affair not longer after their marriage, and Hugo also had several. His most lasting was with Juliette Drouet (born Julienne Josephine Gauvain, 10 April, 1806–11 May, 1883). A talented actress, she abandoned her theatrical career to dedicate her life to her lover. She became Hugo's secretary and travelling companion. For many years she lived a cloistered life, leaving home only in his company. In 1852, she accompanied him in his exile on Jersey, and then in 1855 on Guernsey. She wrote thousands of letters to him throughout her life, which testify to her writing talent.

Hugo was devastated when his oldest and favourite daughter, Léopoldine, died at age 19 in 1843, shortly after her marriage. She was drowned in the Seine, pulled down by her heavy skirts, when a boat overturned. Her young husband died trying to save her. Hugo was travelling with his mistress at the time in the south of France, and learned about Léopoldine's death from a newspaper as he sat in a cafe.

In the 1870s, Hugo suffered a mild stroke, his daughter Adèle's internment in an insane asylum, and the death of his two sons. His wife Adèle had died in 1868. His faithful mistress, Juliette, died in 1883, only two years before his own death.

To Adèle Foucher

Saturday Evening, January, 1820.

 A few words from you, my beloved Adèle, have again changed my state of mind. Yes, you can do anything with me; and to-morrow, were I even dead, the sweet tones of your voice, the tender pressure of your lips, would call me back to life again. How differently I shall feel as I go to sleep to-night from what I did last evening! Yesterday, Adèle, all confidence in the future had abandoned me; I no longer believed that you loved me; yesterday the hour of my death would have been welcome to me. And yet I said to myself: "If it is quite true she does not love me, and nothing in me has deserved her love, that love without which there is no charm left for me in life, is that any reason I should die? Is it for my own personal happiness that I exist? Oh no! My whole existence is devoted to her, shall be hers in spite of herself. And by what right have I aspired to win her love? Am I more than an angel or a deity? I love her, it is true—I—even I! I am ready for her sake to sacrifice everything with joy—even the hope that she may love me; there is no limit to the devotion for her that I am capable of; for one of her looks, for one of her smiles. But could I do otherwise? Is she not the one supreme object in my life? If she shows me indifference, if she even hates me, it will be my misfortune— that is all. What matter can it be, since it does not impair her happiness? Oh! yes; if she cannot love me, I must only blame myself. My duty is to wait upon her steps, to envelop her existence with my own, to be her defence against all perils, to offer her my head to set her foot on, even to place myself between her and every sorrow, without making any claim for myself—without expecting any reward. Too happy if from time to time she deigns to bend upon her slave a look of pity, and, Oh! if only she remembers me, and turns to me in a moment of danger! Alas! would she but permit me to give my life that all her desires might be accomplished, all her caprices attained! Would she but permit me to kiss with devotion and respect her very footsteps; would she but consent to lean upon me sometimes in life's difficult places—then I should have obtained the only happiness to which I have the presumption to aspire. Because I am ready to give everything up for her sake, is that any reason she should owe me any gratitude? Is it her fault that I love her? Must she fancy herself constrained because of that to love me? No! she may make what use she pleases of my devotion, she may pay me with hatred for my services, she may scorn my idolatry, she may treat me with contempt, but I shall have no right whatever to complain of such an angel, nor to cease for a moment to lavish on her the care that she disdains. And when each one of my days shall have been marked by some sacrifice made for her sake, on the day of my death I shall not have paid all the infinite debt that my existence owes to hers."

 Such were my thoughts at this time yesterday, Adèle, my much beloved, and such were the resolutions of my soul. They are the same to-day. Only now I have the certainty of happiness, of a happiness so great that I cannot think of it without trembling, and hardly believe it, even now.

Then is it true you love me, Adèle? Tell me, may I put faith in that most ravishing idea? Does it not strike you that I might become mad with joy if I could pass my whole life at your feet, sure of making you as happy as I should be myself; sure of being adored by you, even as I adore you? Oh! your letter has given me back peace; your words this evening filled me with happiness. Receive my thanks a thousand times; Adèle, my beloved angel, I should like to kneel before you as I would before a divinity. How happy you have made me! Adieu, adieu! I shall have a happy night dreaming of you.

Sleep sweetly, and let your husband take the twelve dear kisses that you promised him, and many more for which you have not yet given him permission.

28 March, 1820.

You ask me for a few words, Adèle, but what can I tell you that I have not told you a thousand and a thousand times? Shall I say over again how much I love you? But expressions fail me... To tell you that I love you better than my life would be a small matter, for you know I care very little for life. Well, I must!... for I must... I forbid you, do you hear? to say anything more to me about my "contempt" my "want of esteem." for you. You will make me seriously angry if you force me to repeat that I could not love you if I did not esteem you. And from what, if you please, could my want of esteem for you arise? If one or other of us is guilty, it assuredly is not my Adèle. But I am afraid you will despise me, because I hope you know the purity of my love for you. I am your husband, or, at least, I consider myself as such. You only can make me give up that name...

Do you know that one thought makes three-quarters of my happiness? I dream that, in spite of all obstacles, I may be permitted yet to be your husband, even though it be only for one day. Suppose we were married to-morrow, and I were to kill myself the next day, I should have been happy for one day, and no one would have any reason to reproach you. You would be my widow. Would it not be possible, my Adèle, under certain circumstances, to arrange matters thus? One day of happiness is worth more than a life of sorrow.

Listen, think of me, my love, for I think of nothing but you. You owe me that. I am trying to become a better man that I may be more worthy of you. If you only knew how much I love you!... Everything I do is somehow connected with you. I am working solely for my wife, my beloved Adèle. Love me a little in return.

One word more. Now that you are the daughter of General Hugo, do nothing unworthy of that station, suffer no one to fail in proper attention and respect to you. Mamma is very particular about such things, and I think my most excellent mother is right. You will fancy I have suddenly grown proud of my social rank, just as you thought I was proud of what people call my success; and yet, my Adèle, God knows that there is only one thing that could make me proud, and that is to be loved by you.

Adieu. You still owe me eight kisses, and I fear you will forever refuse to pay them.

Adieu; all yours and yours alone.

Saturday, 20 October, 1821.

Behold me, alone in this melancholy apartment, counting the hours that divide the morning from the evening. What am I going to write to you? My heart is full, but my mind is blank. My desire is to speak only of yourself, of our love, of our hopes, or of our fears; and did I do this, words would fail me in which to express my thoughts. But it is necessary for us to discuss trivialities, importunate nothings, which are a source of annoyance to you, and for that reason are odious to me. I must make it plain to you that all this gossip is as worthless as the idle moments that it occupies. I must reassure you and console you in regard to trifles which ought not to occasion you either uneasiness or alarm.

What can I say to you seriously, my Adèle? That I am resolved to marry you? Ah, well, are you ashamed of that, or are you in doubt about it? Perhaps you are afraid to own that you love me? If this is so, it is because you do not love me. When one really loves, one is proud of loving.

Do not misunderstand the intention of these words, dear love; I do not intend them to convey the idea that you ought to be proud of the object of your affection—that is an honour which I am far indeed from meriting—but you should be proud of possessing a soul capable of experiencing love, that elevated, noble, and chaste passion. Of all the passions which torment men in life, it is the only one that is eternal. Love in its true and divine conception creates in the being who experiences it all good qualities, as it does in thee; or else it creates in him the desire to possess them, as in myself. A love such as I feel for you, my Adèle, raises every sentiment above the miserable sphere of humanity. It is a union with an angel who draws us steadily upward towards heaven. These expressions would, perhaps, strike an ordinary woman as extravagant; but you are created to understand them, since it is you yourself who inspire them.

We seem to have travelled far from the absurd gossip which was the subject of our discussion. If we were not pledged to each other, Adèle, I would put an end to it by my own withdrawal. It would be the only means of closing people's mouths, and even so it might not be successful. In our case, it is for you to determine whether such a step is necessary; if you decide in favour of it, I will come less often, or I will cease to come altogether, until my fate shall be decided. Your decision in favour of this arrangement will afford me convincing proof that I alone shall suffer in consequence of it, and I will resign myself to do so until such time as the suffering shall cease. I have already told you that only two great events have any place in my future: one is happiness, the other is neither happiness nor misery. In either case, I shall no longer suffer.

These are serious and solemn thoughts upon which I often reflect, but which I make the subject of our conversation with reluctance, because they are only ideas, and ideas, so long as they are not put into action, are a more or less sonorous assemblage of words. Some day my last, most exquisite hope, that of being yours, will either vanish or be fulfilled; in either case you will read these lines again, and you will then be able to judge whether I have spoken truly or falsely. It is in this conviction that I write them.

I see that I am digressing at each moment from the subject of your letter. I am grateful to you, my Adèle, for communicating to me the distress occasioned you by unkind reports repeated with no less malice than foolishness. They only serve to show me more plainly that if you think it right for me to continue to see you, I must use my utmost efforts to hasten the longed-for day of our marriage.

This would in itself be enough to supply a stimulus to exertion, even if my own impatience was not far more than sufficient. Alas! is it possible to desire this happiness more ardently than I do?

If it is within my power to hasten the longed-for moment by abstaining from all unworthy action, I shall have a strong motive for restraint. There are moments, my Adèle, when I feel myself capable of stooping to anything which would enable me to reach this wished-for end more quickly; and then I recover myself, shocked at my own thoughts, and I ask myself whether I should indeed really attain my goal if I reached it by a road unworthy of my better self. Dear love, the position of a young man, independent by his principles, his affections, and his desires, who is nevertheless dependent upon others by reason of his age and of his lack of fortune, is a cruel one. Yes, if I come out of this experience as pure as I entered into it, I shall feel that I am entitled to some measure of self-esteem.

There are many annoyances that I am forced to disregard, for I am obliged to work in spite of continual agitation. Those persons are greatly mistaken who think that among my aims there is a wish for glory, for celebrity or for any of the trivialities with which it is possible to fill a life that is empty of love.

Consider all my words, Adèle, for you will find in them an overpowering affection; and if you love me in return, you will find in them also a source of gladness. I sometimes envy you, in that you are beloved as you are by me. As for you, you love me VERY MUCH, and that is all.

For what reason can your parents be opposed to our intercourse, when they intend, as they have done hitherto, that their daughter shall be my wife? I am aware that they would prefer to have my father's consent; in many respects they are right in this matter, and I will do everything to satisfy them. It certainly will not be I, the most impatient of men, who will preach patience. All my life was settled at Dreux. Some day I will give you an account of that journey to Dreux. You will see then how I have always loved you, even when I believed myself forgotten.

Adieu, dearest love; I embrace thee tenderly.
Victor.

This letter is very grave, my own Adèle, and, therefore, I add one line to tell you, and to repeat to you, how much I love you.

The Same Night.

This letter is very important, Adèle; for the impression that it makes upon you will decide all our happiness. I am about to make an effort to collect some calm ideas, and I shall have no difficulty in contending with sleep to-night. I am going to have a serious and intimate conversation with you, and I wish earnestly that it could be face to face, for then I could at once receive your answer (which I shall expect with the utmost impatience), and I should be able to observe in your countenance the effect that my words may produce upon you—that effect which will decide the happiness of us both.

There is one word, Adèle, which we seem, up to the present moment, to be afraid to pronounce. It is the word love; and yet the feeling that I experience for you is undoubtedly genuine love. It is of importance now to ascertain whether the sentiment that animates you is likewise love.

Listen! There is within us an immaterial being, in exile, as it were, within our bodies, which will survive to all eternity. This being, which is the essence of all in us that is best and purest, is the soul.

It is the soul that is the source of all enthusiasm and all affection, and upon it depend our conceptions of God and of heaven.

I am treating of matters beyond our knowledge, because it is necessary to do so in order to make myself fully understood; but, lest this talk should strike you as unusual, let us speak of things which require only simple but elevated language. To continue. The soul, being superior to the body, with which it is united, would remain on earth in an unbearable isolation, were it not that it is permitted to choose among other human souls a companion with whom it may share the misfortunes of life and the happiness of eternity. When two souls, which for a longer or a shorter time have sought each other amidst the crowd, at length find each other; when they perceive that they belong to each other; when, in short, they comprehend their affinity, then there is established between them a union, pure and ardent as themselves, a union begun upon earth in order that it may be completed in heaven. This union is love; real and perfect love, such love as very few men can adequately conceive; love which is a religion, adoring the being beloved as a divinity; love that lives in devotion and ardour, and for which to make great sacrifices is the purest pleasure. It is such love as this that you inspire in me, and it is such love that you will some day assuredly feel for me, even though, to my ever-present grief, you do not do so now. Your soul is formed to love with the purity and ardour of the angels, but it may be that only an angel can inspire it with love, and when I think this I tremble.

The world, Adèle, does not understand this kind of affection, for it is the appointed lot only of those who are singled out either for happiness or misery; like yourself, in the former instance, or, in the latter, like me. Love, in the eyes of the world, is either a carnal appetite or a vague fancy, which possession extinguishes or absence destroys. That is why it is commonly said, with a strange abuse of words, that passion does not endure. Alas! Adèle, do you know that passion means suffering? And do you seriously believe that there is any suffering in the ordinary love of men, so violent in appearance, so feeble in reality? No; immaterial love is eternal, because that part of our being which experiences it cannot die. It is our souls that love, and not our bodies.

Notice here, however, that nothing should be pushed to an extreme. I do not intend to say that the body has no place in this, the first of our affections. A gracious God perceived that without an intimate personal union, the union of souls could never be made perfect, because two persons who love each other must spend their lives in a community of thought and action. This is, therefore, one of the ends for which God has established that attraction of one sex towards another which, in itself, shows that marriage is divine. Thus it is that in youth personal union serves to ratify the union of souls, and it is our souls, in their turn, which, being ever young and indestructible, maintain the union of persons in their old age and perpetuate it after death.

Do not be alarmed, then, Adèle, in regard to the duration of a passion which it is not within the power of God Himself to extinguish. It is this profound and enduring affection that I feel for you; it is not based on personal charms, but on moral qualities, and it is an affection that leads to heaven or to hell, and which fills life, the whole of life, with delight or with misery.

I have laid bare my soul to you; I have spoken a language that I speak only to those who can understand it. Inquire of yourself, in your turn; ascertain if love expresses for you what it does for me; find out whether your soul is really a sister soul to mine. Do not pause to consider what is said by a foolish world, or what is thought by the little minds that surround you; search your own heart, and listen to its voice. If the thoughts expressed in this letter are real to you, if the affection that you entertain for me is indeed of the same nature as that which I feel for you, my Adèle, then, indeed, I am thine for life, thine for eternity. If you fail to understand my love, if I seem to you extravagant, then adieu. Nothing but death will be left to me, and death will have no terrors when I have no longer any hope upon earth. Do not imagine, however, that I should take my own life without regard to others; so long as there are the stricken to heal, and sacred combats to sustain, suicide is the act of an egoist and a coward. I shall take care that the sacrifice of my life shall be as useful to others as it will be sweet to myself.

These thoughts, perhaps, seem to you a little gloomy, addressed as they are to one for whom my lips have always worn a smile, to one who does not know the tenor of my habitual reflections.

Adèle, I tremble in saying so, but I believe that you do not love me with such love as I offer you, and only a love such as that can satisfy me. If you loved me thus, could you keep asking me, as you do, if I have confidence in your conduct? You do this so lightly that it seems to me to indicate indifference.

Yet you are offended at the most natural questions, and you ask me whether I am under any apprehension that your conduct is blamable. If you loved me as I love you, Adèle, you would understand that there are a thousand things that may be done without criminality, even without real error, which, nevertheless, are of a nature to alarm the sensitive jealousy of my affection. Such love as I have described to you is exclusive. I myself wish for nothing, not even a glance, from any other woman in the world; but I desire that no man should dare to claim anything from the woman who is mine. If I desire her alone, it is because I wish for her wholly and entirely. A glance, a smile, a kiss from you are my greatest happiness; do you really believe that I can patiently endure to see them bestowed on some one else as well? Does this sensitiveness alarm you? If you loved me, it would delight you. Why do you not feel thus towards me?

Love is jealous, and ingenious in self-torture in proportion as it is pure and intense. I have always found it so. Some years ago, I remember, I shuddered instinctively when your little brother, who was then a mere child, chanced to pass the night with you. Age, experience, observation of the world, have only confirmed this disposition in me. It will be my undoing, Adèle, for I perceive that, while it ought to increase your happiness, it does but render you uneasy.

Speak without constraint. Make it plain whether you wish me to be such as I am or no. My future, as well as yours, depends upon this, and while my fate is nothing to me, yours is everything. Remember that, if you do not love me, there is a sure and speedy way of releasing yourself from me; you have only to agree to it. I shall not oppose you. There is one kind of absence, thanks to which we are soon forgotten by those who regard us with indifference. It is an absence from which there is no return.

One word more. If this long letter seems to you sad and depressed, do not be astonished; your own was so cold. You are of opinion that between us passion is out of place! Adèle... I read over again some old letters of yours, in the hope of consolation, but the difference between the old and the new was so great that in place of being consoled... Adieu.

Friday evening, 15 March, 1822.

After the two delightful evenings spent yesterday and the day before, I shall certainly not go out tonight, but will sit here at home and write to you. Besides, my Adèle, my adorable and adored Adèle, what have I not to tell you? O, God! for two days, I have been asking myself every moment if such happiness is not a dream. It seems to me that what I feel is not of earth. I cannot yet comprehend this cloudless heaven.

You do not yet know, Adèle, to what I had resigned myself. Alas, do I know it myself? Because I was weak, I fancied I was calm; because I was preparing myself for all the mad follies of despair, I thought I was courageous and resigned. Ah! let me cast myself humbly at your feet, you who are so grand, so tender and strong! I had been thinking that the utmost limit of my devotion could only be the sacrifice of my life; but you, my generous love, were ready to sacrifice for me the repose of yours!

Adèle, to what follies, what delirium, did not your Victor give way during these everlasting eight days! Sometimes I was ready to accept the offer of your admirable love; I thought that if pushed to the last extremity by the letter from my father, I might realise a little money, and then carry you away—you, my betrothed, my companion, my wife—away from all those who might want to disunite us; I thought we would cross France, I being nominally your husband, and go into some other country which would give us our rights. By day we would travel in the same carriage, at night we would sleep under the same roof. But do not think, my noble Adèle, that I would have taken advantage of so much happiness. Is it not true that you would never have done me the dishonour of thinking so? You would have been the object most worthy of respect, the being most respected, by your Victor; you might on the journey have even slept in the same chamber without fearing that he would have alarmed you by a touch, or have even looked at you. Only I should have slept, or watched wakefully in a chair, or lying on the floor beside your bed, the guardian of your repose, the protector of your slumbers. The right to defend and to watch over you would have been the only one of a husband's rights that your slave would have aspired to, until a priest had given him all the others.

Adèle, when I gave myself up to this delightful dream in the midst of my unhappiness, I forgot everything else... And then came my awakening; and then remorse for having for one moment conceived of such things. I thought of your parents, of your own peace of mind, and of your position, and I reproached myself for having shown you so little devotion as to have been so willing to accept so much, for having been so ungenerous as to consent to so much generosity, when my own dream had always been how to increase your happiness, even if I sacrificed my own! Then I cursed myself—I called myself the evil genius of your life, I remembered all the sufferings I had brought upon you, and I took that mad resolution that yesterday cost you those tears, tears I was inexcusable for having made you shed, and I went in search of a friend unhappy like myself, who, like me, had lost his last hope of happiness, and had nothing more to do with life but to endure its last pangs.

Adèle, oh, do not hate me, do not despise me for having been so weak and abject when you were so strong and so sublime. Think of my bereavements, of my loneliness, of what I expected from my father; think that for a week I had looked forward to losing you, and do not be astonished at the extravagance of my despair. You—a young girl—were admirable. And, indeed, I feel as if it would be flattering an angel to compare such a being to you. You have been privileged to receive every gift from nature, you have both fortitude and tears. Oh, Adèle, do not mistake these words for blind enthusiasm—enthusiasm for you has lasted all my life, and increases day by day. My whole soul is yours. If my entire existence had not been yours, the harmony of my being would have been lost, and I must have died—died inevitably.

These were my meditations, Adèle, when the letter that was to bring me hope or else despair arrived. If you love me, you know what must have been my joy. What I know you may have felt I will not describe.

My Adèle, why is there no word for this but joy? Is it because there is no power in human speech to express such happiness?

The sudden bound from mournful resignation to infinite felicity seemed to upset me. Even now I am still beside myself, and sometimes I tremble lest I should suddenly awaken from this dream divine.

Oh, now you are mine! At last you are mine! Soon—in a few months, perhaps, my angel will sleep in my arms, will awaken in my arms, will live there. All your thoughts at all moments, all your looks, will be for me; all my thoughts, all my moments, all my looks, will be for you! My Adèle!

Ah! I can at last do something to assist my own career! With so much hope, what courage I shall have to work! With courage, what success may I not obtain! What a burden has been lifted from my heart! What!—was it only the day before yesterday! It seems to me a long time since happiness was mine. I have felt so many things these last two days.

And your letter last Wednesday evening. How can I thank you for it, my Adèle? I did not think that at such a moment anything could have increased my happiness, but your letter made me feel that there can be no bounds to love and joy in the human breast. What a noble, tender, and devoted wife is destined for me! How can I ever deserve her? Adèle, I am as nothing beside you. The more I lift my head when I compare myself with other men, the more I sink in my own sight when I compare myself with you.

And now you will belong to me! Now I am called on earth to enjoy celestial felicity! I see you as my young wife, then a young mother, but always the same, always my Adèle, as tender, as adored in the chastity of married life as in the virgin days of our first love. Dear love, answer me—tell me if you can conceive the happiness of love immortal in an eternal union! And that will be ours some day.

This morning I answered my father's letter. There were two things in it which gave me pain. He told me he had formed new ties. My mother might have read what I wrote to him this morning. My excitement did not make me altogether forget what I owed to her memory. You cannot blame me, my noble love. Besides, I hope we may yet be reconciled. I am his son, and I am your husband. All my duty is comprised in those two relationships.

I do not forget that you told me that an account of how I had passed this week would be interesting to you. I own that up to Wednesday I tried in vain to work. The time was passed in struggling with my own emotions. I was full of thoughts of her whom I expected to lose, and all my ideas centred upon that loss. Yesterday I was able to work. Today I have spent in running from one ministerial bureau to another, a task I shall have to resume tomorrow, after having given all my morning to work. In the evening I shall be very happy.

My Adèle, no obstacle will now discourage me, either in my writing or in my attempt to gain a pension, for every step I take to attain success in both will bring me nearer to you. How could anything now seem painful to me? Do not think so ill of me as to believe that, I implore you. What is a little toil, if it conquers so much happiness? Have I not a thousand times implored heaven to let me purchase it at the price of my blood? Oh! how happy I am; how happy I am going to be!

Adieu, my angel, my beloved Adèle! Adieu! I will kiss your hair and go to bed. Still I am far from you, but I can dream of you. Soon perhaps you will be at my side. Adieu; pardon the delirium of your husband who embraces you, and who adores you, both for this life and another.

To Juliette Drouet

31 December, 1851.

You have been wonderful, my Juliette, all through these dark and violent days. If I needed love, you brought it to me, bless you! When, in my hiding places, always dangerous, after a night of waiting, I heard the key of my door trembling in your fingers, peril and darkness were no longer round me—what entered then was light!

We must never forget those terrible, but so sweet, hours when you were close to me in the intervals of fighting. Let us remember all our lives that dark little room, the ancient hangings, the two armchairs, side by side, the meal we ate off the corner of the table, the cold chicken you had brought; our sweet converse, your caresses, your anxieties, your devotion. You were surprised to find me calm and serene. Do you know whence came both calmness and serenity? From you...

David Hume

David Hume (7 May, 1711–25 August, 1776) was a Scottish philosopher, historian, economist, and essayist, known especially for his philosophical empiricism and scepticism. He is regarded as one of the most important figures in the history of Western philosophy and the Scottish Enlightenment. Hume is often grouped with John Locke, George Berkeley, and a handful of others as a British Empiricist. Beginning with his *A Treatise of Human Nature* (1739), Hume strove to create a total naturalistic "science of man" that examined the psychological basis of human nature. In stark opposition to the rationalists who preceded him, most notably Descartes, he concluded that desire rather than reason governed human behaviour, saying famously: "Reason is, and ought only to be the slave of the passions." A prominent figure in the sceptical philosophical tradition and a strong empiricist, he argued against the existence of innate ideas, concluding instead that humans have knowledge only of things they directly experience. He developed the position that mental behaviour is governed by "custom"; our use of induction, for example, is justified only by our idea of the "constant conjunction" of causes and effects. Hume advocated a compatibilist theory of free will that proved extremely influential on subsequent moral philosophy. He was also a sentimentalist who held that ethics are based on feelings rather than abstract moral principles.

Hume never married, and little is known of any romances he may have had. In 1734, he was accused of fathering a child with Agnes Galbraith. He disappeared to France, and she was left with the consequences, including being punished by wearing sackcloth and being committed to the pillory. In the 1760s he forged a close relationship with the Countess Marie-Charlotte de Boufflers (1725–1800). He was in France as the secretary of an English ambassador when they met. She was already the mistress of the Prince of Conti, and hosted men of letters at her salon in Paris. Hume was certainly infatuated, but their relationship was short-lived.

To Madame de Boufflers

3 April, 1766.

It is impossible for me, dear madame, to express the difficulty which I have to bear your absence, and the continual want which I feel of your society. I had accustomed myself, of a long time, to think of you as a friend from whom I was never to be separated during any considerable time; and I had flattered myself that we were fitted to pass our lives in intimacy and cordiality with each other.

Age and natural equality of temper were in danger of reducing my heart to too great indifference about everything, it was enlivened by the charms of your conversation, and the vivacity of your character. Your mind, more agitated both by unhappy circumstances in your situation and by your natural disposition, could repose itself in the more calm sympathy which you found with me.

But behold! Three months are elapsed since I left you; and it is impossible for me to assign a time when I can hope to join you. I still return to my wish, that I never left Paris, and that I had kept out of the reach of all other duties, except that which was so sweet, and agreeable, to fulfil, the cultivating your friendship and enjoying your society. Your obliging expressions revive this regret in the strongest degree; especially where you mention the wounds which, though skinned over, still fester at the bottom.

Oh! my dear friend, how I dread that it may still be long ere you reach a state of tranquillity, in a distress which so little admits of any remedy, and which the natural elevation of your character, instead of putting you above it, makes you feel with great sensibility. I could only wish to administer the temporary consolation, which the presence of a friend never fails to afford...

I kiss your hands with all the devotion possible.

Hume.

James Henry Leigh Hunt

James Henry Leigh Hunt (19 October, 1784–28 August, 1859), best known as Leigh Hunt, was an English critic, essayist, poet and writer. In 1808 he became editor of the *Examiner*, a newspaper founded by his brother, John. Noted for its unusual political independence and vitriolic criticism, in 1812, both brothers were arrested and charged with libel after they published an article criticising the Prince Regent. They were imprisoned for two years. In 1816 he made a mark in English literature with the publication of *The Story of Rimini*. The poem is an optimistic narrative which runs contrary to the tragic nature of its subject. Hunt's flippancy and familiarity, often degenerating into the ludicrous, subsequently made him a target for ridicule and parody. In 1818 appeared a collection of poems entitled *Foliage*, followed in 1819 by *Hero and Leander*, and *Bacchies and Ariadne*. In the same year he reprinted these two works with *The Story of Rimini* and *The Descent of Liberty* with the title of *Poetical Works*, and started the *Indicator* (1819–1821), in which some of his best work appeared. He suffered financial difficulties throughout his life, surviving often on the kindness of friends, especially Lord Byron. The death of his friends John Keats in 1821, Percy Bysshe Shelley in 1822 and Lord Byron in 1824 greatly affected him. In his final years, the history of Hunt's life is a painful struggle with poverty and sickness. He worked unremittingly, but one effort failed after another.

In 1802, Leigh Hunt met and fell in love with Marianne Kent "Marian" (1788–26 January, 1857). Their courtship lasted several years (when they met she was only 14 and he 18), and produced many passionate love letters. She was less educated and literary than he, and though he tried in vain to teach her, she remained oblivious. On 3 July, 1809, they finally married, after much delay and at least one broken engagement. Though their marriage was fraught with difficulties, including poverty, extravagance, his imprisonment and wanderings and her later alcoholism, they had 10 children, 8 of whom survived infancy: Thornton (1810–1873), John Horatio (1812–1846), Mary Florimel (1813–1849), Swinburne Percy (1816–1827), Percy Bysshe Shelley (1817–1899), Henry Sylvan (1819–1876), Vincent Novello (1823–1852), Julia Trelawny (1826–1872), Jacintha Shelley (1828–1914) and Arabella (1829–1830).

London, 1 August, 1803.

My dearest Marian,
I am very uncomfortable; I get up at five in the morning, say a word to nobody, curse my stars till eleven at night, and then creep into bed to curse my

stars for to-morrow; and all this because I love a little black-eyed girl of fifteen, whom nobody knows, with all my heart and soul.

Take notice, that if you do not send me a very long letter to-morrow (it may be as sober and you may talk with as little violence as Mrs. H pleases), I'll be very happy all the rest of the week; and when I do receive one at last, I shall say to the servant looking at the letter sideways;—"Oh, a letter from Brighton; here, lay it down on the table, I am going out to dinner in a great hurry, so I can read it when I return at night."—There's a true lover's malice for you—You think I was offended last Friday evening, you assured me of your affection, you begged pardon of one, who when he utters an unkind word to you, is putting a thousand daggers to his own breast; but you know I was never seriously or beyond a moment offended with you, nor was I then; 'tis true, I stayed but a minute with you when you sent for me, and persisted in leaving the room even when you entreated me to stop: I did not so much as look at you; but it was because I knew, that if I trusted myself with a single glance at the face I doated on, I should have folded you to my bosom, and begged that pardon which I thought I ought not to beg: for you must confess, that if you did leave me, when you came down, for the reason you assigned, yet you might have come down sometime before a quarter to nine, considering I was not to see you for a week. However, you are a dear-affectionate girl; though you must not suppose I love you a bit the better for being fifty miles out of my reach; that is, out of my reach in the day time; for you must know that I travel at a pretty tolerable pace every night, and have held many a happy chat with you about twelve or one o'clock at midnight though you may have forgotten it by this time;

Oft by yon sad and solitary stream
Sweet visions gild the youthful poet's dream;
Calm as he slumbers in the roseate shade,
Unvarying Fancy clasps his absent maid,
Hangs on each charm that captivates the heart,
The smile, the glance too eloquent for art,
The whispers trembling as of love they tell,
And the smooth bosom's undulating swell;
Paints the bright prospect of approaching years,
And all Elysium opens to his pray'rs.

You see lovers can no more help being poets, than poets can help being lovers. ...

I shall see you again, and will pay you prettily for running away from me, for you shall not stir from my side the whole evening; tell Betsey too, that she is a very malicious prophetess, and that if she comes to me again with such ill news as she gave me in her last epistle, I shall pray Heaven to cut at least two inches of plumpness from her round face and at nineteen to give her a husband of ninety. If you are well and have been so at Brighton, you are every thing I could wish you. God bless you and yours; you see I can still pray for myself. Heaven knows, that every blessing bestowed on you is a tenfold one bestowed on your H.

10 February, 1804. 11 at night. London St., Fitzroy Sq.—

I sit down to write to you, Marian, with a beating heart; perhaps it is the last time I may thus address you, but if it is, I shall at least have to thank Heaven, that my last words were those of tenderness and affection, and that if we must part, it will be with the farewell of friendship instead of the anger of disappointment or the petulance of mortified vanity. It is impossible for me to keep silence any longer; my heart is wrapped up in you, and yet I cannot even speak to you, I can neither laugh with you when you are cheerful, nor sympathise with you in your troubles; every body may take an interest in your comfort and your wishes but he, who would be the happiest in rendering you the closest attention and gratifying, where it lies in his power, the slightest of your inclinations.—Once more, Marian, I ask of you your love, and I assure you that I would not ask it, were I not persuaded that it's bestowal would contribute to your own happiness as well as mine: I offer you, with the sincerest tenderness, a heart entirely your own, and ready to devote itself to your comfort and happiness as long as it beats; a head, not naturally devoid of sense, whose errors have been, I trust, conquered by my affection for you and an unceasing wish to become better and wiser for your sake; and a confluence, entire and unlimited, the confidence of a love, which will not nor can enjoy a single gratification without it's sharing it with you.

Without love my heart is like a desert without water, it is in danger of being dried up for want of nourishment; in the little anxieties I may chance to have, in things which would otherwise afford me pleasure, I can find neither consolation nor happiness,—for I am without Her who should share them with me, who would receive me with smiles after the toils of a laborious profession, and be most happy when I was so.—Dearest girl, refuse not what I ask: I would entreat you for the sake of our former love, had I not so miserably forfeited it; but I may ask you for the sake of my constancy, and for the sake of your shewing you know how to forgive when the error is done away.—Perhaps my own wishes have been the means of finding it out, but I sincerely confess to you, that I fancy I have discovered that in your face and your heart, which would encourage my hopes of your returning affection. I have indeed great hopes, though they are mingled and occasionally overpowered by great doubts—dispel this cloud that hangs over me, and take once more to your bosom your again dear Henry, now no longer fretful and melancholy, but prepared to be happy himself and to do every thing he can to make you happy too; and you will be happy, if all that Love can devise can make you so, and I am sure that Love must give the greatest happiness to "that mind, Which Pity and Esteem can move, Which can be just and kind."

Do you remember those lines? How happy was I, when I first read them! I would not give away that slip of paper on which you wrote the song to Myra for all it's author was worth.—I hope I have said what I should in this letter, and that you have not been in the least troubled while reading it: nothing can be further from my intentions than giving pain to a heart, whose pains and pleasures are those of mine. Believe me, I have been as sincere as I would wish to be affectionate, and that I have said all that I think and nothing that I do not.—I shall look for a packet from Titchfield St. with anxiety, and hope you will not keep me long in suspense.—If you once more say you love me, what a heavenly day shall I not pass to-morrow—it will indeed be a day of rest in every sense of the word—if you cannot make me happy, I shall have only to wish that God may bless you and make your future husband as anxious for your happiness and proud of your love, as I should be, if I ever had the joy of calling you my wife. Heaven be with you—have your mother always in your mind, and you will be an excellent woman. God grant I may a thousand times subscribe and more than a thousand times prove myself,

Your own affectionate
Henry

Thomas Jefferson

Thomas Jefferson (13 April, 1743–4 July, 1826) was was the third President of the United States (1801–1809) and the principal author of the Declaration of Independence (1776). An influential Founding Father, Jefferson envisioned America as a great "Empire of Liberty" that would promote republicanism.

Jefferson served as a delegate to the Second Continental Congress beginning in June 1775, soon after the outbreak of the American Revolutionary War. When Congress began considering a resolution of independence in 1776, Jefferson was appointed to a five-man committee to prepare a declaration to accompany the resolution. The committee selected Jefferson to write the first draft probably because of his reputation as a writer. On 4 July, 1776, the Declaration was adopted by the Continental Congress, which announced that the thirteen American colonies then at war with Great Britain were now independent states, and thus no longer a part of the British Empire. Jefferson served as the wartime Governor of Virginia (1779–1781), first United States Secretary of State (1789–1793) under the Presidency of George Washington, and second Vice President of the United States (1797–1801) under John Adams. On 4 March, 1801, he became the third President of the United States. During his tenure he made the Louisiana Purchase (1803), and sent the Lewis and Clark Expedition (1804–1806). In 1807 he signed a bill making slave importation illegal in the United States. Tensions escalated with Britain and France, leading to war with Britain in 1812 shortly after he left office.

On 1 January, 1772, at age 29 Jefferson married the 23-year-old widow Martha *née* Wayles Skelton (30 October, 1748–6 September, 1782). Throughout their almost eleven-year marriage, they appeared to have been wholly devoted to each other. They had six children, only two of whom survived to adulthood. Martha Jefferson died in 1782, after the birth of her last child. Jefferson was at his wife's bedside when she died and was deeply upset for a month after her death. He later destroyed all of their correspondence.

In the spring of 1786, while serving as the US minister to France, Jefferson met and fell in love with Maria *née* Hadfield Cosway (1760–1838), an Anglo-Italian artist. Cosway was also an accomplished composer, musician and society hostess, married to a much older man in what was thought to be a marriage of convenience. Cosway and Jefferson shared an interest in art and architecture and attended exhibits throughout the city and countryside together, and Jefferson soon developed a romantic attachment to her. Just after Cosway left Paris in October, Jefferson composed a remarkable letter to her in which his head argued with his heart. Their letters would continue the rest of Jefferson's life.

As a widower, Jefferson had a long-term, intimate relationship with his slave Sally Hemings (c.1773–1835), which lasted more than three decades. She was three-fourths white, described as pretty and agreeable, and a half-sister to

Jefferson's late wife, as they both had John Wayles as father. Though there has been much controversy surrounding the facts, it is generally understood that Sally Hemings had six children by Jefferson. They all had seven-eighths European ancestry, and of the four who survived to adulthood, three entered white communities.

To Maria Cosway

12–13 October, 1786.

My Dear Madam,—Having performed the last sad office of handing you into your carriage at the pavillon de St. Denis, and seen the wheels get actually into motion, I turned on my heel & walked, more dead than alive, to the opposite door, where my own was awaiting me. Mr. Danquerville was missing. He was sought for, found, & dragged down stairs. We were crammed into the carriage, like recruits for the Bastille, & not having soul enough to give orders to the coachman, he presumed Paris our destination, & drove off. After a considerable interval, silence was broke with a "Je suis vraiment affligé du depart de ces bons gens." This was a signal for a mutual confession of distress. We began immediately to talk of Mr. & Mrs. Cosway, of their goodness, their talents, their amiability; & tho' we spoke of nothing else, we seemed hardly to have entered into matter when the coachman announced the rue St. Denis, & that we were opposite Mr. Danquerville's. He insisted on descending there & traversing a short passage to his lodgings. I was carried home. Seated by my fireside, solitary & sad, the following dialogue took place between my Head & my Heart:

Head. Well, friend, you seem to be in a pretty trim.

Heart. I am indeed the most wretched of all earthly beings. Overwhelmed with grief, every fibre of my frame distended beyond its natural powers to bear, I would willingly meet whatever catastrophe should leave me no more to feel or to fear.

Head. These are the eternal consequences of your warmth & precipitation. This is one of the scrapes into which you are ever leading us. You confess your follies indeed; but still you hug & cherish them; & no reformation can be hoped, where there is no repentance.

Heart. Oh, my friend! This is no moment to upbraid my foibles. I am rent into fragments by the force of my grief! If you have any balm, pour it into my wounds; if none, do not harrow them by new torments. Spare me in this awful moment! At any other I will attend with patience to your admonitions.

Head. On the contrary I never found that the moment of triumph with you was the moment of attention to my admonitions. While suffering under your follies, you may perhaps be made sensible of them, but, the paroxysms over, you fancy it can never return. Harsh therefore as the medicine may be, it is my office to administer it. You will be pleased to remember that when our friend Trumbull used to be telling us of the merits & talents of these good people, I never ceased whispering to you that we had no occasion for new acquaintance; that the greater their merits & talents, the more dangerous their friendship to our tranquillity, because the regret at parting would be greater.

Heart. Accordingly, Sir, this acquaintance was not the consequence of my doings. It was one of your projects which threw us in the way of it. It was you, remember, & not I, who desired the meeting at Legrand & Molinos. I never trouble myself with domes nor arches. The Halle aux bleds might have rotted down before I should have gone to see it. But you, forsooth, who are eternally getting us to sleep with your diagrams & crotchets, must go & examine this wonderful piece of architecture. And when you had seen it, oh! It was the most superb thing on earth. What you had seen there was worth all you had yet seen in Paris! I thought so too. But I meant it of the lady & gentleman to whom we had been presented; & not of a parcel of sticks & chips put together in pens. You then, Sir, & not I, have been the cause of the present distress.

Head. I would have been happy for you if my diagrams & crotchets had gotten you to sleep on that day, as you are pleased to say they eternally do. My visit to Legrand & Molinos had public utility for its object... While I was occupied with these objects, you were dilating with your new acquaintances, & contriving how to prevent a separation from them. Every soul of you had an engagement for the day. Yet all these were to be sacrificed, that you might dine together. Lying messengers were to be despatched into every quarter of the city, with apologies for your breach of engagement. You particularly had the effrontery to send word to the Dutchess Danville that, on the moment we were setting out to dine with her, despatches came to hand which required immediate attention. You wanted me to invent a more ingenious excuse; but I knew you were getting into a scrape, & I would have nothing to do with it. Well, after dinner to St. Cloud, from St. Cloud to Ruggieri, from Ruggieri to Krumfoltz, & if the day had been as long as a Lapland summer day, you would still have contrived means among you to have filled it.

Heart. Oh! My dear friend, how you have revived me by recalling to my mind the transactions of that day! How well I remember them all, & that when I came home at night & looked back to the morning, it seemed to have been a month agone. Go on then, like a kind comforter & paint to me the day we went to St. Germains. How beautiful was every object! The Port de Reuilly, the hills along the Seine, the rainbows of the machine of Marly, the terrace of St. Germains, the chateaux, the gardens, the statues of Marly, the pavillon of Lucienne. Recollect too Madrid, Bagatelle, the Kings garden, the Desert. How grand the idea excited by the remains of such a column! The spiral staircase too was beautiful. Every moment was filled with something agreeable. The wheels of time moved on with a rapidity of which those of our carriage gave but a faint idea. And yet in the evening when one took a retrospect of the day, what a mass of happiness had we travelled over! Retrace all those scenes to me, my good companion, & I will forgive the unkindness with which you were chiding me. The day we went to St. Germains was a little too warm, I think; was it not?

Head. Thou art the most incorrigible of all the beings that ever sinned! I reminded you of the follies of the first day, intending to deduce from thence some useful lessons for you, but instead of listening to these, you kindle at the recollection, you retrace the whole series with a fondness which shews you want nothing but the opportunity to act it over again. I often told you during its course that you were imprudently engaging your affections under circumstances that must have cost you a great deal of pain: that the persons indeed were of the greatest merit, possessing good sense, good humour, honest hearts, honest manners, & eminence in a lovely art; that the lady had moreover qualities & accomplishments, belonging to her sex, which might form a chapter apart for her: such as music, modesty, beauty, & that softness of disposition which is the ornament of her sex & charm of ours, but that all these considerations would increase the pang of separation: that their stay here was to be short; that you rack our whole system when you are parted from those you love, complaining that such a separation is worse than death, inasmuch as this ends our sufferings, whereas that only begins them; & that the separation would in this instance be the more severe as you would probably never see them again.

Heart. But they told me they would come back again the next year.

Head. But in the meantime see what you suffer: & their return too depends on so many circumstances that if you had a grain of prudence you would not count upon it. Upon the whole it is improbable & therefore you should abandon the idea of ever seeing them again.

Heart. May heaven abandon me if I do!

Head. Very well. Suppose then they come back. They are to stay two months, & when these are expired, what is to follow? Perhaps you flatter yourself they may come to America?

Heart. God only knows what is to happen. I see nothing impossible in that supposition. And I see things wonderfully contrived sometimes to make us happy. Where could they find such objects as in America for the exercise of their enchanting art? Especially the lady, who paints landscapes so inimitably. She wants only subjects worthy of immortality to render her pencil immortal. The Failing Spring, the Cascade of Niagara, the Passage of the Potowmac through the Blue Mountains, the Natural bridge. It is worth a voyage across the Atlantic to see these objects; much more to paint, and make them, & thereby ourselves, known to all ages. And our own dear Monticello, where has nature spread so rich a mantle under the eye? Mountains, forests, rocks, rivers. With what majesty do we there ride above the storms! How sublime to look down into the workhouse of nature, to see her clouds, hail, snow, rain, thunder, all fabricated at our feet! And the glorious sun when rising as if out of a distant water, just gilding the tops of the mountains, & giving life to all nature? I hope in God no circumstance may ever make either seek an asylum from grief! With what sincere sympathy I would open every cell of my composition to receive the effusion of their woes! I would pour my tears into their wounds: & if a drop of balm could be found on the top of the Cordilleras, or at the remotest sources of the Missouri, I would go thither myself to seek & to bring it. Deeply practised in the school of affliction, the human heart knows no joy which I have not lost, no sorrow of which I have not drunk! Fortune can present no grief of unknown form to me! Who then can so softly bind up the wound of another as he who has felt the same wound himself?

But Heaven forbid they should ever know a sorrow! Let us turn over another leaf, for this has distracted me...

Head. Let us return then to our point. I wished to make you sensible how imprudent it is to place your affections, without reserve, on objects you must so soon lose, & whose loss when it comes must cost you such severe pangs. Remember that last night you knew your friends were to leave Paris to-day. This was enough to throw you into agonies. All night you tossed us from one side of the bed to the other. No sleep, no rest. The poor crippled wrist too, never left one moment in the same position, now up, now down, now here, now there; was it to be wondered at if its pains returned? The Surgeon then was to be called, & to be rated as an ignoramus because he could not divine the cause of this extraordinary change. In fine, my friend, you must mend your manners. This is not a world to live at random in as you do. To avoid those eternal distresses, to which you are forever exposing us, you must learn to look forward before you take a step which may interest our peace. Everything in this world is a matter of calculation. Advance then with caution, the balance in your hand. Put into one scale the pleasures which any object may offer; but put fairly into the other the pains which are to follow, & see which preponderates. The making an acquaintance is not a matter of indifference. When a new one is proposed to you, view it all round. Consider what advantages it presents, & to what inconveniences it may expose you. Do not bite at the bait of pleasure till you know there is no hook beneath it. The art of life is the art of avoiding pain, & he is the best pilot who steers clearest of the rocks & shoals with which he is beset. Pleasure is always before us; but misfortune is at our side, while running after that, this arrests us. The most effectual means of being secure against pain is to retire within ourselves, & to suffice for our own happiness. Those, which depend on ourselves, are the only pleasures a wise man will count on; for nothing is ours which another may deprive us of. Hence the inestimable value of intellectual pleasures. Even in our power, always leading us to something new, never cloying, we ride serene & sublime above the concerns of this mortal world, contemplating truth & nature, matter & motion, the laws which bind up their existence, & that eternal being who made & bound them up by those laws. Let this be our employ. Leave the bustle & tumult of society to those who have not talents to occupy themselves without them. Friendship is but another name for an alliance with the follies & the misfortunes of others. Our own share of miseries is sufficient, why enter then as volunteers into those of another? Is there so little gall poured into our cup that we must needs help to drink that of our neighbor? A friend dies or leaves us: we feel as if a limb was cut off. He is sick: we must watch over him, & participate of his pains. His fortune is shipwrecked; ours must be laid under contribution. He loses a child, a parent, or a partner: we must mourn the loss as if it were our own.

Heart. And what more sublime delight than to mingle tears with one whom the hand of heaven hath smitten! To watch over the bed of sickness, & to beguile its tedious & its painful moments! To share our bread with one to whom misfortune has left none! This world abounds indeed with misery, to lighten its burthen we must divide it with one another. But let us now try the virtues of your mathematical balance, & as you have put into one scale the burthen of friendship, let me put its comforts into the other. When languishing then under disease, how grateful is the solace of our friends! How are we penetrated with their assiduities & attentions! How much are we supported by their encouragements & kind offices! When heaven has taken from us some object of our love, how sweet is it to have a bosom whereon to recline our heads, & into which we may pour the torrent of our tears! Grief, with such a comfort, is almost a luxury! In a life where we are perpetually exposed to want & accident, yours is a wonderful proposition, to insulate ourselves, to retire from all aid, & to wrap ourselves in the mantle of self-sufficiency! For assuredly nobody will care for him who cares for nobody. But friendship is precious, not only in the shade but in the sunshine of life; & thanks to a benevolent arrangement of things, the greater part of life is sunshine. I will recur for proof to the days we have lately passed. On these indeed the sun shone brightly. How gay did the face of nature appear! Hills, valleys, chateaux, gardens, rivers, every object wore its liveliest hue! Whence did they borrow it? From the presence of our charming companion. They were pleasing, because she seemed pleased. Alone, the scene would have been dull & insipid, the participation of it with her gave it relish. Let the gloomy monk, sequestered from the world, seek unsocial pleasures in the bottom of his cell! Let the sublimated philosopher grasp visionary happiness while pursuing phantoms dressed in the garb of truth! Their supreme wisdom is supreme folly; & they mistake for happiness the mere absence of pain. Had they ever felt the solid pleasure of one generous spasm of the heart, they would exchange for it all the frigid speculations of their lives, which you have been vaunting in such elevated terms. Believe me then my friend, that that is a miserable arithmetic which, could estimate friendship at nothing, or at less than nothing. Respect for you has induced me to enter into this discussion, & to hear principles uttered which I detest & abjure. Respect for myself now obliges me to recall you into the proper limits of your office. When nature assigned us the same habitation, she gave us over it a divided empire. To you she allotted the field of science; to me that of morals. When the circle is to be squared, or the orbit of a comet to be traced; when the arch of greatest strength, or the solid of least resistance is to be investigated, take up the problem; it is yours; nature has given me no cognizance of it. In like manner, in denying to you the feelings of sympathy, of benevolence, of gratitude, of justice, of love, of friendship, she has excluded you from their control. To these she has adapted the mechanism of the heart. Morals were too essential to the happiness of man to be risked on the incertain combinations of the head... I shall never envy nor control your sublime delights. But leave me to decide when & where friendships are to be contracted... I receive no one into my esteem till I know they are worthy of it. Wealth, title, office, are no recommendations to my friendship. On the contrary great good qualities are requisite to make amends for their having wealth, title, & office. You confess that in the present case I could not have made a worthier choice. You only object that I was so soon to lose them. We are not immortal ourselves, my friend; how can we expect our enjoyments to be so? We have no rose without its thorn; no pleasure without alloy. It is the law of our existence; & we must acquiesce. It is the condition annexed to all our pleasures, not by us who receive, but by him who gives them. True, this condition is pressing cruelly on me at this moment. I feel more fit for death than life. But when I look back on the pleasures of which it is the consequence, I am conscious they were worth the price I am paying. Notwithstanding your endeavours too to damp my hopes, I comfort myself with expectations of their promised return. Hope is sweeter than despair, & they were too good to mean to deceive me. In the summer, said the gentleman; but in the spring, said the lady, & I should love her forever, were it only for that! Know then, my friend, that I have taken these good people into my bosom; that I have lodged them in the warmest cell I could find, that I love them, & will continue to love them through life, that if fortune should dispose them on one side the globe, & me on the other, my affections shall pervade its whole mass to reach them. Knowing then my determination, attempt not to disturb it. If you can at any time furnish matter for their amusement, it will be the office of a good neighbor to do it. I will in like manner seize any occasion which may offer to do the like good turn for you with Condorcet, Rittenhouse, Madison, La Cretelle, or any other of those worthy sons of science whom you so justly prize.

I thought this a favorable proposition whereon to rest the issue of the dialogue. So I put an end to it by calling for my night-cap. Methinks I hear you wish to heaven I had called a little sooner, & so spared you the ennui of such a sermon. I did not interrupt them sooner because I was in a mood for hearing sermons. You too were the subject; & on such a thesis I never think the theme long; not even if I am to write it, and that slowly & awkwardly, as now, with the left hand. But that you may not be discouraged from a correspondence which begins so formidably, I will promise you on my honour that my future letters shall be of a reasonable length. I will even agree to express but half my esteem for you, for fear of cloying you with too full a dose. But, on your part, no curtailing. If your letters are as long as the bible, they will appear short to me. Only let them be brimful of affection. I shall read them with the dispositions with which Arlequin, in Les deux billets spelt the words "je taime," and wished that the whole alphabet had entered into their composition.

We have had incessant rains since your departure. These make me fear for your health, as well as that you had an uncomfortable journey. The same cause has prevented me from being able to give you any account of your friends here... As to myself my health is good, except my wrist which mends slowly, & my mind which mends not at all, but broods constantly over your departure. The lateness of the season obliges me to decline my journey into the south of France. Present me in the most friendly terms to Mr. Cosway, & receive me into your own recollection with a partiality & a warmth, proportioned, not to my own poor merit, but to the sentiments of sincere affection & esteem with which I have the honour to be, my dear Madam, your most obedient humble servant.

Franz Kafka

Franz Kafka (3 July, 1883–3 June, 1924) was a culturally influential German-language novelist. Contemporary critics and academics regard Kafka as one of the best writers of the 20th century. The term "Kafkaesque" has become part of the English vernacular. Kafka was born to middle class German-speaking Jewish parents in Prague, Bohemia, then part of the Austro-Hungarian Empire. He worked as an insurance officer for the majority of his adult life, his writing attracting little attention until after his death. From 1912, Kafka began to suffer from tuberculosis, which would require frequent convalescence during which he was supported by his family. During his lifetime, he published mostly short stories. Many collections of the stories have since been published and it is for these that he is now best known. He finished the novella *The Metamorphosis* (1915), but never finished any of his full length novels. Much of Kafka's work was unfinished, or prepared for publication posthumously by his friend Max Brod. The novels *The Castle* (which stopped mid-sentence and had ambiguity on content), *The Trial* (chapters were unnumbered and some were incomplete) and *Amerika* (Kafka's original title was *The Man who Disappeared*) were all prepared for publication by Brod.

In 1912, at Max Brod's home, Kafka met Felice Bauer (1887–1960), who lived in Berlin and worked as a representative for a dictaphone company. Over the next five years they corresponded a great deal, met occasionally, and twice were engaged to be married. Their relationship finally ended in 1917.

From 1919 Kafka developed an intense relationship with Czech journalist and writer Milena Jesenská (10 August, 1896–17 May, 1944). Married, and working as a translator, in 1919 she wrote to Kafka to ask permission to translate one of his stories. The letter launched an intense and increasingly passionate correspondence. Jesenská and Kafka met twice: they spent four days in Vienna and later a day in Gmünd. Eventually Kafka broke off the relationship, partly because Jesenská was unable to leave her husband, and their almost daily communication ceased abruptly in November 1920.

In July, 1923, on vacation in Graal-Müritz on the Baltic Sea, he met Dora Diamant (4 March, 1898–15 August, 1952) and briefly moved to Berlin in the hope of distancing himself from his family's influence to concentrate on his writing. In Berlin, he lived with Diamant, a 25-year-old kindergarten teacher from an orthodox Jewish family, who was independent enough to have escaped her past in the ghetto. She became his lover, and influenced Kafka's interest in the Talmud. Some of his last writings which were in her possession were confiscated by the Gestapo in 1933.

To Felice Bauer

11 November, 1912.

Fräulein Felice!
I am now going to ask you a favour which sounds quite crazy, and which I should regard as such, were I the one to receive the letter. It is also the very greatest test that even the kindest person could be put to. Well, this is it:

Write to me only once a week, so that your letter arrives on Sunday—for I cannot endure your daily letters, I am incapable of enduring them. For instance, I answer one of your letters, then lie in bed in apparent calm, but my heart beats through my entire body and is conscious only of you. I belong to you; there is really no other way of expressing it, and that is not strong enough. But for this very reason I don't want to know what you are wearing; it confuses me so much that I cannot deal with life; and that's why I don't want to know that you are fond of me. If I did, how could I, fool that I am, go on sitting in my office, or here at home, instead of leaping onto a train with my eyes shut and opening them only when I am with you? Oh, there is a sad, sad reason for not doing so. To make it short: my health is only just good enough for myself alone, not good enough for marriage, let alone fatherhood. Yet when I read your letter, I feel I could overlook even what cannot possibly be overlooked.

If only I had your answer now! And how horribly I torment you, and how I compel you, in the stillness of your room, to read this letter, as nasty a letter as has ever lain on your desk! Honestly, it strikes me sometimes that I prey like a spectre on your felicitous name! If only I had mailed Saturday's letter, in which I implored you never to write to me again, and in which I gave a similar promise. Oh God, what prevented me from sending that letter? All would be well. But is a peaceful solution possible now? Would it help if we wrote to each other only once a week? No, if my suffering could be cured by such means it would not be serious. And already I foresee that I shan't be able to endure even the Sunday letters. And so, to compensate for Saturday's lost opportunity, I ask you with what energy remains to me at the end of this letter: if we value our lives, let us abandon it all.

Did I think of signing myself Yours? No, nothing could be more false. No, I am forever fettered to myself, that's what I am, and that's what I must try to live with.
Franz

Night of 15–16 December, 1912.

Well dearest, the doors are shut, all is quiet, I am with you once more. How many things does 'to be with you' mean by now? I have not slept all day, and while I duly went about all the afternoon and early evening with a heavy head and a befogged brain, now, as night sets in, I am almost excited, I feel within me a tremendous desire to write; the demon inhabiting the writing urge begins to stir at most inopportune moments. Let him, I'll go to bed. But if I could spend Christmas writing and sleeping, dearest, that would be wonderful!

I was after you continuously this afternoon, in vain of course. As a matter of fact not quite in vain, for I constantly kept as close as possible to Frau Friedmann, because after all she was close to you for quite a time, because you say 'du' to each other, and because she happens to be the possessor of letters from you, which I certainly begrudge her. But why doesn't she say a word about you while I keep staring at her lips, ready to pounce on the first word? Have you stopped writing to each other? Perhaps she knows nothing new about you? But how is this possible! And if she knows nothing new, why doesn't she talk about you, why doesn't she at least mention your name, as she used to, when she was around before? But no, she won't; instead, she keeps me hanging about, and we talk about incredibly unimportant things, such as Breslau, coughing, music, scarves, brooches, hairstyles, Italian holidays, sleighrides, beaded bags, stiff shirts, cufflinks, Herbert Schottlander, the French language, public baths, showers, cooks, Harden, economic conditions, travelling by night, the Palace Hotel, Schreiberhau, hats, the University of Breslau, relatives—in short about everything under the sun, but the only subject that has, unfortunately, some faint association with you consists of a few words about Pyramidos and aspirin; it is cause for wonder why I pursue this subject for so long, and why I enjoy rolling these two words around my tongue. But really, I am not satisfied with this as the sole outcome of an afternoon, because for hours on end my head hums with the desire to hear the name Felice. Finally, by force, I direct the conversation to the railway connections between Berlin and Breslau, at the same time giving her a menacing look—nothing.

Franz

To Milena

c.1920.

... The most beautiful of your letters (and that means a lot, for as a whole they are, almost in every line, the most beautiful thing that ever happened to me in my life) are those in which you agree with my 'fear' and at the same time try to explain that I don't need to have it. For I too, even though I may sometimes look like a bribed defender of my 'fear,' probably agree with it deep down in myself, indeed it is part of me and perhaps the best part. And as it is my best, it is also perhaps this alone that you love. For what else worthy of love could be found in me? But this is worthy of love.

And when you once asked me how I could have called that Saturday 'good' with that fear in my heart, it's not difficult to explain. Since I love you (and I do love you, you stupid one, as the sea loves a pebble in its depths, this is just how my love engulfs you—and may I in turn be the pebble with you, if Heaven permits), I love the whole world and this includes your left shoulder, no, it was first the right one, so I kiss it if I feel like it (and if you are nice enough to pull the blouse away from it) and this also includes your left shoulder and your face above me in the forest and my resting on your almost bare breast. And that's why you're right in saying that we were already one and I'm not afraid of it, rather it is my only happiness and my only pride and I don't confine it at all only to the forest.

But just between this day-world and that 'half-hour in bed' of which you once spoke contemptuously as 'men's business,' there lies for me an abyss which I cannot bridge, probably because I don't want to. That over there is a concern of the night, thoroughly and in every sense a concern of the night: this here is the world and I possess it and now I'm supposed to leap across into the night in order to take possession of it once more. Can one take possession of anything twice? Does that not mean to lose it? Here is the world which I possess, and I'm supposed to leap across for the sake of a sinister black-magic, of a hocus-pocus, a philosopher's stone, an alchemy, a wish-ring. Away with it, I'm terribly afraid of it.

To try and catch in one night by black magic, hastily, heavily breathing, helpless, obsessed, to try and obtain by black magic what every day offers to open eyes! ('Perhaps' children can't be begotten in any other way, 'perhaps' children too are black magic. Let us leave this question for the moment.) This is the reason why I'm so grateful (to you and to everything) and it is therefore natural that by your side I'm most quiet and most unquiet, most inhibited and most free, and this is also why, after this realisation, I have renounced all other life. Look into my eyes!

c.1920.

The first letter was already sent off when yours arrived. Apart from everything which may be underneath—under such things as 'fear', etc.—and which nauseates me, not because it's nauseating but because my stomach is too weak, apart from this it is perhaps even simpler than you say. Like this, for instance: lonely imperfection has to be endured through every moment, imperfection shared by two does not have to be endured. Hasn't one got eyes to tear them out and a heart for the same purpose? And yet it isn't so bad, it's all an exaggeration and a lie, everything is an exaggeration, only the longing is true, this cannot be exaggerated. But even the truth of longing is not so much its truth, rather is it an expression of the lie of everything else.

This sounds rather crazy, but it is so.

Nor is it perhaps really love when I say that for me you are the most beloved; love is to me that you are the knife which I turn within myself.

Moreover, you say it yourself—'the people who haven't got the strength to love'—shouldn't this be the sufficient distinction between 'animal' and 'human being'?

John Keats

John Keats (31 October, 1795–23 February, 1821) was an English Romantic poet. His first poem, the sonnet *O Solitude* appeared in the *Examiner* in May 1816, while his collection *Lamia, Isabella, The Eve of St Agnes and Other Poems* was published in July 1820. His poetry is characterised by sensual imagery, most notably in the series of odes (1819). Along with Lord Byron and Percy Bysshe Shelley, he was one of the key figures in the second generation of the Romantic movement, despite the fact that his work had been in publication for only four years before his death. During his life, his poems were not generally well received by critics; however, after his death, his reputation grew to the extent that by the end of the 19th century he had become one of the most beloved of all English poets. It is believed that, in his lifetime, sales of his three volumes of poetry amounted to only 200 copies. Today his poems and letters are considered as among the most popular and analysed in English literature.

During 1820, Keats displayed increasingly serious symptoms of tuberculosis. He lost large amounts of blood and was "bled" by the attending physician. Leigh Hunt nursed him in London for much of the summer. At the suggestion of his doctors, he agreed to move to Italy. He died from tuberculosis, in Rome. Knowing he was dying, he wrote in February 1820, "I have left no immortal work behind me—nothing to make my friends proud of my memory—but I have lov'd the principle of beauty in all things, and if I had had time I would have made myself remember'd." However, he has since had a significant influence on a diverse range of later poets and writers.

Letters and poem drafts suggest that Keats first met Frances "Fanny" Brawne (9 August, 1800–4 December, 1865) between September and November 1818. It is likely that the 18-year-old Brawne was visiting the Dilke family at Wentworth Place, where Keats also lived. Like Keats, Brawne was a Londoner. Her grandfather had kept a London inn, as Keats's father had done, and had also lost several members of her family to tuberculosis. Brawne had a talent for dress-making and languages. She describes herself as having "a natural theatrical bent". During November 1818 an intimacy sprang up between Keats and Brawne but was very much shadowed by the impending death of his brother Tom Keats, whom John was nursing. That year, he also met the beautiful, talented and witty Isabella Jones, for whom he also felt a conflicted passion. On 3 April, 1819, Brawne and her widowed mother moved into the other half of Wentworth Place and Keats and Brawne were able to see each other every day. Their engagement, lasting from 1819 until his death in 1821, covered some of the most poetically productive years of Keats's life. None of Brawne's letters to Keats survive, though we have his to her.

Shanklin, Isle of Wight, Thursday.
3 July, 1819.

My dearest Lady—I am glad I had not an opportunity of sending off a letter which I wrote for you on Tuesday night—'twas too much like one out of Rousseau's Heloise. I am more reasonable this morning. The morning is the only proper time for me to write to a beautiful girl whom I love so much: for at night, when the lonely day has closed, and the lonely, silent, unmusical chamber is waiting to receive me as into a sepulchre, then believe me my passion gets entirely the sway, then I would not have you see those rhapsodies which I once thought it impossible I should ever give way to, and which I have often laughed at in another, for fear you should think me either too unhappy or perhaps a little mad.

I am now at a very pleasant cottage window, looking onto a beautiful hilly country, with a glimpse of the sea; the morning is very fine. I do not know how elastic my spirit might be, what pleasure I might have in living here and breathing and wandering as free as a stag about this beautiful coast if the remembrance of you did not weigh so upon me. I have never known any unalloy'd happiness for many days together: the death or sickness of some one has always spoilt my hours—and now when none such troubles oppress me, it is you must confess very hard that another sort of pain should haunt me.

Ask yourself my love whether you are not very cruel to have so entrammelled me, so destroyed my freedom. Will you confess this in the letter you must write immediately, and do all you can to console me in it—make it rich as a draught of poppies to intoxicate me—write the softest words and kiss them that I may at least touch my lips where yours have been. For myself I know not how to express my devotion to so fair a form: I want a brighter word than bright, a fairer word than fair. I almost wish we were butterflies and liv'd but three summer days—three such days with you I could fill with more delight than fifty common years could ever contain. But however selfish I may feel, I am sure I could never act selfishly: as I told you a day or two before I left Hampstead, I will never return to London if my fate does not turn up Pam or at least a court-card. Though I could centre my happiness in you, I cannot expect to engross your heart so entirely—indeed if I thought you felt as much for me as I do for you at this moment I do not think I could restrain myself from seeing you again tomorrow for the delight of one embrace. But no—I must live upon hope and chance. In case of the worst that can happen, I shall still love you—but what hatred shall I have for another!

Some lines I read the other day are continually ringing a peal in my ears:

> *To see those eyes I prize above mine own*
> *Dart favours on another—*
> *And those sweet lips (yielding immortal nectar)*
> *Be gently press'd by any but myself—*
> *Think, think Francesca, what a cursed thing*
> *It were beyond expression!*

J.

Do write immediately. There is no post from this place, so you must address Post Office, Newport, Isle of Wight. I know before night I shall curse myself for having sent you so cold a letter; yet it is better to do it as much in my senses as possible. Be as kind as the distance will permit to your

John Keats

Present my compliments to your mother, my love to Margaret and best remembrances to your Brother—if you please so.

8 July, 1819.

My sweet Girl—Your letter gave me more delight than any thing in the world but yourself could do; indeed I am almost astonished that any absent one should have that luxurious power over my senses which I feel. Even when I am not thinking of you I receive your influence and a tenderer nature stealing upon me. All my thoughts, my unhappiest days and nights have, I find, not at all cured me of my love of beauty, but made it so intense that I am miserable that you are not with me: or rather breathe in that dull sort of patience that cannot be called life.

I never knew before, what such a love as you have made me feel, was; I did not believe in it; my fancy was afraid of it, lest it should burn me up. But if you will fully love me, though there may be some fire, 'twill not be more than we can bear when moistened and bedewed with pleasures.

You mention 'horrid people' and ask me whether it depend upon them whether I see you again. Do understand me, my love, in this. I have so much of you in my heart that I must turn mentor when I see a chance of harm befalling you. I would never see any thing but pleasure in your eyes, love on your lips, and happiness in your steps. I would wish to see you among those amusements suitable to your inclinations and spirits; so that our loves might be a delight in the midst of pleasures agreeable enough, rather than a resource from vexations and cares. But I doubt much, in case of the worst, whether I shall be philosopher enough to follow my own lessons: if I saw my resolution give you a pain I could not.

Why may I not speak of your beauty, since without that I could never have lov'd you? I cannot conceive any beginning of such love as I have for you but beauty. There may be a sort of love for which, without the least sneer at it, I have the highest respect and can admire it in others: but it has not the richness, the bloom, the full form, the enchantment of love after my own heart. So let me speak of your beauty, though to my own endangering; if you could be so cruel to me as to try elsewhere its power.

You say you are afraid I shall think you do not love me—in saying this you make me ache the more to be near you. I am at the diligent use of my faculties here, I do not pass a day without sprawling some blank verse or tagging some rhymes; and here I must confess, that, (since I am on that subject) I love you the more in that I believe you have liked me for my own sake and for nothing else. I have met with women whom I really think would like to be married to a poem and to be given away by a novel. I have seen your comet, and only wish it was a sign that poor Rice would get well whose illness makes him rather a melancholy companion: and the more so as so to conquer his feelings and hide them from me, with a forc'd pun.

I kiss'd your writing over in the hope you had indulg'd me by leaving a trace of honey. What was your dream? Tell it me and I will tell you the interpretation threreof.

Ever yours, my love!
John Keats.

Do not accuse me of delay—we have not here any opportunity of sending letters every day. Write speedily.

27 July, 1819.
Sunday Night

My sweet Girl—I hope you did not blame me much for not obeying your request of a letter on Saturday: we have had four in our small room playing at cards night and morning leaving me no undisturb'd opportunity to write. Now Rice and Martin are gone I am at liberty. Brown to my sorrow confirms the account you give of your ill health. You cannot conceive how I ache to be with you: how I would die for one hour—for what is in the world? I say you cannot conceive; it is impossible you should look with such eyes upon me as I have upon you: it cannot be.

Forgive me if I wander a little this evening, for I have been all day employ'd in a very abstract poem and I am in deep love with you, two things which must excuse me. I have, believe me, not been an age in letting you take possession of me; the very first week I knew you I wrote myself your vassal; but burnt the letter as the very next time I saw you I thought you manifested some dislike to me. If you should ever feel for man at the first sight what I did for you, I am lost. Yet I should not quarrel with you, but hate myself if such a thing were to happen—only I should burst if the thing were not as fine as a man as you are as a woman.

Perhaps I am too vehement, then fancy me on my knees, especially when I mention a part of your letter which hurt me; you say speaking of Mr. Severn 'but you must be satisfied in knowing that I admired you much more than your friend.' My dear love, I cannot believe there ever was or ever could be any thing to admire in me especially as far as sight goes—I cannot be admired, I am not a thing to be admired. You are, I love you; all I can bring you is a swooning admiration of your beauty. I hold that place among men which snub-nos'd brunettes with meeting eyebrows do among women—they are trash to me—unless I should find one among them with a fire in her heart like the one that burns in mine.

You absorb me in spite of myself—you alone: for I look not forward with any pleasure to what is called being settled in the world; I tremble at domestic cares—yet for you I would meet them, though if it would leave you the happier I would rather die than do so.

I have two luxuries to brood over in my walks, your loveliness and the hour of my death. O that I could have possession of them both in the same minute. I hate the world: it batters too much the wings of my self-will, and would I could take a sweet poison from your lips to send me out of it. From no others would I take it. I am indeed astonish'd to find myself so careless of all charms but yours—remembering as I do the time when even a bit of ribband was a matter of interest with me.

What softer words can I find for you after this—what it is I will not read. Nor will I say more here, but in a postscript answer any thing else you may have mentioned in your letter in so many words—for I am distracted with a thousand thoughts. I will imagine you Venus tonight and pray, pray, pray to your star like a Heathen.

Your's ever, fair star,

My seal is mark'd like a family table cloth with my Mother's initial F for Fanny: put between my Father's initials. You will soon hear from me again. My respectful compliments to your Mother. Tell Margaret I'll send her a reef of best rocks and tell Sam I will give him my light bay hunter if he will tie the Bishop hand and foot and pack him in a hamper and send him down for me to bathe him for his health with a necklace of good snubby stones about his neck.

25 College Street.
13 October, 1819.

My dearest Girl,

This moment I have set myself to copy some verses out fair. I cannot proceed with any degree of content. I must write you a line or two and see if that will assist in dismissing you from my mind for ever so short a time. Upon my soul I can think of nothing else—The time is passed when I had power to advise and warn you against the unpromising morning of my life—My love has made me selfish. I cannot exist without you—I am forgetful of every thing but seeing you again—my life seems to stop there—I see no further. You have absorb'd me. I have a sensation at the present moment as though I was dissolving—I should be exquisitely miserable without the hope of soon seeing you. I should be afraid to separate myself far from you. My sweet Fanny, will your heart never change? My love, will it? I have no limit now to my love...

Your note came in just here—I cannot be happier away from you—'T is richer than an Argosy of Pearles. Do not threat me even in jest. I have been astonished that men could die martyrs for religion—I have shudder'd at it—I shudder no more—I could be martyr'd for my religion—Love is my religion—I could die for that—I could die for you. My creed is love and you are its only tenet—You have ravish'd me away by a power I cannot resist: and yet I could resist till I saw you; and even since I have seen you I have endeavoured often "to reason against the reasons of my Love." I can do that no more—the pain would be too great—My Love is selfish—I cannot breathe without you.

Yours for ever

John Keats

March, 1820.

Sweetest Fanny,
You fear, sometimes, I do not love you so much as you wish? My dear Girl I love you ever and ever and without reserve. The more I have known you the more have I lov'd. In every way—even my jealousies have been agonies of Love, in the hottest fit I ever had I would have died for you. I have vex'd you too much. But for Love! Can I help it? You are always new. The last of your kisses was ever the sweetest; the last smile the brightest; the last movement the gracefullest. When you pass'd my window home yesterday, I was fill'd with as much admiration as if I had then seen you for the first time. You uttered a half complaint once that I only lov'd your beauty. Have I nothing else then to love in you but that? Do not I see a heart naturally furnish'd with wings imprison itself with me? No ill prospect has been able to turn your thoughts a moment from me. This perhaps should be as much a subject of sorrow as joy—but I will not talk of that. Even if you did not love me I could not help an entire devotion to you: how much more deeply then must I feel for you knowing you love me. My mind has been the most discontented and restless one that ever was put into a body too small for it. I never felt my mind repose upon anything with complete and undistracted enjoyment—upon no person but you. When you are in the room my thoughts never fly out of window: you always concentrate my whole senses. The anxiety shown about our Love in your last note is an immense pleasure to me; however you must not suffer such speculations to molest you any more: not will I any more believe you can have the least pique against me. Brown is gone out—but here is Mrs Wylie—when she is gone I shall be awake for you.—Remembrances to your Mother.
Your affectionate, J. Keats

May/June, 1820.
Wednesday Morning.

My Dearest Girl,
I have been a walk this morning with a book in my hand, but as usual I have been occupied with nothing but you: I wish I could say in an agreeable manner. I am tormented day and night. They talk of my going to Italy. 'Tis certain I shall never recover if I am to be so long separate from you: yet with all this devotion to you I cannot persuade myself into any confidence of you. Past experience connected with the fact of my long separation from you gives me agonies which are scarcely to be talked of. When your mother comes I shall be very sudden and expert in asking her whether you have been to Mrs Dilke's, for she might say no to make me easy. I am literally worn to death, which seems my only recourse. I cannot forget what has pass'd. What? nothing: with a man of the world, but to me deathful. I will get rid of this as much as possible. When you were in the habit of

flirting with Brown you would have left off, could your own heart have felt one half of one pang mine did. Brown is a good sort of man—he did not know he was doing me to death by inches. I feel the effect of every one of those hours in my side now; and for that cause, though he has done me many services, though I know his love and friendship for me, though at this moment I should be without pence were it not for his assistance, I will never see or speak to him until we are both old men, if we are to be. I will resent my heart having been made a football. You will call this madness. I have heard you say that it was not unpleasant to wait a few years—you have amusements—your mind is away—you have not brooded over one idea as I have, and how should you? You are to me an object intensely desireable—the air I breathe in a room empty of you is unhealthy. I am not the same to you—no—you can wait—you have a thousand activities—you can be happy without me. Any party, any thing to fill up the day has been enough. How have you pass'd this month? Who have you smil'd with? All this may seem savage in me. You do not feel as I do—you do not know what it is to love—one day you may—your time is not come. Ask yourself how many unhappy hours Keats has caused you in loneliness. For myself I have been a martyr the whole time, and for this reason I speak; the confession is forc'd from me by the torture. I appeal to you by the blood of that Christ you believe in: Do not write to me if you have done anything this month which it would have pained me to have seen. You may have altered—if you have not—if you still behave in dancing rooms and other societies as I have seen you—I do not want to live—if you have done so I wish this coming night may be my last. I cannot live without you, and not only you but chaste you; virtuous you. The sun rises and sets, the day passes, and you follow the bent of your inclination to a certain extent—you have no conception of the quantity of miserable feeling that passes through me in a day. Be serious! Love is not a plaything—and again do not write unless you can do it with a crystal conscience. I would sooner die for want of you than—

Yours for ever

J. Keats

Henry von Kleist

Henry von Kleist (born Bernd Heinrich Wilhelm von Kleist, 18 October, 1777–21 November, 1811) was a German poet, dramatist, novelist and short story writer. He entered the Prussian Army in 1792, served in the Rhine campaign of 1796, and retired from the service in 1799 with the rank of lieutenant. He studied law and philosophy at the Viadrina University and in 1800 received a subordinate post in the Ministry of Finance at Berlin. In the following year, Kleist's roving, restless spirit got the better of him, he visited Paris and then settled in Switzerland. In the autumn of 1802, he returned to Germany; visited friends Goethe, Schiller, and Wieland in Weimar, stayed for a while in Leipzig and Dresden, again proceeded to Paris, and returning in 1804 to his post in Berlin was transferred to Königsberg. On a journey to Dresden in 1807, Kleist was arrested by the French as a spy. On regaining his liberty, he proceeded to Dresden, where, in conjunction with Adam Heinrich Müller, he published the journal *Phöbus* in 1808.

His first major work was a gloomy tragedy, *The Schroffenstein Family* (*Die Familie Schroffenstein*, 1803); the material for the second, *Penthesilea* (1808), is taken from a Greek source about the queen of the Amazons and presents a picture of wild passion. More successful than either of these was his romantic play, *Käthchen of Heilbronn* (*Das Käthchen von Heilbronn*, 1808), a poetic drama full of medieval bustle and mystery, which has retained its popularity. In comedy, Kleist made a name with *The Broken Jug* (*Der Zerbrochne Krug*, 1808). Of his other dramas, *Die Hermannsschlacht* (1809) and *The Prince of Homburg* (*Prinz Friedrich von Homburg oder die Schlacht bei Fehrbellin*, 1810), are among his best works.

Little is known of Kleist's love life. There has been speculation that he was homosexual or bisexual, due to many mysteries in his life, disguises and close friendships to Ernst von Pfuel (1779–1866) and others. Sometime around 1800 he became engaged to Wilhelmine von Zenge (1780–1852) and shortly thereafter disappeared with a male friend on a trip to Würzburg. The engagement lasted for three years. In 1809, he made the acquaintance of Adolfine Sophie Henriette Vogel (c.1780–21 November, 1811). She was an accomplished musician, actress and intellectual. Married, she had a young daughter. Their friendship blossomed into a mutual respect, sharing a love for music and the arts. The relationship between the two became more intimate in 1811, but by then she was dying of cancer. In the autumn of 1811, Kleist and Adolfine agreed to a suicide pact. They travelled together to an inn near Wannsee Lake, and on 21 November, climbed a hill and had a picnic, after which Kleist shot Vogel and then himself. He left two suicide notes, one to his sister, Ulrike and another to his cousin Marie. One read "I am going, since there is nothing left for me either to learn or gain in this life."

To Wilhelmine von Zenge

11 January, 1801.

    In so many instances I have observed this truth: that love always brings about the most unbelievable changes in people... in most cases this begins with their clothes... then begins the reform of their physical natures, and perhaps it would progress no further, but if the love were of a higher kind, only then would the great evolution of the soul commence: desires, hopes, prospects, all are changed, the coarse satisfactions overthrown, replaced by the more refined... all that is beautiful, noble, good and great are comprehended with a more open, receptive soul, and so they feel it more fully within themselves, their hearts expand, their souls uplift in their breasts, they embrace some high ideal against which they begin to measure themselves...

22 March, 1801.

    If everyone wore green glasses instead of eyes, they would have to judge that the things they saw through them were green—and they could never decide whether their eyes showed them things as they are or whether something had been added that belonged not to the thing but to the eyes. So it is with the understanding. We cannot decide whether what we call truth is truly the truth, or whether it only seems so to us. Ah, Wilhelmine, if the point of this thought does not strike your heart, do not smile at another, who feels himself wounded in the depths of his inmost soul. My only, my highest goal has fallen, and now I have none.

To Ernst von Pfuel

7 January, 1805.

    You exercise—you good, dear boy—a strange power over my heart with your eloquence, and whether I give you the whole insight into my being or not, at times you show me a picture of myself so close to my very soul that I am moved, as before the newest occurrence in the world. I shall never forget that solemn night when you abused me in a manner that was truly sublime, in the worst hole in all of France, almost like the archangel abused his fallen brother in the Messiad. Why can't I worship you, whom I still love above all, as my master? Oh how we flew into one another's arms a year ago in Dresden! How the world has opened up, like a racetrack, before us, trembling with desire and longing for the contest! And now we have plunged in, lying there one above the another, with our view of the race to the goal that never seemed so shining to us as now, enveloped in the dust of our downfall. Mine, mine, is the blame, I entangled you in this, oh I can't tell you how I feel it. My dear Pfuel, of what use are all these tears to me? To pass the time each minute as they fall, I would, like the naked King Richard, hollow out a grave with them and in that grave bury you and me and our endless pain. Perhaps we shall never embrace again! Not even if one day, recovered from our plunge into ruin—for what is there from which man does not recover—we meet again, walking on crutches.

At one time we loved in one another the highest qualities of mankind; because we loved our true nature developing like a few lucky plants. We felt—or at least I did—the sweet enthusiasm of friendship! You reawakened the times of ancient Greece to my heart, I could sleep with you, dear boy; thus my whole soul embraces you. Often, as you waded into the Lake at Thun, I would gaze upon your beautiful body with truly girlish feelings. I could really be as an artist for the study. I would have found, if I had been one, perhaps the inspiration for a God. Your small, curly head, a sturdy neck, two broad shoulders, a sinewy body: the whole an image of strength, as though you had been designed after the most beautiful young bull ever sacrificed to Zeus. All the laws of Lykurgus, as well as his concept of the love of youths, have become clear to me through the feelings you have woken up in me. Come to me!

Listen, I want to tell you. I have come to love Altenstein, I have been entrusted with the drawing up of some transcripts and I do not doubt that the expectation is for me to complete them. I can solve differential equations and I can write verses; are these not the two limits of human capability? They will surely employ me, and soon, and with a wage: come with me to Ansbach and let us enjoy our sweet friendship. Let me have achieved something from all these battles that makes my life at least bearable. You have shared with me in Leipzig, or you wanted to, which amounts to the same thing; accept the same from me!

I shall never marry—be thou wife to me, and children, and grandchildren! Do not go further on the road you are walking on, do not throw fate under your feet, it can hurt and crush you. Let one victim be enough. Preserve the ruins of your soul, we will forever remember with pleasure the romantic part of our lives. And if war calls you to the battlefield to fight for your homeland, then go, you will feel your worth when the need must be. Accept my proposal. If you do not, I shall feel that nobody loves me in all the world. I should like to say more, but it is not suited for a letter. Adieu. In person once more.

Heinrich v. Kleist

To Adolfine Henriette Vogel

Berlin, after St. Michael's day, 1810.

My Henriette, my darling, my love, my little dove, my life, my dear sweet life, light of my life, my all, my wealth and possessions, my castles, fields, meadows and vineyards, oh sun of my life, sun, moon and stars, heaven and earth, my past and my future, my bride, my girl, my dear friend, my innermost, my heart's blood, my intestines, my shining star, oh dearest, how do I call you?

My golden child, my pearl, my precious stone, my crown, my queen and empress. You dear darling of my heart, my highest and most precious, my all and everything, my wife, the baptism of my children, my tragic play, my posthumous reputation. Ah! You are my second better self, my virtues, my merits, my hope, the forgiveness of my sins, my future sanctity. Oh! Little daughter of heaven, my child of God, my intercessor, my guardian angel, my cherubim and seraph, how I love you!

D. H. Lawrence

David Herbert Richards Lawrence (11 September, 1885–2 March, 1930) was an English novelist, poet, playwright, essayist and literary critic. He is perhaps best known for his novels *Sons and Lovers* (1913), *The Rainbow* (1915), *Women in Love* (1920) and *Lady Chatterley's Lover* (1928). His collected works represent an extended reflection upon the dehumanising effects of modernity and industrialisation. In them, Lawrence confronts issues relating to emotional health and vitality, spontaneity, and instinct. His opinions earned him many enemies and he endured official persecution, censorship, and misrepresentation of his creative work throughout the second half of his life, much of which he spent in a voluntary exile he called his "savage pilgrimage." At the time of his death, his public reputation was that of a pornographer who had wasted his considerable talents. E. M. Forster, in an obituary notice, challenged this widely held view, describing him as, "The greatest imaginative novelist of our generation." Later, the influential Cambridge critic F. R. Leavis championed both his artistic integrity and his moral seriousness, placing much of Lawrence's fiction within the canonical "great tradition" of the English novel. Lawrence is now valued by many as a visionary thinker and significant representative of modernism in English literature.

An early engagement to Louisa "Louie" Burrows (1888–1962), an old friend from his days in Nottingham and Eastwood, ended in 1911. In March, 1912, Lawrence met Frieda Freiin *née* von Richthofen Weekley (11 August, 1879–11 August, 1956), with whom he was to share the rest of his life. She was six years older than he, married to his former modern languages professor at Nottingham University, Ernest Weekley, and with three young children. Within two months they had eloped to her parents' home in Metz, a garrison town then in Germany near the disputed border with France. Their stay included Lawrence's first brush with militarism, when he was arrested and accused of being a British spy, before being released following an intervention from Frieda's father. After this encounter Lawrence left for a small hamlet to the south of Munich, where he was joined by Weekley. From Germany they walked south, across the Alps to Italy, returning to England in 1913. Eventually, Weekley obtained her divorce, and shortly before the outbreak of World War I they were married, on 13 July, 1914. They intended to return to the continent, but the outbreak of war kept them in England, where they endured official harassment and censorship. They also struggled with limited resources and D. H. Lawrence's already frail health. Leaving post-war England at the earliest opportunity, they travelled widely, eventually settling at the Kiowa Ranch near Taos, New Mexico and, in Lawrence's last years, at the Villa Mirenda, near Scandicci in Tuscany. After her husband's death in Vence, France in 1930, Frieda returned to Taos to live with her third husband, Angelo Ravagli.

To Louie Burrows

20 December, 1910.

My dear—it is ten minutes to post time—been to the kiddies party at school. Don't let me sadden you—I could not bear to do so.

I told Jessie she could marry me if she'd ask me. Unawares I had let our affair run on: what could I do! But she wouldn't have me so—thank God. I don't want to marry her—though she is a very dear friend. She has not any very intrinsic part of me, now —no, not at all.

As for the other 3—you were one, and Jessie another: well, I lied. They only liked me and flattered me. I am a fool. One is a jolly nice girl who is engaged now, and whom I hope you will know. She's a school-mistress in Yorkshire. One is a little bitch, and I hate her: and she plucked me, like Potiphar's wife: and one is nothing. I'll tell you verbatim when you ask me.

I am wild and sudden by nature—but I shall be true and try to make you happy—I am as sure of myself as I can be sure of anything. I have a tiresome character. But don't doubt me—don't. I do love you. When we are together, and quiet, it will be beautiful. I do want you to be peaceful with, to grow with, to slowly and sweetly develop with—it's only now and then passionate. Oh dear—I wonder if you'll ever wish you'd had Court[18]. I wish I were just like ordinary men. I am a bit different—and god knows, I regret it.

Nay my love, don't doubt me. I love you truly.
D. H. Lawrence

To Frieda Weekley

Queen's Square, Eastwood, March, 1912.

You are the most wonderful woman in all England.

D. H. Lawrence

Eastwood, 30 April, 1912.

I feel so horrid and helpless. I know how it all sickens you, and you are almost at the end of the tether. And what was decent yesterday will perhaps be frightfully indecent today. But it's like being ill: there's nothing to do but shut one's teeth and look at the wall and wait.

You say you're going to Gladys tomorrow. But even that is uncertain. And I must know about the trains. What time are you going to Germany, what day, what

---

[18] Ernest Court, her friend.

hour, which railway, which class? Do tell me as soon as you can, or else what can I do? I will come any time you tell me—but let me know.

You must be in an insane whirl in your mind. I feel helpless and rudderless, a stupid scattered fool. For goodness sake tell me something and something definite. I would do anything on earth for you, and I can do nothing. Yesterday I knew would be decent, but I don't like my feeling today—presentiment. I am afraid of something low, like an eel which bites out of the mud, and hangs on with its teeth. I feel as if I can't breathe while we're in England. I wish I could come and see you, or else you me.

D. H. Lawrence

Hotel Deutscher Hof, Metz, 7 May, 1912.

Now I can't stand it any longer, I can't. For two hours I haven't moved a muscle—just sat and thought. I have written a letter to Ernst. You needn't, of course, send it. But you must say to him all I have said. No more dishonour, no more lies. Let them do their—silliest—but no more subterfuge, lying, dirt, fear. I feel as if it would strangle me. What is it all but procrastination? No, I can't bear it, because it's bad. I love you. Let us face anything, do anything, put up with anything. But this crawling under the mud I cannot bear.

I'm afraid I've got a fit of heroics. I've tried so hard to work—but I can't. This situation is round my chest like a cord. It mustn't continue. I will go right away, if you like. I will stop in Metz till you get Ernst's answer to the truth. But no, I won't utter or act or willingly let you utter or act, another single lie in the business.

I'm not going to joke, I'm not going to laugh, I'm not going to make light of things for you. The situation tortures me too much. It's the situation, the situation I can't stand—no, and I won't. I love you too much.

Don't show this letter to either of your sisters—no. Let us be good. You are clean, but you dirty your feet. I'll sign myself as you call me

—Mr Lawrence

Don't be miserable—if I didn't love you I wouldn't mind when you lied. But I love you, and Lord, I pay for it.

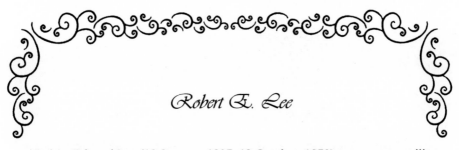

Robert E. Lee

Robert Edward Lee (19 January, 1807–12 October, 1870) was a career military officer who is best known for having commanded the Confederate Army of Northern Virginia in the American Civil War. The son of U.S. Revolutionary War hero, Henry ("Light Horse Harry") Lee III, and a top graduate of West Point, Robert E. Lee distinguished himself as an exceptional officer and combat engineer in the United States Army for 32 years. In early 1861, with the Civil War looming, President Abraham Lincoln invited Lee to take command of the entire Union Army. Lee declined because his home state of Virginia was, despite his wishes, seceding from the Union, and Lee chose to follow his home state. Lee's eventual role in the newly established Confederacy was to serve as a senior military adviser to Confederate President Jefferson Davis. Lee soon emerged as the shrewdest battlefield tactician of the war, after he assumed command of the Confederate eastern army. His abilities as a tactician have been praised by many military historians. They were made evident in his many victories. In the spring of 1864, the new Union commander, Ulysses S. Grant, began a series of campaigns to wear down Lee's army. In the final months of the Civil War, Lee's depleted forces were overwhelmed at Petersburg; he abandoned Richmond and retreated west as Union forces encircled his army. Lee surrendered to Grant at Appomattox Court House on 9 April, 1865, marking the end of Confederate hopes; the remaining armies soon capitulated. Lee rejected as folly the starting of a guerrilla campaign against the Yankees and called for reconciliation between the North and the South. He became a post-war icon of the South's "lost cause," and is still admired to this day.

In the summer of 1829, Lee courted Mary Anna Randolph Custis (1 October, 1808–5 November, 1873), great-granddaughter of Martha Washington, whom he had known as a child. Lee obtained permission to write to her, though Mary warned him to be "discreet" in his writing, as her mother read her letters, especially from men. Custis refused Lee the first time he asked to marry her; her father, George Washington Custis did not believe he was a suitable man for his daughter. She accepted him, with her father's consent, in September, 1830, while he was on summer leave, and the two were wed on 30 June, 1831, at the Custis home, Arlington House. They had three sons and four daughters: George Washington "Custis" (1832–1913), Mary (1835–1918), William Henry Fitzhugh "Rooney" (1837–1891), Anne Carter "Annie" (1839–1862), Eleanor Agnes (1841–1873), Robert Edward (1843–1914) and Mildred Childe "Milly" (1846–1905). He was a devoted husband and father, and wrote continuously to his wife and children during his long absences.

Louisville, 5 June, 1839.

My dearest Mary

I arrived here last night, and before going out this morning, will inform you of my well-doing thus far.

After leaving Staunton, I got on very well, but did not reach Guyandotte till Sunday afternoon, where, before alighting from the stage, I espied a boat descending the river, in which I took passage to Cincinnati...

You do not know how much I have missed you and the children, my dear Mary. To be alone in a crowd is very solitary. In the woods I feel sympathy with the trees and birds, in whose company I take delight, but experience no pleasure in a strange crowd.

I hope you are all well and will continue so, and therefore must urge you to be very prudent and careful of those dear children. If I could only get to squeeze at that little fellow turning up his sweet mouth to 'keese baba!' You must not let him run wild in my absence, and will have to exercise firm authority over all of them. This will not require severity, or even strictness, but constant attention and an unwavering course. Mildness and forbearance, tempered by firmness and judgment, will strengthen their affection for you, while it will maintain your control over them.

Richmond, 2 April, 1860.

...I am very anxious about you. You have to move and make arrangements to go to some point of safety, which you must select. The Mount Vernon plate and pictures ought to be secured. Keep quiet while you remain and in your preparation. War is inevitable, and there is no telling when it will burst around you. Virginia, yesterday, I understand, joined the Confederate States. What policy they may adopt I cannot conjecture. May God bless and preserve you, and have mercy upon all our people, is the constant prayer of your affectionate husband,

Robert Lee

Abraham Lincoln

Abraham Lincoln (12 February, 1809–15 April, 1865) was the 16th President of the United States, from 1861, until his assassination in 1865. Reared in a poor family on the western frontier, Lincoln was mostly self-educated. He became a country lawyer, an Illinois state legislator, and a one-term member of the United States House of Representatives, but failed in two attempts at a seat in the United States Senate. Lincoln was an outspoken opponent of the expansion of slavery in the United States, which he deftly articulated in his campaign debates and speeches. As a result, he secured the Republican nomination and was elected the 16th President of the United States on 6 November, 1860. He successfully led the country through its greatest constitutional, military and moral crisis—the American Civil War—by preserving the Union by force while ending slavery and promoting economic modernisation. He issued his Emancipation Proclamation in 1863, and promoted the passage of the Thirteenth Amendment to the United States Constitution, abolishing slavery. His Gettysburg address, one of the most quoted speeches in history, was delivered at the dedication of the Soldiers' National Cemetery in Gettysburg, Pennsylvania, on the afternoon of Thursday, 19 November, 1863. In 1865 Lincoln began his second term as President, but was shot and killed that April.

Lincoln's first romantic interest was Ann Rutledge (7 January, 1813–25 August, 1835), whom he met in New Salem; by 1835, they were in a relationship but not formally engaged. Ann wanted to notify a former love before "consummating the engagement to Mr. L. with marriage." Rutledge died, however, on 25 August, most likely of typhoid fever. In the early 1830s, he met Mary Owens (1808–1877) from Kentucky when she was visiting her sister. Late in 1836, Lincoln agreed to a match with Mary if she returned to New Salem. Mary did return in November, 1836, and Lincoln courted her for a time; however, they both had second thoughts about their relationship. On 16 August, 1837, Lincoln wrote to Mary suggesting he would not blame her if she ended the relationship. She never replied, and the courtship was over.

In 1840, Lincoln became engaged to Mary Ann Todd (13 December, 1818–16 July, 1882), who was from a wealthy slave-holding family in Lexington, Kentucky. They met in Springfield in December, 1839, and were engaged shortly after. A wedding was set for 1 January, 1841, but the couple split as the wedding approached. They later met at a party, and then married on 4 November, 1842, in the Springfield mansion of Mary's married sister. While preparing for the nuptials and having cold feet again, Lincoln, when asked where he was going, replied, "To hell, I suppose." Mary worked diligently in their home, assuming household duties which had been performed for her in her own family. She also made efficient use of the limited funds available from her husband's law practice. The Lincolns had a budding family, with the birth of four sons: Robert Todd (1843–1926), Edward

Baker (1846–1850), William Wallace (1850–1862) and Thomas (1853–1871). Robert was the only child to live past the age of 18. The death of their sons had profound effects on both parents. Later in life, Mary struggled with the stresses of losing her husband and sons; Robert Lincoln committed her to a mental health asylum in 1875.

To Mary Owens

7 May, 1837.

This thing of living in Springfield is rather a dull business after all, at least it is so to me. I am quite as lonesome here as ever was anywhere in my life. I have been spoken to by but one woman since I've been here, and should not have been by her, if she could have avoided it. I've never been to church yet, nor probably shall not be soon. I stay away because I am conscious I should not know how to behave myself.

I am often thinking about what we said of your coming to live at Springfield. I am afraid you would not be satisfied. There is a great deal of flourishing about in carriages here, which it would be your doom to see without shareing in it. You would have to be poor without the means of hiding your poverty. Do you believe you could bear that patiently? Whatever woman may cast her lot with mine, should any ever do so, it is my intention to do all in my power to make her happy and contented; and there is nothing I can imagine, that would make me more unhappy than to fail in the effort. I know I should be much happier with you than the way I am, provided I saw no signs of discontent in you. What you have said to me may have been in jest, or I may have misunderstood it. If so, then let it be forgotten; if otherwise, I much wish you would think seriously before you decide. For my part I have already decided. What I have said I will most positively abide by, provided you wish it. My opinion is that you had better not do it. You have not been accustomed to hardship, and it may be more severe than you now imagine. I know you are capable of thinking correctly on any subject; and if you deliberate maturely upon this, before you decide, then I am willing to abide your decision.

16 August, 1837.

My dear Mary
You must know that I cannot see you or think of you with entire indifference; and yet it may be that you are mistaken in regard to what my real feelings toward you are. If I knew that you were not, I should not trouble you with this letter. Perhaps any other man would know enough without further information, but I consider it my peculiar right to plead ignorance and your bounden duty to allow the plea. I want in all cases to do right, and most particularly so in all cases with

women. I want at this particular time more than anything else to do right with you, and if I knew it would be doing right, as I rather suspect it would, to let you alone, I would do it. And for the purpose of making the matter as plainly as possible I now say you can drop the subject, dismiss your thoughts—if you ever had any—from me forever, and leave this letter unanswered without calling forth one accusing murmur from me. And I will even go further and say that if it will add anything to your comfort and peace of mind to do so, it is my sincere wish that you should.

Do not understand by this that I wish to cut your acquaintance. I mean no such thing. What I do wish is that our further acquaintance should depend upon yourself. If such further acquaintance would contribute nothing to your happiness, I am sure it would not to mine. If you feel yourself in any degree bound to me, I am now willing to release you, provided you wish it; while, on the other hand, I am willing and even anxious to bind you faster, if I can be convinced that it will in any degree add to your happiness. This indeed is the whole question with me. Nothing would make me more miserable than to believe you miserable; nothing more happy than to know you were so.

In what I have now said I cannot be misunderstood; and to make myself understood is the only object of this letter. If it suits you best not to answer this, farewell. A long life and a merry one attend you. But if you conclude to write back, speak as plainly as I do. There can be neither harm nor danger in saying to me anything you think just in the manner you think it.

Your friend,
A. Lincoln

To Mary Todd Lincoln

Executive Mansion
Washington, 8 August, 1863.

My dear Wife.
All is well as usual, and no particular trouble any way. I put the money into the Treasury at five per cent, with the privilege of withdrawing it any time upon thirty days notice. I suppose you are glad to learn this. Tell dear Tad, poor "Nanny Goat," is lost; and Mrs. Cuthbert & I are in distress about it.

The day you left, Nanny was found resting herself, and chewing her little cud, on the middle of Tad's bed. But now she's gone! The gardener kept complaining that she destroyed the flowers, till it was concluded to bring her down to the White House. This was done, and the second day she had disappeared, and has not been heard of since. This is the last we know of poor "Nanny."

The weather continues dry, and excessively warm here.

Nothing very important occurring. The election in Kentucky has gone very strongly right. Old Mr. Wickliffe got ugly, as you know, ran for Governor, and is terribly beaten. Upon Mr. Crittendens death, Brutus Clay, Cassius' brother, was put on the track for Congress, and is largely elected. Mr. Menzies, who, as we

thought, behaved very badly last session of Congress, is largely beaten in the District opposite Cincinnati, by Green Clay Smith, Cassius Clay's nephew. But enough. Affectionately
    A. Lincoln

Franz Liszt

Franz Liszt (22 October, 1811–31 July, 1886) was a 19th century Hungarian composer, virtuoso pianist and teacher. Liszt became renowned throughout Europe during the 19th century for his great skill as a performer. He was said by his contemporaries to have been the most technically advanced pianist of his age and perhaps the greatest pianist of all time. He was also an important and influential composer, a notable piano teacher, a conductor who contributed significantly to the modern development of the art, and a benefactor to other composers and performers, notably Richard Wagner, Hector Berlioz, Camille Saint-Saëns, Edvard Grieg and Alexander Borodin. As a composer, Liszt was one of the most prominent representatives of the "Neudeutsche Schule" ("New German School"). He left behind an extensive and diverse body of work, in which he influenced his forward-looking contemporaries and anticipated some 20th-century ideas and trends. Some of his most notable contributions were the invention of the symphonic poem, developing the concept of thematic transformation as part of his experiments in musical form and making radical departures in harmony.

In 1828, Liszt fell in love with one of his pupils, Caroline de Saint-Cricq, the daughter of Charles X's minister of commerce. However, her father insisted that the affair be broken off. In the following years Liszt had many love affairs, leading in 1833, to his relationship with the Countess Marie Catherine Sophie *née* de Flavigny d'Agoult (31 December, 1805–5 March, 1876). In 1835 the Countess left her husband and family to join Liszt in Geneva; their daughter Blandine Rachel (18 December, 1835–11 September, 1862) was born there. For the next four years Liszt and the Countess lived together, mainly in Switzerland and Italy—where, in Como, their daughter, Cosima Francesca Gaetana (24 December, 1837–1 April, 1930), was born—with occasional visits to Paris. In 1839, their only son, Daniel (9 May, 1839–13 December, 1859), was born, but that autumn relations between them became strained. The Countess returned to Paris with the children, while Liszt gave six concerts in Vienna, then toured Europe, spending holidays with the Countess and their children on the island of Nonnenwerth on the Rhine. In spring 1844 the couple finally separated.

In February, 1847, Liszt played in Kiev. There he met the Princess Carolyne zu Sayn-Wittgenstein (8 February, 1819–9 March, 1887), who dominated most of the rest of his life. She persuaded him to concentrate on composition, which meant giving up his career as a travelling virtuoso. He spent the winter with the Princess at her estate in Woronince, and they then lived together in Weimar. She eventually wished to marry Liszt, but since she had been previously married and her husband was still alive, she had to convince the Roman Catholic authorities that her marriage to him had been invalid. After huge efforts and a monstrously intricate process, she was temporarily successful (September, 1860). It was planned that the couple would marry in Rome, on 22 October, 1861, Liszt's 50th birthday. Liszt having arrived in Rome the day before, the Princess nevertheless declined, by the late evening, to marry him. It appears that both her husband and the Tsar of Russia had managed to quash permission for the marriage at the Vatican. The Russian government also impounded her several estates in the Polish Ukraine, which made her later marriage to anybody unfeasible.

The 1860s were a period of great sadness in Liszt's private life, and by 1863 he had announced that he would retreat to a solitary living.

To the Countess Marie d'Agoult

Thursday morning, December, 1834.

My heart overflows with emotion and joy! I do not know what heavenly languor, what infinite pleasure permeates it and burns me up. It is as if I had never loved!!! Tell me whence these uncanny disturbances spring, these inexpressible foretastes of delight, these divine tremors of love. Oh! all this can only spring from you, sister, angel, woman, Marie! All this can only be, is surely nothing less than a gentle ray streaming from your fiery soul, or else some secret poignant teardrop which you have long since left in my breast.

My God, my God, never force us apart, take pity on us! But what am I saying? Forgive my weakness, how couldst Thou divide us! Thou wouldst have nothing but pity for us... No no! It is not in vain that our flesh and our souls quicken and become immortal through Thy Word, which cries out deep within us Father, Father... out Thy hand to us, that our broken hearts seek their refuge in Thee... O! we thank, bless and praise Thee, O God, for all that Thou has given us, and all that Thou hast prepared for us....

This is to be—to be!

Marie! Marie!

Oh let me repeat that name a hundred times, a thousand times over; for three days now it has lived within me, oppressed me, set me afire. I am not writing to you, no, I am close beside you. I see you, I hear you. Eternity in your arms... Heaven, Hell, everything, all is within you, redoubled... Oh! Leave me free to rave in my delirium. Drab, tame, constricting reality is no longer enough for me. We must live our lives to the full, loving and suffering to extremes!... Oh! you believe me capable of self-sacrifice, chastity, temperance and piety, do you not? But let no more be said of this... it is for you to question, to draw conclusions, to save me as you see fit. Let me be mad, senseless since you can do nothing, nothing at all for me. It is good for me to speak to you now. This is to be! To be!!!

Franz

Jack London

John Griffith "Jack" (Chaney) London (12 January, 1876–22 November, 1916) was an American author, journalist, and social activist. Raised by an ex-slave after his mother had tried to kill herself while pregnant with him, he became an oyster pirate, worked on ships, and became a tramp and sailor before joining the Klondike Gold Rush in 1897. His experiences influenced many of his stories. He was a passionate advocate of unionization, socialism, and the rights of workers and wrote several powerful works dealing with these topics such as his non-fiction exposé, *The People of the Abyss* (1903) and his dystopian novel, *The Iron Heel* (1908). However he is best remembered as the author of novels *The Call of the Wild* (1903), set in the Klondike Gold Rush, his most-read, and generally considered his best book; *The Sea-Wolf* (1904) and *White Fang* (1906), which was also incredibly popular, about a wild wolfdog's journey to domestication. He was a pioneer in the then-burgeoning world of commercial magazine fiction and was one of the first fiction writers to obtain worldwide celebrity and a large fortune from his fiction alone.

London first met Anna Strunsky (1877–1964), in 1899. They spent a great deal of time together discussing social and political issues, and became dear friends. Anna and her sister Rose became leading members of the turn of the 20th century San Francisco intellectual scene, part of a radical group of young Californian writers and artists known as "The Crowd", which included London. On 7 April, 1900, London married Elizabeth "Bess" Maddern (c.1876–1948). Bess had been part of his circle of friends for a number of years. London admitted that his reason for marrying her was not love, but science. London's pet name for Bess was "Mother-Girl" and Bess's for London was "Daddy-Boy". Their first child, Joan, was born on 15 January, 1901, and their second, Bessie (later called Becky), on 20 October, 1902. While London had pride in his children, the marriage was under strain. It was implied by London that his wife, "devoted to purity", mistrusted him, and would no longer share a bed with him. On 24 July, 1903, London told Bess he was leaving and moved out. During 1904 London and Bess negotiated the terms of a divorce, and the decree was granted on 11 November, 1904. During the marriage, London continued his friendship with Anna Strunsky, even co-authoring *The Kempton-Wace Letters* in 1903, an epistolary novel contrasting two philosophies of love. She may have been the cause of his marital problems, but they were never together formally and in 1905 she met and fell in love with William English Walling, marrying him in 1906.

After divorcing Bess, London married Charmian Kittredge (27 November, 1871–14 January, 1955) on 19 November, 1905. London was introduced to Kittredge in 1900 by his MacMillan publisher, George Platt Brett, Sr., while Kittredge served as Brett's secretary. His attraction to her may also have affected his decision to leave Bess. Their time together included numerous trips. They attempted to have children. One child died at birth, and another pregnancy ended in a miscarriage.

To Anna Strunsky

Oakland, 3 April, 1901.

> *Dear Anna*
> *Did I say that the human might be filed in categories? Well, and if I did, let me qualify—not all humans. You elude me. I cannot place you, cannot grasp you. I may boast that of nine out of ten, under given circumstances, I can forecast their action; that of nine out of ten, by their word or action, I may feel the pulse of their hearts. But of the tenth I despair. It is beyond me. You are that tenth.*
>
> *Were ever two souls, with dumb lips, more incongruously matched! We may feel in common—surely, we oftimes do—and when we do not feel in common, yet do we understand; and yet we have no common tongue. Spoken words do not come to us. We are unintelligible. God must laugh at the mummery.*
>
> *The one gleam of sanity through it all is that we are both large temperamentally, large enough to often understand. True, we often understand but in vague glimmering ways, by dim perceptions, like ghosts, which, while we doubt, haunt us with their truth. And still, I, for one, dare not believe; for you are that tenth which I may not forecast.*
>
> *Am I unintelligible now? I do not know. I imagine so. I cannot find the common tongue.*
>
> *Large temperamentally—that is it. It is the one thing that brings us at all in touch. We have, flashed through us, you and I, each a bit of universal, and so we draw together. And yet we are so different.*
>
> *I smile at you when you grow enthusiastic? It is a forgivable smile—nay, almost an envious smile. I have lived twenty-five years of repression. I learned not to be enthusiastic. It is a hard lesson to forget. I begin to forget, but it is so little. At the best, before I die, I cannot hope to forget all or most. I can exult, now that I am learning, in little things, in other things; but of my things, and secret things doubly mine, I cannot, I cannot. Do I make myself intelligible? Do you hear my voice? I fear not. There are poseurs. I am the most successful of them all.*
> *Jack*

Count Honoré Gabriel de Mirabeau

Honoré Gabriel Riqueti, Comte de Mirabeau (9 March, 1749–2 April, 1791) was a French revolutionary, as well as a writer, diplomat, freemason, journalist and French politician. He was a popular orator and statesman. During the French Revolution, he was a moderate, favouring a constitutional monarchy built on the model of Great Britain. He unsuccessfully conducted secret negotiations with the French monarchy in an effort to reconcile it with the Revolution. Mirabeau however, is most notorious for the scandals which followed him around, especially his love affairs and writings. In his *Secret History of the Court of Berlin* (1787), he denounced the Prussian court as scandalous and corrupt, described the King of Prussia as weak and overly emotional, and labelled Prince Henry of Prussia, brother of Frederick the Great, narrow-minded and incompetent. The resulting uproar was an extreme embarrassment for the French government, which quickly censored the book but could not prevent its widespread notoriety.

Mirabeau's love affairs were well-known. In the late 1760s he won the heart of the lady to whom his colonel was attached; this led to such scandal that his own father obtained a *lettre de cachet* (an official document signed by the King), and Mirabeau was imprisoned on the Ile de Ré. On being released, the young Count obtained leave to accompany the French expedition to Corsica as a volunteer. During the Corsican expedition, Mirabeau contracted gambling debts and engaged in other scandalous love affairs. In 1772 he married a rich heiress, Marie Marguerite Emilie de Covet (c.1752–1800). Emilie, who was 19 years old, was apparently engaged to a much older nobleman. Nonetheless, Mirabeau pursued her for several months expecting that his marriage to her would benefit him from the allowance that the couple would receive from their parents. After several months of failed attempts at being introduced to the heiress, Mirabeau bribed one of Emilie's maids to let him into their residence, where he pretended to have had a sexual encounter with Emilie. To avoid losing face, her father saw that they got married just a couple of days after the incident.

Mirabeau, who was still facing financial trouble and increasing debt, could not keep up with the expensive lifestyle his wife was used to and their extravagances forced his father to send him into semi-exile in the country, where he wrote his earliest extant work, the *Essai sur le Despotisme* (1775). The couple had a son who died early, mostly due to the poor living conditions they experienced during that time. In 1775 in a house of a friend he met Marie Thérèse Sophie Richard de Ruffey, Marquise de Monnier (9 January, 1754–8 September, 1789). She was married to a much older man, and the two began an affair. Mirabeau escaped to Switzerland, where Sophie joined him; they then went to the Netherlands. Meanwhile Mirabeau had been condemned to death at Pontarlier for seduction and abduction, and in May, 1777, he was seized by the Dutch police, sent to France and imprisoned in the castle of Vincennes. Sophie was pregnant, and was placed in a nursing home. Their child, Sophie Gabrielle, died aged 2. The early part of his confinement is marked by the indecent letters to Sophie (first published in 1793), and the obscene *Erotica Biblion* and *Ma Conversion*.

Upon his release in August, 1782, he found that his Sophie had consoled herself with a young officer. He then met Henriette Amélie, Madame de Nehra (1765–1818). She was an educated, refined woman, capable of appreciating Mirabeau's good points. His life was strengthened by her love, his adopted son, Lucas de Montigny, and his little dog, Chico.

To Sophie

August, 1777.

Yes, my dearest, yes, my candour has always prevailed with you, and never will it play me false. It is so natural a quality of mine that I trust it overmuch, with my enemies, for instance, and those who are unworthy of my confidence. My countenance speaks for me, even when I do not speak myself; and you must often have seen how carefully I have to prepare myself in advance, when I wish to adopt a disguise. Unless I keep myself well in hand, I am bound to reveal my true self; for every movement that I make helps to reveal what is passing in my mind. It is the inevitable result of possessing in excess what is really a very estimable quality; I must certainly endeavour to correct the defect; I have in part succeeded already; but never with my Sophie need I look to conceal my true self; I have everything to gain by showing her the innermost workings of my heart, where she reigns supreme and alone. The traces of jealousy which she finds there will seem to her no more than a fresh mark of homage, which she will take in good part. I shall not even keep from you things that may afflict you, because I know so well that it is a true consolation for you to know all my misery and just how wretched I am. Doubts and fears augment our ills a thousandfold, and it is impossible to shape our lives by that which is not clearly defined, but only to be seen through the veil of some dense fog...

Change? Ah, no! it is not possible; never will Gabriel have need to clear himself from the charge of so atrocious a crime, of which, indeed, it is impossible for you even to imagine him capable without yourself affording him a proof that you hold him in utter contempt. But pray do not imagine that considerations of duty and of honour have aught to do with my constancy. I love you because I live. Love is the breath of my life. To think of ceasing to adore you seems to me as absurd as to think of continuing to live without a heart to pump the blood through my veins or without lungs wherewith to breathe. My Sophie, I can take no more merit to myself for loving you, than the streams for flowing into the sea or the fire for burning; it is my nature, the very essence of my life. I would assuredly still love you were I free to choose between indifference or love, between constancy or

inconstancy; but I have no such freedom; I love you, for I cannot do otherwise...
Love me likewise, if you can; but not in gratitude to me, for I deserve none...

Ah! how true it is that the more one really feels the simpler is one's
language!... It is an easy matter to decide whether a woman is really in love,
especially when we take care to consider her in her relations with other men. A
heart filled with the object of its affection is not susceptible to anything else. Love
is so delicate a flower that the least puff of a strange wind kills it; and I shall
never believe that a woman who can find pleasure in the society of other men and
in listening without repugnance to their chaff and silly gossip would ever be
capable of loving one man tenderly and constantly. My opinion should count for
something in the matter of love and sensibility; I may without arrogance say that
I know how to love. You cannot believe what pleasure you gave me with your neat
epigram: 'My heart is too full of you to be able to attach myself'. I have always
been convinced that even a keen friendship was a kind of infidelity to love, not, of
course, criminal, but one which reveals the feebleness of love's tie. Moreover, I
have to think thus, dear heart of mine, to justify myself; for, since I have loved
you, I have loved nothing else; I am susceptible to feelings of emotion, of pity, of
eagerness to oblige, but feelings of affection for others are entirely strange to me.
When once the heart is on fire it is either quite insensible to what is only
lukewarm, or lukewarmness gives actual pain...

Yes, dear Sophie, I feel, from the depths of my soul, that our hearts were made
for one another; you alone can keep me constant, you alone have taught me what
love is; for you must not think, O my beloved, that I had ever known love ere you
came to me. The fever in my blood had no more in common with the transports
with which you fill me than you yourself have with the women to whom I paid
homage before you. I have told you again and again, that the perfume of your
breath as you press your lips to mine stirs me a thousand times more deeply than
any emotions, however poignant, that I have ever felt in the arms of other women.
It is a triumph that you may not fully appreciate, my dearest, but it consoles me
when I think of how I have laid my homage at the feet of so many other beautiful
women, by showing me the difference between the desires of nature and those of
love; proving to me, consequently, that I have never loved any but you. My dear,
you know most of my experiences in the search after pleasure. The vigour of my
constitution would appear to have been established beyond question by the
multiplicity and the variety of what I am pleased to call my enjoyments. Never did
I keep long to one woman; only once, by her wantonness, did a certain Messalina
(whom I need not name) think to put an end to my life. The rest of my existence
has been but as that of other men, until you came. Those laurels that I thought I
had won so gloriously, senseless fool that I was, has not love completely
shrivelled them up! How lovely the garlands of flowers that now take the place of
a few dry blades of grass! Into what a frenzy of delight have you thrown me!
What victories have I not won! O Sophie, Sophie! how I love to think of it, and to
think, too, that it was my strength only that fell short of my desire! But the ardour
that fires my senses is not the best proof that I have never loved before. It is the
union of our souls that puts a seal upon our love; it is this unbounded devotion,
this great passion, without equal in the world, that makes the universe seem in

our eyes no more than a tiny atom; that causes all other interests to fade before our love, or rather, should I say, to be mingled with it; that makes all sacrifice a pleasure, all duty a sentiment; that renders virtue and vice, honour and shame, happiness and misfortune, now and for ever meaningless, except in so far as they serve love or stand in her way, delight my Sophie-Gabriel or offend her! O my love! call to mind all the tenderest words I have ever written to you, all the most ardent, the most enthusiastic, conjure them up to make a picture of them; refresh your heart with the sight; store it away in your memory; it will be only a sketch, the roughest sketch of what your lover really feels, even at times when he seems least to think of you! Ah! tell me, tell me yet again, that you have never loved as you now love, that I alone am he whom you could ever love! Tell me this, that I may strive to believe it, O my dearest love! Above all, do not worry about what I said of those men; I had my reasons for saying what I did, believe me; had it been only that I felt suspicious, I should have held my peace. Jealous I cannot be. I know well enough that you will not see them, besides, you are not able to see them. But tell me everything, I implore you; and deny everything, either in regard to this matter, or that concerning M. P... to all others save myself...

Since I received your letters my dreams have been happier, often quite delicious; formerly I had such terrible dreams. I can recall one in particular, so awful that I sprang from my bed in terror. At present, every night in my sleep I recall some episode of our love's history; often the illusion is so strong that I hear you, see you, touch you. Three days ago I had a vision of the very day on which you decided to make me happy. Everything came before my eyes, down to the minutest detail. Dear God! I tremble even now to think of it. Your head resting on my arms... Your lovely neck, your snowy bosom... Desire burnt in my blood; my hand, my happy hand, daring to wander where it would; I remove the barriers you had till then so carefully set up... Your beautiful eyes are closed... You gasp, you shiver... Sophie... dare I? O my dearest! will you make me happy? You make no reply... You hide your face upon my breast... Love intoxicates you, but modesty withholds you... I am consumed with desire; I expire... I come to life again... I raise you in my arms... futile efforts... the floor recedes before my eyes... I gaze eagerly on your charms, but may not enjoy them... Love renders the victory more difficult that it may be the greater prize! Ah! how useless it all was... Importunate neighbours deprived me of all my resources... What moments! What delights! What ineffable constraint! What transports strangled at their birth! What pleasure-fruit all but tasted! Yes, my beloved, I went through it all again; in my dream I leaned with you against my couch, which later on became the witness of my happy triumph... At length I awoke from my troubled sleep, full of agitation, and realised how far I had been borne in my frenzy. Are you sometimes happy, O dearly beloved? Do you in your dreams seem to realise all that my love means to you? Do you feel my kisses on your lips, do you press your own to mine in an abandonment of tenderness? Do your burning caresses thaw, if ever so slightly, the cold tract that keeps us apart? My darling, you tell me you dream, but you do not describe your dreams. Ought you not to render account to me of the night as well as of the day? Yes, yes, certainly you ought. The nights are more to me; they are everything to me. Recount me your illusions, O my beloved wife! Let absence be cheated; embrace your dear; let him see that he holds your imagination as well as your heart. Your soul burns so fiercely for love of me! Shall your senses be of ice, spellbound? No, no, nature has endowed you liberally; your feelings are as exquisite as your sentiments are delicate; at least, so I am pleased to think; therein rest the very foundations of my self-respect; I have none but through you, and all I have is in you. Farewell, dear, dear and matchless love; farewell, my heart's bride, the well-beloved of Gabriel; farewell, my all, my goddess, my soul, my life, my universe. Accept as many kisses as you would give. I spread them over your lovely body; not a spot is left uncovered!

Monday, 7 September, 1777.

Sophie,

To be with the people one loves, says La Bruyere, is enough—to dream you are speaking to them, or not speaking to them, thinking of them, or thinking of the most indifferent things, but by their side, nothing else matters. O my love, how true that is! and it is also true that when one acquires such a habit, it becomes a necessary part of one's existence.

Alas! I well know, I should know too well, since the three months that I sigh, far away from thee, that I possess thee no more, than my happiness has departed. However, when every morning I wake up, I look for you, it seems to me that half of myself is missing, and that is too true.

Twenty times during the day, I ask myself where you are; judge how strong the illusion is, and how cruel it is to see it vanish. When I go to bed, I do not fail to make room for you; I push myself quite close to the wall and leave a great empty space in my small bed. This movement is mechanical, these thoughts are involuntary. Ah! how one accustoms oneself to happiness. Alas! one only knows it well when one has lost it, and I'm sure we have only learnt to appreciate how necessary we are to each other, since the thunderbolt has parted us. The source of our tears has not dried up, dear Sophie; we cannot become healed; we have enough in our hearts to love always, and, because of that, enough to weep always...

Wolfgang Amadeus Mozart

Wolfgang Amadeus Mozart (born Johannes Chrysostomus Wolfgangus Theophilus Mozart, 27 January, 1756–5 December, 1791), was a prolific and influential Austrian composer of the Classical era. He composed over 600 works, many acknowledged as pinnacles of symphonic, concertante, chamber, piano, operatic, and choral music. He is among the most enduringly popular of classical composers. Mozart showed prodigious ability from his earliest childhood in Salzburg. Already competent on keyboard and violin, he composed from the age of five and performed before European royalty. By 1772, aged 16, Mozart had already composed 25 symphonies and two string quartets. At 17, he was engaged as a court musician in Salzburg, but grew restless and travelled in search of a better position, always composing abundantly. While visiting Vienna in 1781, he was dismissed from his Salzburg position. He chose to stay in the capital, where he achieved fame but little financial security. Mozart wrote most of his best work in the years that followed: 12 piano concertos (1784–86); six quartets; and the operas *The Marriage of Figaro* (1786), *Don Giovanni* (1787), and *Cosi Fan Tutte* (1790). During his final years in Vienna, he composed many of his best-known symphonies, concertos, and operas, including *The Magic Flute* and portions of the *Requiem*, which was largely unfinished at the time of his death. His influence on subsequent Western music is profound. Beethoven wrote his own early compositions in the shadow of Mozart.

Mozart first fell in love with Aloysia Weber, one of four daughters in a musical family, in 1777. A year later he again encountered Aloysia, now a very successful singer, but she made it plain that she was no longer interested in him. Mozart's interest shifted to her sister, Constanze (5 January, 1762–6 March, 1842). The courtship did not go entirely smoothly; surviving correspondence indicates that Mozart and Constanze briefly broke up in April, 1782. Mozart also faced a very difficult task in getting his father's permission for the marriage, writing to him to him on 31 July, 1782, "All the good and well-intentioned advice you have sent fails to address the case of a man who has already gone so far with a maiden. Further postponement is out of the question." The couple were finally married on 4 August, 1782, in St. Stephen's Cathedral. They had six children, of whom only two survived infancy: Raimund Leopold (June–August, 1783), Karl Thomas (1784–1858), Johann Thomas Leopold (October–November, 1786), Theresa Constanzia Adelheid Friedericke Maria Anna (1787–1788), Anna Maria (died soon after birth, 1789) and Franz Xaver Wolfgang (1791–1844).

With substantial returns from his concerts and elsewhere, he and Constanze adopted a rather plush lifestyle. They moved to an expensive apartment, sent their son Karl to an expensive boarding school, and kept servants. Saving was therefore impossible, and the short period of financial success did nothing to soften the hardship the Mozarts were later to experience. He died suddenly, aged just 35.

Constanze's business skills came into fruition: she obtained a pension from the Emperor, organised profitable memorial concerts, and embarked on a campaign to publish her husband's works.

Dresden, 16 April, 1789, 11.30 P.M.

> *My Darling Sweet Little Wife,—*
> *How? still in Dresden? Yes, my love... On Monday last, after breakfasting at Neumann's, we all went to the Elector's private chapel; the mass was by Neumann (who himself conducted) and a very indifferent one it was... We afterwards went to the opera, which is truly miserable. Do you know who is one of the singers? Rosa Manservisi. You may conceive her delight at seeing me. Still the prima donna, Madame Allegrandi, is far better than Ferrarese, but that is not saying much. After the opera we went home. Then came the happiest of all moments for me; I found the long and ardently wished-for letter from you, my darling, my beloved! Duschek and Neumann were with me as usual; I carried off the letter in triumph to my room, and kissed it over and over again before I broke it open, and then rather devoured than read it. I stayed a long time in my room, for I could not read over your letter often enough, or kiss it often enough. When I rejoined the party, Neumann asked me if I had received a letter from you, and on my saying that I had, they cordially congratulated me, because I had been daily lamenting that I had heard nothing from you. The Neumanns are admirable people. Now for your dear letter. You shall receive by the next post the account of my visit here till we leave this.*
> *Darling wife, I have a number of requests to make to you:—*
> *1st. I beg you will not be melancholy.*
> *2d. That you will take care of yourself, and not expose yourself to the spring breezes.*
> *3d. That you will not go out to walk alone—indeed, it would be better not to walk at all.*
> *4th. That you will feel entirely assured of my love. I have not written you a single letter without placing your dear portrait before me.*
> *5th. I beg you not only to be careful of your honour and mine in your conduct, but to be equally guarded as to appearances. Do not be angry at this request; indeed, it ought to make you love me still better, from seeing the regard I have for my honour.*
> *6th. Lastly, I wish you would enter more into details in your letters. I should like to know whether my brother-in-law, Hofer, arrived the day that I set off; whether he comes often, as he promised he would; whether the Langes call on you; whether the portrait is progressing; what your mode of life is—all things which naturally interest me much. Now farewell, my best beloved! Remember that every night before going to bed I converse with your portrait for a good half-hour, and the same when I awake. We set off on the 18th, the day after to-*

morrow. Continue to write to me, Poste Restante, Berlin. I kiss and embrace you 1,095,060,437,082 times, (this will give you a fine opportunity to exercise yourself in counting) and am ever your most faithful husband and friend,

W. A. Mozart.

The account of the close of our Dresden visit shall follow next time. Good night!

Frankfort-on-Maine, 30 September, 1790.

My Best Beloved Wife,—

If I only had a letter from you, then all would be right. I hope you received mine from Efferding and Frankfort... I am as happy as a child at the thought of returning to you. If people could see into my heart, I should almost feel ashamed—all there is cold, cold as ice. Were you with me, I should possibly take more pleasure in the kindness of those I meet here, but all seems to me so empty. Adieu, my love! I am ever your loving,

Mozart.

P. S.—While writing the last page, many a tear has fallen on it. But now let us be merry. Look! Swarms of kisses are flying about—quick! catch some! I have caught three, and delicious they are. You have still time to reply to this letter, but it is safer to address to me at Linz, Poste Restante, as I am not yet certain whether I go to Ratisbon or not, for I can fix nothing at present. Write on the letter, "to be left till called for." Adieu, my dearest sweetest wife! Be careful of your health, and do not go into the town on foot. Write to me how you like your new quarters. Adieu! I send you a million kisses.

Alfred de Musset

Alfred Louis Charles de Musset-Pathay (11 December, 1810–2 May, 1857) was a French dramatist, poet, and novelist. After attempts at careers in medicine (which he gave up owing to a distaste for dissections), law, drawing, English and piano, he became one of the first Romantic writers, with his first collection of poems, *Contes d'Espagne et d'Italie* (*Tales of Spain and Italy*, 1829). By the time he reached the age of 20, his rising literary fame was already accompanied by a fiery reputation. His most famous plays include *Les Caprices de Marianne* (*The Moods of Marianne*, 1833), *Lorenzaccio* (1833), *Fantasio* (1834) and *On ne Badine pas avec l'Amour* (*No Trifling with Love*, 1834). For many years he was the librarian of the French Ministry of the Interior under the July Monarchy. He received the Légion d'Honneur on 24 April, 1845, at the same time as Balzac, and was elected to the Académie Française in 1852 (after two failures to do so in 1848 and 1850).

The great love affair of his life began in June, 1833, when he met George Sand, the author. Amantine Aurore Lucile Dupin, Baroness Dudevant (1 July, 1804–8 June, 1876), had married a Baron in 1822 and had two children. In early 1831, she left her prosaic husband and entered upon a four-or five-year period of 'romantic rebellion.' She conducted affairs of varying duration with poets, authors and composers, and in 1832 began writing under the pseudonym George Sand. In 1833 Musset was busy making a name for himself both as a womaniser and a talented poet and critic. Sand and Musset first met at a literary dinner and quickly recognised in each other a like minded love of literature. At first their relationship remained platonic, but soon the pair embarked on a tumultuous affair which led them to Venice. After a month there, Alfred became very ill and a doctor was called. Unfortunately, while Alfred was incapacitated, the doctor and Sand began an amour of their own. She eventually moved in with the doctor, and having recovered, Alfred returned to Paris alone, in despair. Sand and Musset's celebrated love affair lasted from 1833 to 1835 and is told from his point of view in his autobiographical novel, *La Confession d'un Enfant du Siècle* (*The Confession of a Child of the Century*, 1836), and from her point of view in her *Elle et Lui* (*She and Him*, 1859). Musset's *Nuits* (*Nights*, 1835–1837) trace the emotional upheaval of his love for Sand, from early despair to final resignation.

In 1837 Musset became engaged to Aimée d'Alton (20 September, 1804–1880), but the relationship ended within a year. She later married his brother Paul, in 1861. In 1838, he met and courted the 17 year old Pauline García (18 July, 1821–18 May, 1910) after having earlier been taken with her sister Maria. Some sources say he asked for Pauline's hand in marriage, but she declined. However, she remained on good terms with him for many years. Her friend George Sand had a role in discouraging her from accepting Musset's proposal.

Throughout the rest of his life, Musset had numerous affairs, frequented prostitutes and used opium. His health quickly began to fail. For the years 1848–1850 he had a relationship with the actress Louise Rosalie Allan-Despreaux (1810–March 1856).

To George Sand

1833.

> *My dear George,*
> *I have something stupid and ridiculous to tell you. I am foolishly writing to you instead of having told you this, I do not know why, when returning from that walk. To-night I shall be annoyed at having done so. You will laugh in my face, will take me for a maker of phrases in all my relations with you hitherto. You will show me the door and you will think I am lying. I am in love with you. I have been thus since the first day I called on you. I thought I should cure myself in seeing you quite simply as a friend. There are many things in your character which could cure me; I have tried to convince myself of that as much as I could. But I pay too dearly for the moments I pass with you. I prefer to tell you and I have done well, because I shall suffer much less if I am cured by your showing me the door now. This night during which...[19] I had decided to let you know that I was out of town, but I do not want to make a mystery of it nor have the appearance of quarrelling without a reason. Now George, you will say: "Another fellow, who is about to become a nuisance", as you say. If I am not quite the firstcomer for you, tell me, as you would have told me yesterday in speaking of somebody else, what I ought to do. But I beg of you, if you intend to say that you doubt the truth of what I am writing, then I had rather you did not answer me at all. I know how you think of me, and I have nothing to hope for in telling you this. I can only foresee losing a friend and the only agreeable hours I have passed for a month. But I know that you are kind, that you have loved, and I put my trust in you, not as a mistress, but as a frank and loyal comrade. George, I am an idiot to deprive myself of the pleasure of seeing you the short time you have still to spend in Paris, before your departure for Italy, where we would have spent such beautiful nights together, if I had the strength. But the truth is that I suffer, and that my strength is wanting.*
> *Alfred de Musset*

---

[19] George Sand, who edited the letter for publication, deleted a small section here.

Baden, 1 September, 1834.

But do you know what it is to wait five months for a kiss? Do you know what a poor heart endures, that for five months has felt, day by day, hour by hour, life abandon it, the cold of the tomb descend lowly in the solitude, death and oblivion, falling drop by drop like snow? Do you know what it feels like for a heart that has almost ceased to beat, to dilate for a moment, to re-open like a poor dying flower, to drink again a drop of heaven-sent dew?...

Never did man love as I love you. I am lost; behold! I am drowned, overwhelmed with love. I love you, my flesh and my bones and my blood. Of love I am dying, and of a love endless, nameless, insensate, desperate, beyond redemption. You are loved, adored, idolised to death. No; I shall not get well, I shall not attempt to live, and I prefer it so; and to die loving you is worth more than to live. I am, indeed, concerned at what people say. They will say that you have another lover, I know. I am dying with it, but I love I love. Let them stop me from loving!...

But let me have this letter, containing nothing but your love; and tell me that you give me your lips, your hair, all that face that I have possessed, and tell me that we embrace—you and I!

O God, O God, when I think of it, my throat closes, my sight is troubled; my knees fail, ah, it is horrible to die, it is also horrible to love like this! What longing, what longing I have for you! I beg you to let me have the letter I ask. I am dying.

Farewell.

Horatio, Lord Nelson

Horatio Nelson, 1st Viscount Nelson, 1st Duke of Bronté, KB (29 September, 1758–21 October, 1805) was an English flag officer famous for his service in the Royal Navy. He developed a reputation in the service through his personal valour and firm grasp of tactics. He was noted for his ability to inspire and bring out the best in his men: the "Nelson touch".

With the outbreak of the French Revolutionary Wars, Nelson was particularly active. In 1797, he took part in the Battle of Santa Cruz de Tenerife, where his attack was defeated and he was badly wounded, losing his right arm, and was forced to return to England to recuperate. The following year, he won a decisive victory over the French at the Battle of the Nile and remained in the Mediterranean to support the Kingdom of Naples against a French invasion. In 1801, he was dispatched to the Baltic and won another victory, this time over the Danes at the Battle of Copenhagen. He subsequently commanded the blockade of the French and Spanish fleets at Toulon and, after their escape, chased them to the West Indies and back but failed to bring them to battle. After a brief return to England, he took over the Cádiz blockade in 1805. On 21 October, 1805, the Franco-Spanish fleet came out of port, and Nelson's fleet engaged them at the Battle of Trafalgar. The battle was Britain's greatest naval victory, but during the action Nelson was fatally wounded. His body was brought back to England where he was accorded a state funeral. His death at Trafalgar secured his position as one of Britain's most heroic figures. Numerous monuments, including Nelson's Column in Trafalgar Square, London, have been created in his memory and his legacy remains highly influential.

Nelson met Frances "Fanny" Nisbet (1761–4 May, 1831), a young widow from a Nevis plantation family, sometime in the mid-1780s. Nelson and Nisbet were married at Montpelier Estate on the island of Nevis on 11 March, 1787, shortly before the end of his tour of duty in the Caribbean. Nelson returned to England in July, with Fanny following later. She was by all accounts a devoted wife, putting up with his long absences dutifully. However, in 1793, in Naples, while serving in the Mediterranean, Nelson met British ambassador, William Hamilton and his new wife, Emma *née* Hart (born Amy Lyon, 26 April, 1765–15 January, 1815). Within the year he had fallen deeply in love with her, but work forced him away. He returned to Naples five years later, in 1798 after having lost an arm and most of his teeth. Emma nursed Nelson under her husband's roof, and arranged a party to celebrate his 40th birthday. Their affair seems to have been tolerated, and perhaps even encouraged, by the elderly Hamilton. Nelson and the Hamiltons sailed from Naples on a brief cruise around Malta aboard the *Foudroyant* in April, 1800. It was on this voyage that Horatio and Emma's illegitimate daughter Horatia was probably conceived. Hamilton was recalled to Britain, adding a further incentive for Nelson to return. It was during this period that Fanny and Emma met for the first time. Nelson was reported as being cold and distant to his wife and his attention to Emma became the subject of gossip. Events came to a head around Christmas, when according to Nelson's solicitor, Fanny issued an ultimatum on whether he was to choose her or Emma. Nelson replied: "I love you sincerely but I cannot forget my obligations to Lady Hamilton or speak of her otherwise than with affection and admiration." The two never lived together again after this. Divorce was impossible. It would have tainted her for life, and, even worse, tainted Nelson. On 29 January, 1801, Emma gave birth to their daughter, Horatia. Their second child, a girl, died a few weeks after her birth in 1804. Nelson's affair with Emma Hamilton was widely remarked upon and disapproved of, to the extent that Emma was denied permission to attend Nelson's funeral and was subsequently ignored by the government. She died in poverty.

To Emma Hamilton

San Josef, 8 February, 1801.

    My Dear Lady,
    ... I am not in very good spirits; and, except that our country demands all our services and abilities, to bring about an honourable peace, nothing should prevent my being the bearer of my own letter. But, my dear friend, I know you are so true and loyal an Englishwoman, that you would hate those who would not stand forth in defence of our King, laws, religion, and all that is dear to us.
    It is your sex that make us go forth; and seem to tell us—"None but the brave deserve the fair!" and, if we fall, we still live in the hearts of those females. You are dear to us. It is your sex that rewards us; it is your sex who cherish our memories; and you, my dear, honoured friend, are, believe me, the first, the best, of your sex.
    I have been the world around, and in every corner of it, and never yet saw your equal, or even one which could be put in comparison with you. You know how to reward virtue, honour, and courage; and never to ask if it is placed in a Prince, Duke, Lord, or Peasant: and I hope, one day, to see you, in peace, before I set out for Bronte, which I am resolved to do.
    Only tell me, how I can be useful to you and Sir William; and believe, nothing could give me more pleasure: being, with the greatest truth, my dear Lady, your most obliged and affectionate friend,
    Nelson & Bronte.

26 August, 1803.
Wrote several days past.

My Dearest Emma,

By the Canopus, Admiral Campbell, I have received all your truly kind and affectionate letters, from 20th May to 3d July; with the exception of one, dated 31st May, sent to Naples.

This is the first communication I have had with England since we sailed.

All your letters, *my dear letters*, are so entertaining! and which paint so clearly what you are after, that they give me either the greatest pleasure or pain. It is the next best thing, to being with you.

I only desire, my dearest Emma, that you will always believe, that Nelson's your own; Nelson's Alpha and Omega is Emma! I cannot alter; my affection and love is beyond even this world! Nothing can shake it, but yourself; and that, I will not allow myself to think, for a moment, is possible.

I feel, that you are the real friend of my bosom, and dearer to me than life; and, that I am the same to you. But, I will neither have P.'s nor Q.'s come near you! No; not the slice of Single Gloster! But, if I was to go on, it would argue that want of confidence which would be injurious to your honour.

I rejoice that you have had so pleasant a trip into Norfolk; and I hope, one day, to carry you there by a nearer tie in law, but not in love and affection, than at present.

I wish, you would never mention that person's name! It works up your anger, for no useful purpose. Her good or bad character, of me or thee, no one cares about.

This letter will find you at dear Merton; where we shall one day meet, and be truly happy.

I do not think it can be a long war; and, I believe, it will be much shorter than people expect: and I shall hope to find the new room built; the grounds laid out, neatly but not expensively; new Piccadilly gates; kitchen garden; &c. Only let us have a plan, and then all will go on well. It will be a great source of amusement to you; and Horatia shall plant a tree. I dare say, she will be very busy. Mrs. Nelson, or Mrs. Bolton, &c. will be with you; and time will pass away, till I have the inexpressible happiness of arriving at Merton. Even the thought of it vibrates through my nerves; for, my love for you is as unbounded as the ocean!...

Victory, 5 May, 1804.

I find, my Dearest Emma, that your picture is very much admired by the French Consul at Barcelona; and that he has not sent it to be admired—which, I am sure, it would be—by Bonaparte.

They pretend, that there were three pictures taken. I wish, I had them: but they are all gone, as irretrievably as the dispatches; unless we may read them in a book, as we printed their correspondence from Egypt.

But, from us, what can they find out! That I love you, most dearly; and hate the French, most damnably.

Dr. Scott went to Barcelona, to try to get the private letters; but, I fancy, they are all gone to Paris. The Swedish and American Consuls told him, that the French Consul had your picture, and read your letters; and, Doctor thinks, one of them probably read the letters.

By the master's account of the cutter, I would not have trusted a pair of old shoes in her. He tells me, she did not sail, but was a good sea-boat.

I hope, Mr. Marsden will not trust any more of my private letters in such a conveyance; if they choose to trust the affairs of the public in such a thing, I cannot help it.

I long for the invasion being over; it must finish the war, and I have no fears for the event.

I do not say, all I wish; and which, my dearest beloved Emma—(read that, whoever opens this letter; and, for what I care, publish it to the world)—your fertile imagination can readily fancy I would say: but this I can say, with great truth, that I am, FOR EVER, YOUR'S

19 October, 1805.

My dearest, beloved Emma, the dear friend of my bosom, the signal has been made that the enemy's combined fleet are coming out of port. We have very little wind, so that I have no hopes of seeing them before to-morrow. May the God of Battles crown my endeavours with success; at all events, I will take care that my name shall ever be most dear to you and Horatia, both of whom I love as much as my own life; and as my last writing before the battle will be to you, so I hope in God that I shall live to finish my letter after the Battle. May Heaven bless you prays your Nelson and Bronte.

20 October, 1805.

In the morning, we were close to the mouth of the straits, but the wind had not come far enough to the westward to allow the combined fleets to weather the shoals off Trafalgar; but they were counted as far as forty sail of ships of war, which I suppose to be thirty-four of the line, and six frigates. A group of them was seen off the lighthouse of Cadiz this morning, but it blows so very fresh and thick weather, that I rather believe they will go into the harbour before night. May God Almighty give us success over these fellows, and enable us to get a Peace.[20]

---

[20] At the end of the letter, Emma wrote "This letter was found open on his desk, & brought to Lady Hamilton by Captain Hardy. Oh, miserable, wretched Emma! Oh, glorious & happy Nelson!"

Thomas Otway

Thomas Otway (3 March, 1652–14 April, 1685) was an English dramatist of the Restoration period. After a short stint at Oxford University, Otway journeyed to London where he made the acquaintance of Aphra Behn, who in 1672 cast him as the old king in her play, *Forc'd Marriage; or, The Jealous Bridegroom*, at the Dorset Garden Theatre. However, he had a bad attack of stage fright, and never made a second appearance. His first play, *Alcibiades*, a tragedy, was produced in 1675 at the Dorset Garden, followed swiftly by *Don Carlos, Prince of Spain* (1676). He adapted several plays from the French and in 1678 he produced an original comedy, *Friendship in Fashion*, which was very successful. In February, 1680, the first of Otway's two tragic masterpieces, *The Orphan; or, The Unhappy Marriage*, was produced, followed by *The History and Fall of Caius Marius*, produced in the same year. In 1680 Otway also published *The Poets Complaint of his Muse; or, A Satyr Against Libells*, in which he retaliated on his literary enemies. An indifferent comedy, *The Soldier's Fortune* (1681), was followed in February, 1682, by *Venice Preserv'd, or A Plot Discover'd*, for which he is now best known. The play won instant success and was translated into almost every modern European language.

Otway's one great love was the actress Elizabeth Barry (1658–7 November, 1713), who played many of the leading parts in his plays. A popular actress, she was trained by her married lover, John Wilmot, 2nd Earl of Rochester. She achieved remarkable success and public approval, especially considering that she was a single woman in London in the late 17th century, was unmarried and had had a child with Rochester. Otway cast her in *Alcibiades* when she was just 17 and he quickly became infatuated with her. Barry seems to have flirted with Otway, but had no intention of permanently offending Rochester. Otway's love for her left him wretched. In 1678, driven to desperation by her, Otway obtained a commission through Charles, Earl of Plymouth, a natural son of Charles II, in a regiment serving in the Netherlands. He returned to London within 2 years.

Six letters to her survive, written c.1680–1682. One mentions that he has loved her for seven years, and we know that they had met by at least 1675. The last refers to a broken appointment in the Mall. All six have been included here.

My Tyrant!—I endure too much torment to be silent, and have endured it too long not to make the severest complaint. I love you, I dote on you; desire makes me mad when I am near you; and despair, when I am from you. Sure, of all miseries, love is to me the most intolerable. It haunts me in my sleep, perplexes me when waking; every melancholy thought makes my fears more powerful; and every delightful one makes my wishes more unruly. In all other uneasy chances of

a man's life, there is an immediate recourse to some kind of succour or another. In wants we apply ourselves to our friends; in sickness to physicians. But love, the sum, the total of all misfortunes, must be endured with silence; no friend so dear to trust with such a secret, nor remedy in art so powerful to remove its anguish. Since the first day I saw you, I have hardly enjoyed one hour of perfect quiet. I loved you early, and no sooner had I beheld that soft, bewitching face of yours but I felt in my heart the very foundation of all my peace give way. But when you become another's, I must confess that I did then rebel, had foolish pride enough to promise myself I would in time recover my liberty. In spite of my enslaved nature, I swore against myself, I would not love you. I affected a resentment, stifled my spirit, and would not let it bend, so much as once to upbraid you, each day it was my chance to see or to be near you. With stubborn sufferance I resolved to bear and brave your power. Nay, did it often too, successfully. Generally, with wine or conversation I diverted or appeased the demon that possessed me; but when at night, returning to my unhappy self, to give my heart an account why I had done it so unnatural a violence, it was then I always paid a treble interest for the short moments of ease which I had borrowed; then every treacherous thought rose up and took your part, nor left me till they had thrown me on my bed and opened those sluices of tears that were to run till morning. This has been for some years my best condition; nay, time itself, that decays all things else, has but increased and added to my longings. I tell you and charge you to believe it, as you are generous (for sure you must be, for everything, except your neglect of me, persuades me that you are so), even at this time, though other arms have held you, and so long trespassed on those dear joys that only were my due; I love you with all that tenderness of spirit, that purity of truth, and that sincerity of heart, that I could sacrifice the nearest friends or interest I have on earth, barely but to please you. If I had all the world, it should be yours; for with it I could be but miserable if you were not mine. I appeal to you for justice, if through the whole actions of my life I have done any one thing that might not let you see how absolute your authority was over me. Your commands have always been sacred to me; your smiles have always transported me; and your frowns awed me. In short, you will quickly become to me the greatest blessing or the greatest curse that ever man was doomed to. I cannot so much as look upon you without confusion; wishes and fears rise up in war within me, and work a cursed distraction through my soul that must, I am sure, in time have wretched consequences. You only can with that healing cordial love, assuage and calm my torments; pity the man then who would be proud to die for you and cannot live without you, and allow him thus far to boast too, that (take out Fortune from the balance) you never were beloved or courted by creature that had a nobler or juster pretense to your heart, than the unfortunate (and even at this time) weeping,

    Otway.

    In value of your quiet, though it would be the utter ruin of my own, I have endeavoured this day to persuade myself never more to trouble you with a passion that has tormented me sufficiently already, and is so much more a torment to me, in that I perceive it has become one to you, who are much dearer to me than my own self. I have laid all the reasons my distracted conditions would let me have recourse to before me. I have consulted my pride whether after a rival's possession, I ought to ruin all my peace for a woman that another has been more blessed in, though no man ever loved as I did. But love, victorious love, overthrows all that, and tells me it is his nature never to remember; he still looks forward from the present hour, expecting still new dawns, new rising happiness; never looks back, never regards what is past and left behind him, but buries and forgets it quite in the hot, fierce pursuit of joy before him. I have consulted too my very self, and find how careless nature was in framing me; seasoned me hastily with all the most violent inclinations and desires, but omitted the ornaments that should make those qualities become me. I have consulted too my lot of fortune and find how foolishly I wish possession of what is so precious, all the world's too cheap for it; yet still I love, still I dote on, and cheat myself, very content because the folly pleases me. It is pleasure to think how fair you are, though at the same time worse than damnation to think how cruel. Why should you tell me you have shut your heart up forever? It is an argument unworthy of yourself, sounds like reserve, and not so much sincerity as sure I may claim even from a little of your friendship. Can your age, your face, your eyes, and your spirit bid defiance to that sweet power? No, you know better to what end Heaven made you, know better how to manage youth and pleasure than to let them die and pall upon your hands. 'Tis me, 'tis only me you have barred your heart against. My sufferings, my diligence, my sighs, complaints and tears are of no power with your haughty nature; yet sure you might at least vouchsafe to pity them, not shift me off with gross, thick home-spun friendship, the common coin that passes betwixt worldly interest. Must that be my lot! Take it, ill-natured, take it, give it to him who would waste his fortune for you, give it to the man who would fill your lap with gold, court with offers of vast rich possessions, give it the fool who hath nothing but his money to plead for him. Love will have a much nearer relation, or none. I ask for glorious happiness ; you bid me welcome to your friendship; it is like seating me at your side-table, when I have the best pretense to the right-hand at the feast. I love, I dote, I am mad, and know no measure, nothing but extremes can give me ease; the kindest love, or most provoking scorn. Yet even your scorn would not perform the cure; it might indeed take off the edge of hope, but damned despair will gnaw my heart forever. If then I am not odious to your eyes, if you have charity enough to value the well-being of a man who holds you dearer than you the child your bowels are most fond of, by that sweet pledge of your first softest love, I charm and here conjure you to pity the distracting pangs of mine; pity my unquiet days and restless nights; pity the frenzy that has half possessed my brain already, and makes me write to you thus ravingly. The poor wretch in Bedlam is more at peace than I am! And if I must never possess the heaven I wish for, my next desire is (and the sooner the better) a clean swept cell, a merciful keeper, and your compassion when you find me there. Think and be generous.

Since you are going to quit the world, I think myself obliged, as a member of the world, to use the best of my endeavours to divert you from so ill-natured an inclination. Therefore, by reason your visits will take up so much of this day, I have debarred myself the opportunity of waiting on you this afternoon, that I may take a time you are more mistress of, and when you shall have more leisure to hear, if it be possible for any arguments of mine to take place in a heart I am afraid too much hardened against me. I must confess it may look a little extraordinary, for one under my circumstances to endeavour the confirming your good opinion of the world, when it had been better for me, one of us had never seen it. For nature disposed me from my creation to love, and my ill-fortune has condemned me to dote on one who certainly could never have been deaf so long to so faithful a passion, had nature disposed her from her creation to hate anything but me. I beg you forgive this trifling, for I have so many thoughts of this nature that 'tis impossible for me to take pen and ink in my hand, and keep 'em quiet, especially when I have the least pretense to let you know you are the cause of the severest disquiets that ever touched the heart of

Otway.

Could I see you without passion, or be absent from you without pain, I need not beg your pardon for thus renewing my vows that I love you more than health, or any happiness here or hereafter.

Everything you do is a new charm to me, and though I have lanquished for seven long tedious years of desire, jealously despairing, yet every minute I see you I still discover something new and more bewitching. Consider how I love you; what would I not renounce or enterprise for you?

I must have you mine, or I am miserable, and nothing but knowing which shall be the happy hour can make the rest of my years that are to come tolerable. Give me a word or two of comfort, or resolve never to look on me more, for I cannot bear a kind look and after it a cruel denial.

This minute my heart aches for you; and, if I cannot have a right in yours, I wish it would ache till I could complain to you no longer.

Remember poor Otway.

You cannot be but sensible that I am blind, or you would not so openly discover what a ridiculous tool you make of me. I should be glad to discover whose satisfaction I was sacrificed to this morning; for I am sure your own ill-nature would not be guilty of inventing such an injury to me, merely to try how much I could bear, were it not for the sake of some ass that has the fortune to please you. In short, I have made it the business of my life to do you service, and please you, if possible, by any way to convince you of the unhappy love I have for seven years toiled under; and your whole business is to pick ill-natured conjectures out of my harmless freedom of conversation to vex and gall me with, as often as you are pleased to divert yourself at the expense of my quiet. Oh, thou tormenter! Could I think it were jealousy, how should I humble myself to be justified; but I cannot bear the thought of being made a property either of another man's good-fortune or the vanity of a woman that designs nothing but to plague me. There may be means found, some time or other, to let you know your mistaking.

You were pleased to send me word you would meet me in the Mall this evening, and give me further satisfaction in the matter you were so unkind to charge me with; I was there, but found you not; and therefore beg of you, as you ever would wish yourself to be eased of the highest torment it were possible your nature to be sensible of, to let me see you sometime to-morrow, and send me word by this bearer, where, and at what hour, you will be so just as either to acquit or condemn me; that I may hereafter, for your sake, either bless all your bewitching sex, or as often as I henceforth think of you, curse woman-kind forever.

Ovid

Publius Ovidius Naso (20 March, 43 BC–c.18 AD), known as Ovid in the English-speaking world, was a Roman poet who is best known as the author of the three major collections of erotic poetry: *Heroides* (*The Heroines*), *Amores* (*The Loves*), and *Ars Amatoria* (*The Art of Love*). He is also well known for the *Metamorphoses*, a mythological hexameter poem; the *Fasti* (*The Festivals*), about the Roman calendar; and the *Tristia* (*Sorrows*) and *Epistulae ex Ponto* (*Letters from the Black Sea*), two collections written in exile on the Black Sea. Ovid was also the author of several smaller pieces, the *Remedia Amoris* (*The Cure for Love*), the *Medicamina Faciei Femineae* (*Women's Facial Cosmetics*), and the long curse-poem *Ibis*. He also authored a lost tragedy, *Medea*. He is considered a master of the elegiac couplet, and is traditionally ranked alongside Virgil and Horace as one of the three canonic poets of Latin literature. The scholar Quintilian considered him the last of the canonical Latin love elegists. His poetry, much imitated during late Antiquity and the Middle Ages, decisively influenced European art and literature and remains as one of the most important sources of classical mythology.

Ovid was very popular at the time of his early works, but was later exiled by Augustus in 8 AD. He was banished to Tomis, on the Black Sea, in present day Romania, where he remained until his death. Ovid wrote that the reason for his exile was *carmen et error*—"a poem and a mistake", claiming that his crime was worse than murder, more harmful than poetry. Ovid died at Tomis after some ten years.

Ovid married three times and divorced twice by the time he was thirty years old. He married his first wife at age 16 and divorced at 18. His second bore him his only child, a daughter who eventually bore him grandchildren. Her fate is unknown. His last wife was connected in some way to the influential Fabian house and was a friend of the Empress Livia. They married sometime between 2 BC and 1 AD. While in exile, Ovid composed the *Epistulae ex Ponto*, a series of letters to friends in Rome asking them to effect his return. The first three books were published in 13 AD and the fourth book between 14 and 16 AD. They are particularly emotive and personal. In the *Epistulae* he claims friendship with the natives of Tomis (in the *Tristia* they are frightening barbarians). He pined for Rome and for his third wife, as many of the letters are to her.

c.8 AD

I plowed the vast ocean on a frail bit of timber; the ship that bore the son of Jason was strong... The furtive arts of Cupid aided him; arts which I wish that Love had not learned from me. He returned home; I shall die in these lands, if the heavy wrath of the offended God shall be lasting.

My burden, most faithful wife, is a harder one than that which the son of Jason bore. You, too, whom I left still young at my departure from the City, I can believe to have grown old under my calamities. Oh, grant it, ye Gods, that I may be enabled to see you, even if such, and to give the joyous kiss on each cheek in its turn; and to embrace your emaciated body in my arms, and to say, "'twas anxiety, on my account, that caused this thinness"; and, weeping, to recount in person my sorrows to you in tears, and thus enjoy a conversation that I had never hoped for; and to offer the due frankincense, with grateful hand, to the Caesars, and to the wife that is worthy of a Caesar, Deities in real truth!

Oh, that the mother of Menon, that Prince being softened, would with her rosy lips, speedily call forth that day.

c.16 AD

Lyde was not so dear to Antimachus, nor Bittis so loved by her Philetas, as you, my wife, clinging to my heart, worthy of a happier, but not truer husband. You are the support on which my ruins rest, if I am still anyone, it is all your gift. It is your doing that I am not despoiled, stripped bare by those who sought the planks from my shipwreck. As a wolf raging with the goad of hunger, eager for blood, catches the fold unguarded, or as a greedy vulture peers around to see if it can find an unburied corpse, so someone, faithless, in my bitter trouble, would have come into my wealth, if you had let them.

Your courage, with our friends, drove them off, bravely, friends I can never thank as they deserve. So you are proven, by one who is as true as he is wretched, if such a witness carries any weight. Neither Andromache, nor Laodamia, companion of her husband in death, exceeds you in probity. If you had been given to Homer, the Maonian bard, Penelope's fame would be second to yours: either you owe it to your own self, not being taught loyalty by some teacher, but through the character granted you at birth, or, if it is allowed to compare the small and great, Livia, first lady, honoured by you all those years, teaches you to be the model of a good wife, becoming like her, through long-acquired habit.

Alas, my poetry has no great powers, my lips are inadequate to sing your worth!—If I had any inborn vigour long ago, it is extinct, quenched by enduring sorrows!—Or you would be first among the sacred heroines, seen to be first, for the virtues of your heart. Yet in so far as my praise has any power, you will still live, for all time, in my verse.

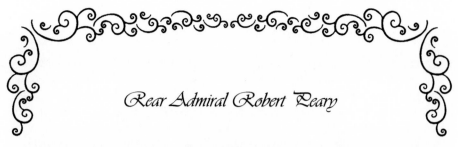

Rear Admiral Robert Peary

Robert Edwin Peary, Sr. (6 May, 1856–20 February, 1920) was an American explorer who claimed to have been the first person, on 6 April, 1909, to reach the geographic North Pole. Peary made several expeditions to the Arctic, exploring Greenland by dogsled in 1886 and 1891 and returning three times in the 1890s. He twice attempted to cross northwest Greenland over the ice cap. During the course of his explorations, he had eight toes amputated. In 1906 Peary's new ship *Roosevelt* battled its way through the ice between Greenland and Ellesmere Island to an American hemisphere farthest north by ship. The 1906 "Peary System" dogsled drive for the pole across the rough sea ice of the Arctic Ocean resulted in his claim to have achieved a farthest North world record at 87°06'. On 15 December, 1906, the National Geographic Society, which was primarily known for publishing a popular magazine, certified Peary's 1905–6 expedition with its highest honour, the Hubbard Gold Medal.

For his final assault on the pole, Peary and 23 men set off from New York City aboard the *Roosevelt* under the command of Captain Robert Bartlett on 6 July, 1908. They wintered near Cape Sheridan on Ellesmere Island and from Ellesmere departed for the pole on 28 February–1 March, 1909. The last support party was turned back from "Bartlett Camp" on 1 April, 1909, in latitude no greater than 87°45' north. On the final stage of the journey towards the North Pole only five of Peary's men remained. On 6 April, he established "Camp Jesup" allegedly within 5 miles (8.0 km) of the pole. In his diary for 7 April, Peary wrote: "The Pole at last!!! The prize of three centuries, my dream and ambition for twenty-three years. Mine at last." Peary was unable to enjoy the fruits of his labours to the full extent when, upon returning to civilization, he learned that Dr. Frederick A. Cook, who had been a surgeon on an 1891–92 Peary expedition, claimed to have reached the pole the year before. Peary's claim was widely credited for most of the 20th century, though it was criticised even in its own day and is today widely doubted.

Peary was the author of several books, the most famous being *Northward over the Great Ice* (1898) and *The North Pole* (1910). He retired in 1911 with the rank of Rear Admiral.

In 1888 Peary married Josephine Diebitsch (22 May, 1863–19 December, 1955), the daughter of a linguist at the Smithsonian Institution. She accompanied him on several of his expeditions, including in June, 1891, to northern Greenland which she wrote about in *My Arctic Journal* (1893). She was with him again in 1893, when she gave birth to their daughter Marie Ahnighito Peary (1893–1978), nicknamed the "The Snow Baby" by the local Inuits and by the press. Josephine recorded the story of her daughter's birth in her next book, *The Snow Baby* (1901).

Peary and other members of his crew also fathered children with Inuit women. Peary started a relationship with an Inuit woman named Aleqasina (Alakahsingwah) when she was about 14 years old. In 1900, when Josephine became stranded in Greenland after the ship she was on was damaged, the two women met. Aleqasina was pregnant, and gave birth to their son, Anaukkaq. Josephine had recently suffered the loss of their second daughter. Aleqasina became sick, and Josephine nursed her, while writing a 26 page letter to her unfaithful husband. However, she remained devoted to her husband throughout the rest of his life and after. She later bore him a son, Robert E. Peary, Jr. (1903–1994). It has been claimed that Aleqasina bore him several.

S.S. Roosevelt
17 August, 1908.

My Darling Josephine: Am nearly through with my writing. Am brain weary with the thousand and one imperative details and things to think of. Everything thus far has gone well, too well I am afraid, and I am (solely on general principles) somewhat suspicious of the future. The ship is in better shape than before; the party and crew are apparently harmonious; I have 21 Eskimo men (against 23 last time) but the total of men, women and children is only 50 as against 67 before owing to a more careful selection as to children... I have landed supplies here, and leave two men ostensibly on behalf of Cook.

As a matter of fact I have established here the sub-base which last I established at Victoria Head, as a precaution in event of loss of the Roosevelt either going up this fall or coming down next summer. In some respects this is an advantage as on leaving here there is nothing to delay me or keep me from taking either side of the Channel going up. The conditions give me entire control of the situation...

You have been with me constantly, sweetheart. At Kangerdlooksoah I looked repeatedly at Ptarmigan Island and thought of the time we camped there. At Nuuatoksoah I landed where we were. And on the 11th we passed the mouth of Bowdoin Bay in brilliant weather, and as long as I could I kept my eyes on Anniversary Lodge. We have been great chums dear. Tell Marie to remember what I told her, tell Mister Man to remember "straight and strong and clean and honest", obey orders, and never forget that Daddy put Mut in his charge till he himself comes back to take her.

In fancy I kiss your dear eyes and lips and cheeks sweetheart; and dream of you and my children, and my home till I come again. Kiss my babies for me. Aufwiedersehen.

Love, Love, Love. Your Bert

P.S. August 18, 9 a.m. ... Tell Marie that her fir pillow perfumes me to sleep.

Pliny the Younger

Gaius Plinius Caecilius Secundus (61 AD–c.112 AD), better known as Pliny the Younger, was a lawyer, author, and magistrate of Ancient Rome. Pliny's uncle, Pliny the Elder, helped raise and educate him and they were both witnesses to the eruption of Vesuvius on 24 August, 79 AD.

Pliny was a notable figure, considered an honest and moderate man. He was active in the Roman legal system, especially in the sphere of the Roman centumviral court, which dealt with inheritance cases. Later, he was a well-known prosecutor and defender at the trials of a series of provincial governors. His career is commonly considered as a summary of the main Roman public charges and is the best-documented example from this period, offering proof for many aspects of imperial culture. He served as an imperial magistrate under Trajan (reigned 98 AD–117 AD) and rose through a series of Imperial civil and military offices. He was a friend of the historian Tacitus and employed the biographer Suetonius in his staff. Pliny also came into contact with many other well-known men of the period, including the philosophers Artemidorus and Euphrates during his time in Syria.

As a litterateur, Pliny started writing at the age of fourteen, penning a tragedy in Greek. In the course of his life he wrote a quantity of poetry, most of which was lost despite the great affection he had for it. Also known as a notable orator, he professed himself a follower of Cicero, but his prose was certainly more magniloquent and less direct than Cicero's. The only oration that now survives is the *Panegyricus Traiani*. This was pronounced in the Senate in 100 AD and is a description of Trajan's figure and actions in an adulatory and emphatic form, especially contrasting him with the Emperor Domitian. It is, however, a relevant document that allows us to know many details about the Emperor's actions in several fields of his administrative power such as taxes, justice, military discipline, and commerce. Pliny defined it as an essay about the *optimus princeps* (best leader).

The largest body of Pliny's work which survives is his *Epistulae* (*Letters*), a series of personal missives directed to his friends and associates, for which he is well known. The letters are an invaluable historical source for the period. Many are addressed to reigning emperors or to notables such as Tacitus.

Pliny the Younger married three times, firstly when he was very young, about 18, to a stepdaughter of Veccius Proculus, of whom he became a widower at age 37, secondly to the daughter of Pompeia Celerina, at an unknown date and thirdly to Calpurnia, daughter of Calpurnius and granddaughter of Calpurnus Fabatus of Comum. Letters survive in which Pliny records this latter marriage taking place, as well as his attachment to Calpurnia and his sadness when they were unable to have children.

To Calpurnia

Rome
c.100 AD

 You say that you are feeling my absence very much, and your only comfort when I am not there is to hold my writings in your hand and often put them in my place by your side. I like to think that you miss me and find relief in this sort of consolation. I, too, am always reading your letters, and returning to them again and again as if they were new to me—but this only fans the fire of my longing for you. If your letters are so dear to me, you can imagine how I delight in your company; do write as often as you can, although you give me pleasure mingled with pain.

c.100 AD

 You will not believe what a longing for you possesses me. The chief cause of this is my love; we have not grown used to be apart. So it comes to pass that I lie awake a great part of the night, thinking of you; and that by day, when the hours return at which I was wont to visit you, my feet take me, as it is so truly said, to your chamber, but not finding you there, I return, sick and sad at heart, like an excluded lover. The only time that is free from these torments is when I am being worn out at the bar, and in the suits of my friends. Judge you what must be my life when I find my repose in toil, my solace in wretchedness and anxiety. Farewell.

Edgar Allan Poe

Edgar Allan Poe (19 January, 1809–7 October, 1849) was an American author, poet, editor and literary critic, considered part of the American Romantic Movement. His publishing career began humbly, with an anonymous collection, *Tamerlane and Other Poems* (1827), credited only to "a Bostonian". Poe switched his focus to prose and spent the next several years working for literary journals and periodicals, becoming known for his own style of literary criticism. *The Baltimore Saturday Visiter* awarded Poe a prize in October, 1833, for his short story "MS. Found in a Bottle". His work forced him to move between several cities, including Baltimore, Philadelphia, and New York City. In January, 1845, Poe published his poem "The Raven" to instant success.

Best known for his tales of mystery and the macabre, Poe was one of the earliest American practitioners of the short story and is considered the inventor of the detective-fiction genre. He is further credited with contributing to the emerging genre of science fiction. He was the first well-known American writer to try to earn a living through writing alone, resulting in a financially difficult life and career. Poe and his works influenced literature in the United States and around the world, as well as in specialised fields, such as cosmology and cryptography. Poe and his work appear throughout popular culture in literature, music, films, and television.

Poe's first love was Sarah Elmira Royster (1810–11 February, 1888). Neighbours and friends since 1825, they soon became secretly engaged. Her father did not approve however and intercepted and destroyed letters from Poe to her so that she thought he had forgotten her. In 1826, Poe returned home from the University of Virginia to learn that she was engaged to someone else. In Baltimore in 1833, Poe became smitten by a neighbour named Mary Devereaux (also known as Mary Starr). Their flirtation was quashed by her family who disapproved. In 1835 Poe was living with a great aunt and two cousins. One, the youngest Virginia Eliza Clemm (15 August, 1822–30 January, 1847), he wished to marry. She was 13. In August, 1835, Edgar wrote an emotional letter to her mother, Maria, declaring that he was "blinded with tears while writing... I have no wish to live another hour... I love Virginia passionately devotedly", and pleading that she allow Virginia to make her own decision. Encouraged by his employment at the *Southern Literary Messenger*, Poe offered to provide financially for Maria, Virginia and her brother Henry if they moved to Richmond. Poe secretly married his cousin, Virginia, on 22 September, 1835, with the ceremony being held on 16 May, 1836. Poe was 26, and Virginia was 13, though she is listed on the marriage certificate as being 21. Virginia and Poe were by all accounts a happy and devoted couple. A few years after their wedding, Poe was involved in a substantial scandal involving Frances Sargent Osgood and Elizabeth F. Ellet. Rumours about amorous improprieties abounded. In 1845, Poe had begun a flirtation with Frances Sargent

Osgood, a married 34-year-old poet. At the same time, another poet, Elizabeth F. Ellet, became enamoured of Poe and jealous of Osgood, and began rumours so as to drag Poe's name through the mud. The scandal affected Virginia so much that on her deathbed she claimed that Ellet had murdered her. Virginia contracted tuberculosis in 1842 and died of the disease in January, 1847, at the age of 24 in the family's cottage outside New York City.

Increasingly unstable after his wife's death, Poe attempted to court the poet Sarah Helen Whitman (19 January, 1803–27 June, 1878). The two exchanged letters and poetry for some time before discussing engagement. After Poe lectured in Providence in December, 1848, reciting a poem by Edward Coote Pinkney directly to Whitman, she agreed to an "immediate marriage". Poe agreed to remain sober during their engagement—a vow he violated within only a few days. Whitman broke off the engagement, though they had planned a wedding for later that month. There is also strong evidence that Whitman's mother intervened and did much to derail their relationship. Poe then returned to his first love, Sarah Elmira *née* Royster Shelton, a widow with 2 children. Poe hoped to marry her. He said goodbye to her, left Richmond on 27 September, 1849, and died mysteriously only two weeks later.

To Virginia Eliza Clemm

29 August, 1835.

My love, my own sweetest Sissy, my darling little wifey, think well before you break the heart of your Cousin, Eddy.

To Sarah Helen Whitman

Fordham, Sunday night, 1 October, 1848.

I have pressed your letter again and again to my lips, sweetest Helen— bathing it in tears of joy, or of a "divine despair." But I—who so lately, in your own presence, vaunted the "power of words"—of what avail are mere words to me now? Could I believe in the efficiency of prayers to the God of Heaven, I would kneel—humbly kneel—at this the most earnest epoch of my life—kneel in entreaty for words—but for words that should disclose to you that might enable me to lay bare to you my whole heart. All thoughts—all passions seem now merged in that one consuming desire—the mere wish to make you comprehend— to make you see that for which there is no human voice—the unutterable fervor of my love for you—for so well do I know your poet-nature, oh Helen, Helen! that I feel sure if you could but look down now into the depths of my soul with your pure spiritual eyes you could not refuse to speak to me that, alas! you still resolutely leave unspoken—you would love me if only for the greatness of my love. Is it not something in this cold, dreary world, to be loved?—Oh, if I could but burn into your spirit the deep the true meaning which I attach to those three syllables underlined!—but, alas! the effort is all in vain and "I live and die unheard."

When I spoke to you of what I felt, saying that I loved now for the first time, I did not hope you would believe or even understand me: nor can I hope to convince you now—but if, throughout some long, dark summer night, I could but have held you close, close to my heart and whispered to you the strange secrets of its passionate history, then indeed you would have seen that I have been far from attempting to deceive you in this respect. I could have shown you that it was not, and could never have been, in the power of any other than yourself to have moved me as I am now moved—to oppress me with this ineffable emotion—to surround and bathe me in this electric light, illumining and enkindling my whole nature— filling my soul with glory, with wonder, and with awe. During our walk in the cemetery I said to you, while the bitter, bitter tears sprang into my eyes—"Helen I love now—now—for the first time and only time." I said this, I repeat, in no hope, that you could believe me, but because I could not help feeling how unequal were the heart-riches we might offer each to each:—I, for the first time, giving my all, at once, and for ever, even while the words of your poem were yet ringing in my ears:

Oh then, beloved, I think on thee
And on that life so strangely fair,
Ere yet one cloud of Memory
Had gathered in Hope's golden air.
I think on thee and thy lone grave
On the green hillside far away
I see the wilding flowers that wave
Around thee as the night winds sway;
And still, though only clouds remain
On Life's horizon, cold and drear,
The dream of Youth returns again
With the sweet promise of the year.

Ah Helen, these lines are indeed beautiful, beautiful—but their very beauty was cruelty to me. Why—why did you show them to me? There seemed, too, so very especial a purpose in what you did.

I have already told you that some few casual words spoken of you... by Miss Lynch, were the first in which I had heard your name mentioned. She described you, in some measure, personally. She alluded to what she called your "eccentricities" and hinted at your sorrows. Her description of the former strangely arrested her allusion to the latter enchained and riveted, my attention. She had referred to thoughts, sentiments, traits, moods which I knew to be my own, but which, until that moment, I had believed to be my own solely unshared by any human being. A profound sympathy took immediate possession of my soul. I cannot better explain to you what I felt than by saying that your unknown heart seemed to pass into my bosom—there to dwell forever—while mine, I thought, was translated into your own. From that hour I loved you. Yes, I now feel it was then—on that evening of sweet dreams—that the very first dawn of human love burst upon the icy night of my spirit. Since that period I have never seen or heard your name without a shiver, half of delight, half of anxiety. The impression, left, however, upon my mind by Miss Lynch (whether through my own fault or her design I knew not) was that you were a wife now and a most happy one, and it is only within the last few months that I have been undeceived in this respect. For this reason I shunned your presence and even the city in which you lived.—You may remember that once, when I passed through Providence with Mrs. Osgood, I positively refused to accompany her to your house, and even provoked her into a quarrel by the obstinacy and seeming unreasonableness of my refusal. I dared neither go nor say why I could not. I dared not speak of you—much less see you. For years your name never passed my lips, while my soul drank in, with a delirious thirst, all that was uttered in my presence respecting you. The merest whisper that concerned you awoke in me a shuddering sixth sense, vaguely compounded of fear, ecstatic happiness, and a wild, inexplicable sentiment that resembled nothing so nearly as the consciousness of guilt.—Judge, then, with what wondering, unbelieving joy I received, in your wellknown MS., the Valentine which first gave me to see that you knew me to exist. The idea of what men call Fate lost then for the first time, in my eyes, its character of futility. I felt that nothing here after was to be doubted, and lost myself, for many weeks, in one continuous, delicious dream, where all was a vivid yet indistinct bliss.— Immediately after reading the Valentine, I wished to contrive some mode of acknowledging—without wounding you by seeming directly to acknowledge—my sense—oh, my keen—my profound—my exulting—my ecstatic sense of the honor you had conferred on me. To accomplish, as I wished it, precisely what I wished, seemed impossible, however; and I was on the point of abandoning the idea, when my eyes fell upon a volume of my own poems; and then the lines I had written, in my passionate boyhood to the first, purely ideal love of my soul—to the Helen Stannard[21] of whom I told you—flashed upon my recollection. I turned to them. They expressed all—all that I would have said to you—so fully—so accurately—and so conclusively, that a thrill of intense superstition ran at once throughout my frame. Read the verses and then take into consideration the peculiar need I had, at the moment, for just so seemingly unattainable a mode of communicating with you as they afforded. Think of the absolute appositeness with which they fulfilled that need—expressing not only all that I would have said of your person, but all that of which I most wished to assure you, in the lines commencing "On desperate seas long wont to roam." Think, too, of the rare agreement of name—Helen and not the far more usual Ellen—think of all those coincidences, and you will no longer wonder that, to one accustomed as I am to the Calculus of Probabilities, they wore an air of positive miracle. There was but one difficulty—I did not wish to copy the lines in my own MS, nor did I wish you to trace them to my volume of poems, I hoped to leave at least something of doubt on your mind as to how, why, and especially whence they came. And now, when,

---

[21] Subject of his poem "To Helen" published in 1831. She was the mother of one of his friends, and died of a brain tumor in 1824.

on accidentally turning the leaf, I found even this difficulty obviated, by the poem happening to be the last in the book, thus having no letter-press on its reverse—I yielded at once to an overwhelming sense of Fatality. From that hour I have never been able to shake from my soul the belief that my Destiny, for good or for evil, either here or here after, is in some measure interwoven with your own.—Of course, I did not expect on your part any acknowledgement of the printed lines "To Helen," and yet, without confessing it even to myself, I experienced an undeniable sorrow in your silence. At length, when I thought you had time fully to forget me (if indeed you had ever really remembered) I sent you the anonymous lines in MS. I wrote them, first, through a pining, burning desire to communicate with you in some way—even if you remained in ignorance of your correspondent. The mere thought that your dear fingers would press—your sweet eyes dwell upon characters which I had penned—characters which had welled out upon the paper from the depths of so devout a love—filled my soul with a rapture which seemed then all sufficient for my human nature. It then appeared to me that merely this one thought involved so much of bliss that here on earth I could have no right ever to repine—no room for discontent.—If ever, then, I dared to picture for myself a richer happiness, it was always connected with your image in Heaven. But there was yet another idea which impelled me to send you those lines:—I said to myself—The sentiment—the holy passion which glows within my spirit for her, is of Heaven, heavenly, and has no taint of the earth. Thus there must lie, in the recesses of her own pure bosom, at least the germ of a reciprocal love; and if this be indeed so, she will need no earthly clew—she will instinctively feel who is her correspondent.—In this case, then, I may hope for some faint token, at least, giving me to understand that the source of the poem is known and its sentiments comprehended even if disapproved. Oh God—how long—how long I waited in vain—hoping against Hope—until at length I became possessed with a spirit far sterner—far more reckless than Despair.—I explained to you—but without detailing the vital influence they wrought upon my fortune—though singular additional yet seemingly trivial fatalities by which you happened to address your lines to Fordham in place of New York—by which my aunt happened to get notice of their being in the West Farms Post-Office and by which it happened that, of all my set of the "Home Journal," I failed in receiving only that individual number which contained your published verses; but I have not yet told you that your MS lines reached me in Richmond on the very day in which I was about to depart on a tour and an enterprize which would have changed my very nature—fearfully altered my very soul—steeped me in a stern, cold, and debasing, although brilliant gigantic ambition—and borne me "far, far away" and forever from you, sweet, sweet Helen, and from this divine dream of your Love.

And now, in the most simple words at my command, let me paint to you the impression made upon me by your personal presence.—As you entered the room, pale, timid, hesitating, and evidently oppressed at heart; as your eyes rested appealingly, for one brief moment, upon mine, I felt, for the first time in my life, and tremblingly acknowledged, the existence of spiritual influences altogether out of the reach of reason. I saw that you were Helen—my Helen—the Helen of a thousand dreams—she whose visionary lips had so often lingered upon my own in the divine trance of passion—she whom the great Giver of all Good preordained to be mine—mine only—if not now, alas! then at least hereafter and forever in the Heavens.—You spoke falteringly and seemed scarcely conscious of what you said. I heard no words only the soft voice, more familiar to me than my own, and more melodious than the songs of the angels. Your hand rested within mine, and my whole soul shook with a tremulous ecstasy. And then but for very shame—but for the fear of grieving or oppressing you—I would have fallen at your feet in as pure—in as real a worship as was ever offered to Idol or to God. And when, afterwards, on those two successive evenings of all—Heavenly delights, you passed to and fro about the room—now sitting by my side, now far away, now standing with your hand resting on the back of my chair, while the preternatural thrill of your touch vibrated even through the senseless wood into my heart— while you moved thus restlessly about the room—as if a deep Sorrow or a more profound Joy haunted your bosom—my brain reeled beneath the intoxicating spell of your presence, and it was with no human senses that I either saw or heard you. It was my soul only that distinguished you there. I grew faint with the luxury of your voice and blind with the voluptuous lustre of your eyes...

14 November, 1848.

My dearest Helen

So kind, so true, so generous (—so unmoved by all that would have moved one who had been less an angel beloved of my heart, of my imagination, of my intellect, life of my life, soul of my soul)—dear dearest Helen, how shall I ever thank you as I ought—I am calm and tranquil and but for a strange shadow of coming evil which haunts me I should be happy. That I am not supremely happy, even when I feel your dear love at my heart terrifies me. What can this mean? Perhaps, however, it is only the necessary reaction after such terrible excitements.

It is five o'clock and the boat is just being made fast to the wharf. I shall start in the train that leaves New York at 7 for Fordham. I write this to show you that I have not dared to break my promise to you. And now, dearest Helen, be true to me.

Alexander Pope

Alexander Pope (21 May, 1688–30 May, 1744) was an eighteenth-century English poet, best known for his satirical verse and for his translation of Homer. He is the third most frequently quoted writer in *The Oxford Dictionary of Quotations*, after Shakespeare and Tennyson, and is also known for his use of the heroic couplet.

In May, 1709, Pope's *Pastorals* were published, bringing him instant fame. This was followed by *An Essay on Criticism* (1711), which was equally well received. Pope's most well known poem was *The Rape of the Lock*; first published in 1712, with a revised version published in 1714. During Pope's friendship with Joseph Addison, he contributed to Addison's play *Cato* as well as writing for *The Guardian* and *The Spectator*. Pope began to grow discontented with the ministry of Robert Walpole and drew closer to the opposition led by Bolingbroke, who had returned to England in 1725. Inspired by Bolingbroke's philosophical ideas, Pope wrote *An Essay on Man* (1733–4). He published the first part anonymously, in a cunning and successful ploy to win praise from his fiercest critics and enemies.

From the age of 12, he suffered numerous health problems, such as Pott's disease (a form of tuberculosis that affects the bone) which deformed his body and stunted his growth, leaving him with a severe hunchback. He never grew beyond 1.37m (4ft 6in) tall. His tuberculosis infection caused other health problems including respiratory difficulties, high fevers, inflamed eyes, and abdominal pain. Pope was already removed from society because he was Catholic; his poor health only alienated him further.

Although Pope never married, he had many female friends to whom he wrote witty letters. In 1711 he met the Blount sisters, Teresa (1688–1759) and Martha (1690–1762), both of whom would remain lifelong friends. They first became acquainted at White Knights, the house of their grandfather, a great lover of poetry and admirer of Pope. With Martha he maintained a close companionship which has long been speculated on. He remembered her in his will, leaving her money, furniture and books. With his neighbour, Lady Mary Wortley Montagu (15 May, 1689–21 August, 1762), Pope formed an attachment. He was impressed by her wit and intelligence and they entered into a long correspondence while she was in the Orient with her husband. He wrote her a series of extravagant letters, which appear to have been chiefly exercises in the art of writing gallant epistles. Very few letters passed between them after Lady Mary's return, and various reasons have been suggested for the subsequent estrangement and violent quarrel. It has been alleged that Pope had made Lady Mary a declaration of love, which she had received with an outburst of laughter. Pope responded by mocking and attacking her in his writing.

To Martha Blount

1714.

Most Divine!—
It is some proof of my sincerity towards you, that I write when I am prepared by drinking to speak truth; and sure a letter after twelve at night must abound with that noble ingredient. That heart must have abundance of flames, which is at once warmed by wine and you: wine awakens and refreshes the lurking passions of the mind, as varnish does the colours that are sunk in a picture, and brings them out in all their natural glowings. My good qualities have been so frozen and locked up in a dull constitution at all my former sober hours, that it is very astonishing to me, now I am drunk, to find so much virtue in me.
In these overflowings of my heart I pay you my thanks for those two obliging letters you favoured me with of the 18th and 24th instant. That which begins with "My charming Mr. Pope!" was a delight to me beyond all expression: you have at last entirely gained the conquest over your fair sister.
It is true you are not handsome, for you are a woman, and think you are not: but this good-humour and tenderness for me has a charm that cannot be resisted. That face must needs be irresistible, which was adorned with smiles even when it could not see the coronation.[22] I do suppose you will not show this epistle out of vanity, as I doubt not your sister does all I write to her. Indeed, to correspond with Mr. Pope, may make any one proud who lives under a dejection of heart in the country.
Every one values Mr. Pope, but every one for a different reason: one for his adherence to the Catholic faith; another for his neglect of Popish superstition; one for his grave behaviour, another for his whimsicalness; Mr. Titcomb, for his pretty atheistical jests; Mr. Caryll, for his moral and Christian sentences; Mrs. Teresa, for his reflections on Mrs. Patty; and Mrs. Patty, for his reflections on Mrs. Teresa...
I am your most faithful admirer, friend, servant, any thing, &c.
I send you Gay's poem on the princess. She is very fat. God help her husband.
Alexander Pope

To Teresa Blount

7 August, 1716.

Madam,
I have so much esteem for you, and so much of the other thing, that were I a handsome fellow, I should do you a vast deal of good: but as it is, all I am good for is to write a civil letter, or to make a fine speech. The truth is, that considering how often & how openly I have declared love to you, I am astonished (and a little

---

[22] of George I, September, 1714.

affronted) that you have not forbid my correspondence, & directly said, see my face no more. It is not enough, Madam, for your reputation that you keep your hands pure, from the strain of such ink as might be shed to gratify a male correspondent. Alas! while your heart consents to encourage him in this lewd liberty of writing, you are not (indeed you are not) what you would so fain have me think you, a prude! I am vain enough to conclude (like most young fellows) that a fine lady's silence is consent, and I write on.

But in order to be as innocent as possible in this epistle, I'll tell you news. You have asked me news a thousand times at the first word you spoke to me, which some would interpret as if you expected nothing better from my lips; and truly 'tis not a sign two lovers are together, when they can be so impertinent as to enquire what the world does? All I mean by this, is, that either you or I cannot be in love with the other; I leave you to guess which of the two is that stupid & insensible creature, so blind to the others excellencies and charms...

To Lady Mary Wortley Montague

June, 1717.

Madam,
If to live in the memory of others have any thing desirable in it, 'tis what you possess with regard to me, in the highest sense of the words. There is not a day in which your figure does not appear before me; your conversations return to my thoughts, and every scene, place, or occasion, where I have enjoyed them, are as livelily painted, as an imagination equally warm and tender can be capable to represent them. Yet how little accrues to you from all this, when not only my wishes, but the very expressions of them, can hardly ever arrive to be known to you? I cannot tell whether you have seen half the letters I have writ; but if you had, I have not said in them half of what I designed to say; and you can have seen but a faint, slight, timorous eschantillon of what my spirit suggests, and my hand follows slowly, and imperfectly, indeed unjustly, because discreetly and reservedly. When you told me there was no way left for our correspondence, but by merchant ships, I watched ever since for any that set out, and this is the first I could learn of, I owe the knowledge of it to Mr. Congreve (whose letters with my Lady Rich's, accompany this). However I was impatient enough to venture two from Mr. Methuen's office; they have miscarried, you have lost nothing but such words and wishes as I repeat every day in your memory, and for your welfare. I have had thoughts of causing what I write for the future to be transcribed, and to send copies by more ways than one, that one at least might have a chance to reach you. The letters themselves would be artless and natural enough to prove there could be no vanity in this practice, and to shew it proceeded from the belief of their being welcome to you, not as they came from me, but from England. My eyesight is grown so bad, that I have left off all correspondence except with yourself; in which methinks I am like those people who abandon and abstract themselves from all that are about them (with whom they might have business and

198 ~ The Love Letters of Great Men

intercourse), to employ their addresses only to invisible and distant beings, whose good offices and favours cannot reach them in a long time, if at all. If I hear from you, I look upon it as little less than a miracle, or extraordinary visitation from another world; 'tis a sort of dream of an agreeable thing, which subsists no more to me; but however it is such a dream as exceeds most of the dull realities of my life. Indeed, what with ill-health and ill-fortune, I am grown so stupidly philosophical as to have no thought about me that deserves the name of warm or lively, but that which sometimes awakens me into an imagination that I may yet see you again. Compassionate a poet, and (which is more) a young poet, who has lost all manner of romantic ideas; except a few that hover about the Bosphorus and Hellespont, not so much for the fine sound of their names as to raise up images of Leander, who was drowned in crossing the sea to kiss the hand of fair Hero. This were a destiny less to be lamented, than what we are told of the poor Jew, one of your interpreters, who was beheaded at Belgrade as a Spy. I confess such a death would have been a great disappointment to me; and I believe Jacob Tonson will hardly venture to visit you, after this news.

You tell me, the pleasure of being nearer the sun has a great effect upon your health and spirits. You have turned my affections so far eastward, that I could almost be one of his worshippers: for I think the sun has more reason to be proud of raising your spirits, than of raising all the plants, and ripening all the minerals in the earth. It is my opinion, a reasonable man might gladly travel three or four thousand leagues, to see your nature, and your wit, in their full perfection. What may not we expect from a creature that went out the most perfect of this part of the world, and is every day improving by the sun in the other! If you do not write and speak the finest things imaginable, you must be content to be involved in the same imputation with the rest of the east, and be concluded to have abandoned yourself to extreme effeminacy, laziness, and lewdness of life.

I make not the least question but you could give me great eclaircissements upon many passages in Homer since you have been enlightened by the same sun that inspired the father of poetry. You are now glowing under the climate that animated him; you may see his images rising more boldly about you, in the very scenes of his story and action; you may lay the immortal work on some broken column of a hero's sepulchre; and read the fall of Troy in the shade of a Trojan ruin. But if, to visit the tomb of so many heroes, you have not the heart to pass over that sea where once a lover perished; you may at least, at ease, in your own window, contemplate the fields of Asia, in such a dim and remote prospect, as you have of Homer in my translation.

I send you therefore with this, the third volume of the Iliad, and as many other things as fill a wooden box, directed to Mr. Wortley. Among the rest, you have all I am worth, that is, my works: there are few things in them but what you have already seen, except the Epistle of Eloisa to Abelard, in which you will find one passage, that I cannot tell whether to wish you should understand, or not...

The last I received from your hands was from Peterwaradin; it gave me the joy of thinking you in good health and humour: one or two expressions in it are too generous ever to be forgotten by me. I writ a very melancholy one just before, which was sent to Mr. Stanyan, to be forwarded through Hungary. It would have informed you how meanly I thought of the pleasures of Italy, without the qualification of your company, and that mere statues and pictures are not more cold to me, than I to them. I have had but four of your letters; I have sent several, and I wish I knew how many you have received. For God's sake, Madam, send to me as often as you can; in the dependance that there is no man breathing more constantly, or more anxiously mindful of you. Tell me that you are well, tell me that your little son is well, tell me that your very dog (if you have one) is well. Defraud me of no one thing that pleases you; for whatever that is, it will please me better than any thing else can do. I am always yours.

1 September, 1718.

    Madam,

    ... I prodigiously long for your sonnets, your remarks, your Oriental learning; but I long for nothing so much as your Oriental self. You must of necessity be advanced so far back into true nature and simplicity of manners, by these three years' residence in the east, that I shall look upon you as so many years younger than you was, so much nearer innocence (that is, truth) and infancy (that is, openness). I expect to see your soul as much thinner dressed as your body; and that you have left off, as unwieldy and cumbersome, a great many d—d European habits. Without offence to your modesty, be it spoken, I have a burning desire to see your soul stark naked, for I am confident 'tis the prettiest kind of white soul in the universe.—But I forget whom I am talking to; you may possibly by this time believe, according to the prophet, that you have none; if so, show me that which comes next to a soul; you may easily put it upon a poor ignorant Christian for a soul, and please him as well with it;—I mean your heart; Mahomet, I think, allows you hearts; which (together with fine eyes and other agreeable equivalents) are worth all the souls on this side the world. But if I must be content with seeing your body only, God send it to come quickly; I honour it more than the diamond-casket that held Homer's Iliads; for in the very twinkle of one eye of it there is more wit, and in the very dimple of one cheek of it there is more meaning, than in all the souls that ever were casually put into women since men had the making them.

1719.

    I might be dead, or you in Yorkshire, for any thing that I am the better for your being in town. I have been sick ever since I saw you last, and now have a swelled face, and very bad; nothing will do me so much good as the sight of dear Lady Mary; when you come this way let me see you, for indeed I love you.

Sir Walter Raleigh

Sir Walter Raleigh (c.1552–29 October, 1618) was an English aristocrat, writer, poet, soldier, courtier, spy, and explorer. He is also well known for popularising tobacco in England.

Raleigh was born to a Protestant family in Devon. Little is known for certain of his early life, though he spent some time in Ireland, in Killua Castle, Clonmellon, County Westmeath, taking part in the suppression of rebellions and participating in a massacre at Smerwick. Later he became a landlord of properties confiscated from the Irish rebels. He rose rapidly in Queen Elizabeth I's favour, being knighted in 1585, appointed warden of the stannaries, that is of the mines of Cornwall and Devon, Lord Lieutenant of Cornwall, and vice-admiral of the two counties. Both in 1585 and 1586, he sat in parliament as member for Devonshire. He was involved in the early English colonisation of Virginia under a royal patent. In 1594 Raleigh heard of a "City of Gold" in South America and sailed to find it, publishing an exaggerated account of his experiences in a book, *The Discovery of Guiana* (1596), that contributed to the legend of "El Dorado". From 1600 to 1603, as Governor of the Channel Island of Jersey, Raleigh modernised its defences. This included construction of a new fort protecting the approaches to Saint Helier, Fort Isabella Bellissima, or Elizabeth Castle. After Queen Elizabeth died in 1603 Raleigh was imprisoned in the Tower of London for allegedly being involved in the Main Plot against King James I, who was not favourably disposed toward him. He remained imprisoned until 1616, when he was released in order to conduct a second expedition in search of El Dorado. This was unsuccessful and men under his command ransacked a Spanish outpost. He returned to England and, to appease the Spanish, was arrested and executed in 1618.

In 1591 Raleigh secretly married Elizabeth "Bess" Throckmorton (16 April 1565–c.1647), one of the Queen's ladies-in-waiting, without the Queen's permission which was required. She was thirteen years his junior, and was pregnant at the time. She gave birth to a son, believed to be named Damerei, who was given to a wet nurse at Durham House, but died in October, 1591, of plague. Bess resumed her duties to the Queen. The following year, the unauthorised marriage was discovered and the Queen ordered Raleigh imprisoned in the Tower and Bess dismissed from court. He was released to divide the spoils from the captured Spanish ship *Madre de Dios* (Mother of God), after which they retired to his estate at Sherborne, Dorset. The couple remained devoted to each other. During Raleigh's absences, Bess proved a capable manager of the family's fortunes and reputation. They had two more sons, Walter (known as Wat) (1593–1616) and Carew (c.1604–1666) who was conceived and born while Raleigh was imprisoned in the Tower.

1603.

You shall now receive (my dear wife) my last words in these my last lines. My love I send you that you may keep it when I am dead, and my counsel that you may remember it when I am no more.

I would not by my will present you with sorrows (dear Besse) let them go to the grave with me and be buried in the dust. And seeing that it is not God's will that I should see you any more in this life, bear it patiently, and with a heart like thy self.

First, I send you all the thanks which my heart can conceive, or my words can rehearse for your many travails, and care taken for me, which though they have not taken effect as you wished, yet my debt to you is not the less; but pay it I never shall in this world.

Secondly, I beseech you for the love you bear me living, do not hide yourself many days, but by your travails seek to help your miserable fortunes and the right of your poor child. Thy mourning cannot avail me, I am but dust.

Thirdly, you shall understand, that my land was conveyed bona fide to my child; the writings were drawn at midsummer was twelve months, my honest cousin Brett can testify so much, and Dolberry too, can remember somewhat therein. And I trust my blood will quench their malice that have cruelly murdered me: and that they will not seek also to kill thee and thine with extreme poverty.

To what friend to direct thee I know not, for all mine have left me in the true time of trial. And I perceive that my death was determined from the first day. Most sorry I am God knows that being thus surprised with death I can leave you in no better estate. God is my witness I meant you all my office of wines or all that I could have purchased by selling it, half of my stuff, and all my jewels, but some one for the boy, but God hath prevented all my resolutions. That great God that ruleth all in all, but if you live free from want, care for no more, for the rest is but vanity. Love God, and begin betimes to repose your self upon him, and therein shall you find true and lasting riches, and endless comfort: for the rest when you have travailed and wearied your thoughts over all sorts of worldly cogitations, you shall but sit down by sorrow in the end.

Teach your son also to love and fear God while he is yet young, that the fear of God may grow with him, and then God will be a husband to you, and a father to him; a husband and a father which cannot be taken from you.

Baily oweth me 200 pounds, and Adrian Gilbert 600. In Jersey I also have much owing me besides. The arrearages of the wines will pay my debts. And howsoever you do, for my souls sake, pay all poor men. When I am gone, no doubt you shall be sought for by many, for the world thinks that I was very rich. But take heed of the pretences of men, and their affections, for they last not but in honest and worthy men, and no greater misery can befall you in this life, than to become a prey, and afterwards to be despised. I speak not this (God knows) to dissuade you from marriage, for it will be best for you, both in respect of the world and of God. As for me, I am no more yours, nor you mine, death hath cut us asunder: and God hath divided me from the world, and you from me.

Remember your poor child for his father's sake, who chose you, and loved you in his happiest times. Get those letters (if it be possible) which I wrote to the Lords, wherein I sued for my life; God is my witness it was for you and yours that I desired life, but it is true that I disdained my self for begging of it: for know it (my dear wife) that your son is the son of a true man, and one who in his own respect despiseth death and all his misshapen and ugly forms.

I cannot write much, God he knows how hardly I steal this time while others sleep, and it is also time that I should separate my thoughts from the world. Beg my dead body which living was denied thee; and either lay it at Sherburne or in Exeter Church, by my Father and Mother; I can say no more, time and death call me away.

The everlasting God, powerfull, infinite, and omnipotent God, That Almighty God, who is goodness itself, the true life and true light keep thee and thine: have mercy on me, and teach me to forgive my persecutors and false accusers, and send us to meet in his glorious Kingdom. My dear wife farewell. Bless my poor boy. Pray for me, and let my good God hold you both in his arms.

Written with the dying hand of sometimes thy Husband, but now alas overthrown. Yours that was, but now not my own.

Walter Raleigh

John Ruskin

John Ruskin (8 February, 1819–20 January, 1900) was an English art critic and social thinker, also remembered as a poet and artist. His essays on art and architecture were extremely influential in the Victorian and Edwardian eras. Ruskin first came to widespread attention for his support of the work of J. M. W. Turner and his defence of naturalism in art. He went on to publish the first volume of one of his major works, *Modern Painters*, in 1843, under the anonymous identity "An Oxford Graduate". Ruskin followed it with a second volume, developing his ideas about symbolism in art. He then turned to architecture, writing *The Seven Lamps of Architecture* (1849) and *The Stones of Venice* (1851–3), both of which argued that architecture cannot be separated from morality. *Modern Painters* subsequently extended to nine volumes.

Ruskin came into contact with Sir John Everett Millais, 1st Baronet, PRA (8 June, 1829–13 August, 1896) following the controversy over Millais' painting *Christ in the House of His Parents*, which was considered blasphemous at the time. Millais, with his colleagues William Holman Hunt and Dante Gabriel Rossetti, had established the Pre-Raphaelite Brotherhood in 1848. The Pre-Raphaelites were influenced by Ruskin's theories. As a result, the critic wrote letters to *The Times* defending their work, later meeting them and putting his weight behind the Pre-Raphaelite movement. He supported many of them financially. His later writings turned increasingly to complex and personal explorations of the interconnection of cultural, social and moral issues, and were influential on the development of Christian socialism.

Ruskin's range was vast. He wrote over 250 works which started from art history, but expanded to cover topics ranging over science, geology, ornithology, literary criticism, the environmental effects of pollution, and mythology. After his death Ruskin's works were collected together in a massive "library edition", completed in 1912 by his friends Edward Cook and Alexander Wedderburn. Its index is famously elaborate, attempting to articulate the complex interconnectedness of his thought.

In 1848, Ruskin married "Effie" Euphemia Chalmers Gray (1828–23 December, 1897), for whom he had written the early fantasy novel *The King of the Golden River* (1841). Their marriage was notoriously unhappy, eventually being annulled in 1854 on grounds of his "incurable impotency," a charge Ruskin later disputed, even going so far as to offer to prove his virility at the court's request. In court, the Ruskin family counter-attacked Effie as being mentally unbalanced. Effie later married John Everett Millais, who had been Ruskin's protégé, in July, 1855, and bore him eight children.

11 November, 1847.

When we are alone—You and I—together—Mais—c'est inconceivable—I was just trying—this evening after dinner—to imagine our sitting after dinner at Keswick—vous et moi... I couldn't do it—it seemed so impossible that I should ever get you all to myself—I shall not be able to speak a word—I shall be running round you—and kneeling to you and holding up my hands to you as Dinah does her paws—speechless—I shan't do it so well as Dinah though—I shall be clumsy and mute—at once perfectly oppressed with delight—if you speak to me I shall not know what you say—you will have to pat me—and point to something for me to fetch and carry for you—or make me lie down on a rug and be quiet—or send me out of the room until I promise to be a good dog; and when you let me in again—I shall be worse—what shall I do?

Folkestone
30 November, 1847.

My beloved Effie,
I never thought to have felt time pass slowly anymore—but—foolish that I am, I cannot help congratulating myself on this being the last day of November— Foolish, I say—for what pleasure soever may be in store for us, we ought not to wish to lose the treasure of time—nor to squander away the heap of gold even though its height should keep us from seeing each for a little while. But your letter of last night shook all the philosopher out of me. That little undress bit! Ah—my sweet Lady—What naughty thoughts had I. Dare I say?—I was thinking—thinking, naughty—happy thoughts, that you would soon have— someone's arms to keep you from being cold! Pray don't be angry with me. How could I help it?—how can I? I'm thinking so just now, even. Oh—my dearest—I am not so 'scornful' neither, of all that I hope for—Alas—I know what I would not give for one glance of your fair eyes—your fair—saucy eyes. You cruel, cruel girl—now that was just like you—to poor William at the Ball. I can see you at this moment—hear you. 'If you wanted to dance with me, William! If!' You saucy— wicked—witching—malicious—merciless—mischief loving—torturing—martyrizing —unspeakably to be feared and fled—mountain nymph that you are—'If!' When you knew that he would have given a year of his life for a touch of your hand. Ah's me—what a world this is, when its best creatures and kindest—will do such things. What a sad world. Poor fellow—How the lights of the ballroom would darken and its floor sink beneath him—Earthquake and eclipse at once, and to be 'if'd' at by you, too; Now—I'll take up his injured cause—I'll punish you for that—Effie—some time—see if I don't—If I don't. It deserves—oh—I don't know what it doesn't deserve—nor what I can do.
P.S. Ah—my mysterious girl—I forgot one little bit of the letter—but I can't forget all, though 'a great many things.'
My heart is yours—my thoughts—myself—all but my memory, but that's mine. Now it is cool—as you say—to give me all that pain—and then tell me—'Never

mind, I won't do it again.' Heaven forbid! How could you—puss? You are not thinking of saying that you have 'been thinking about it—' or 'writing to a friend'—and that you won't have me now! Are you?

December, 1847.

I don't know anything dreadful enough to liken to you—you are like a sweet forest of pleasant glades and whispering branches—where people wander on and on in its playing shadows they know not how far—and when they come near the centre of it, it is all cold and impenetrable—and when they would fain turn, lo— they are hedged with briars and thorns and cannot escape...

You are like the bright—soft—swelling—lovely fields of a high glacier covered with fresh morning snow—which is heavenly to the eye—and soft and winning on the foot—but beneath, there are winding clefts and dark places in its cold—cold ice—where men fall, and rise not again.

Friedrich von Schiller

Johann Christoph Friedrich von Schiller (10 November, 1759–9 May, 1805) was a German poet, philosopher, historian, and playwright. At school, he wrote his first play, *The Robbers*, which was performed in Mannheim, in 1781. The play's critique of social corruption and its affirmation of proto-revolutionary republican ideals astounded its original audience. Schiller became an overnight sensation. He was arrested, sentenced to 14 days of imprisonment, and forbidden from publishing any further works. Later, Schiller would be made an honorary member of the French Republic because of this play. He fled Stuttgart in 1782, going via Frankfurt, Mannheim, Leipzig, and Dresden to Weimar, where he settled in 1787. In 1789, he was appointed professor of History and Philosophy in Jena, where he wrote only historical works.

During the last seventeen years of his life (1788–1805), Schiller struck up a productive, if complicated, friendship with the already famous and influential Johann Wolfgang von Goethe. They frequently discussed issues concerning aesthetics, and Schiller encouraged Goethe to finish works he left as sketches. This relationship and these discussions led to a period now referred to as Weimar Classicism. They also worked together on *Die Xenien*, a collection of short satirical poems in which both Schiller and Goethe challenge opponents to their philosophical vision. He and Goethe founded the Weimar Theatre, which became the leading theatre in Germany. Their collaboration helped lead to a dramatic renaissance in Germany. Schiller's most famous works include the plays *Intrigue and Love* (*Kabale und Liebe*, 1784), *Don Carlos* (1787) and the philosophical work *On the Aesthetic Education of Man in a Series of Letters* (*Über die ästhetische Erziehung des Menschen in einer Reihe von Briefen*, 1794).

In 1784 Schiller conducted a hopeless love-affair with a married woman, Charlotte von Kalb (1761–1843). Their romance lasted until the next year, when Schiller left for Leipzig, and they were briefly reunited in Weimar in 1787, but the relationship went no further. On 22 February, 1790, Schiller married Charlotte "Lotte" Luise Antoinette von Lengefeld (22 November, 1766–9 July, 1826). Lengefeld first met Schiller, then a little-known and impoverished poet, in 1785. They began a correspondence in 1788, and, aided by the Lengefelds, Schiller took up residence near Rudolstadt shortly thereafter. He seems to have made his affections clear to her that year. The Schillers had four children: Karl Ludwig Friedrich (1793–1857), Ernst Friedrich Wilhelm (1796–1841), Karoline Luise Friederike (1799–1850) and Emilie Henriette Luise (1804–1872).

To Charlotte von Lengefeld

3 August, 1789.

    Is it true, dearest Lotte? may I hope that Karoline has read in your soul and has answered me out of your heart what I did not have the courage to confess? Oh, how hard this secret has become for me, that I, as long as we have known each other, have had to conceal! Often, when we still lived together, I collected my whole courage and came to you with the intentions to disclose it to you—but this courage always forsook me. I thought to discover selfishness in my wish, I feared that I had only my happiness in view, and that thought drove me back. Could I not become to you what your were to me, then my suffering would have distressed you, and I would have destroyed the most beautiful harmony of our friendship through my confession. I would have also lost that, what I had, your true and sisterly friendship. And yet again there come moments, when my hope arose afresh, wherein the happiness, which we could give each other, seemed to me exalted above every, every consideration, when I considered it even as noble to sacrifice everything else to it. You could be happy without me—but not become unhappy through me. This I felt alive in me—and thereupon I built my hopes.

    You could give yourself to another, but none could love you more purely or more completely than I did. To none could your happiness be holier, as it was to me, and always will be. My whole existence, everything that lives within me, everything, my most precious, I devote to you, and if I try to ennoble myself, that is done, in order to become ever worthier of you, to make you ever happier. Nobility of souls is a beautiful and indestructible bond of friendship and of our love. Our friendship and love become indestructible and eternal like the feelings upon which we establish them.

    Now forget everything that could put constraint on your heart, and allow your feelings to speak alone. Confirm to me, what Karoline had allowed me to hope. Tell me that you will be mine and that my happiness costs you no sacrifice. Oh, assure me of that, it needs only a single word. Our hearts have a long time been close to each other. Allow the only foreign element which has hitherto been between us to vanish, and nothing to disturb the free communication of our souls. Farewell, dearest Lotte! I yearn for a quiet moment, to portray to you all the feeling of my heart, which, during that long period that this longing alone dwells in my heart, has made me happy and then again unhappy... Do not delay to banish my unrest for ever and always, I give all the pleasures of my life into your hand...

    Farewell, my most precious!

Robert Schumann

Robert Schumann (8 June, 1810–29 July, 1856) was a German composer, aesthete and influential music critic. He is regarded as one of the greatest and most representative composers of the Romantic era. Schumann left the study of law intending to pursue a career as a virtuoso pianist. He had been assured by his teacher, Friedrich Wieck, that he could become the finest pianist in Europe, but a hand injury allegedly caused by a device he created with the false belief that it would help increase the size of his hands prevented that. One of the most promising careers as a pianist thus came to an end. Schumann then focused his musical energies on composing. Schumann's published compositions were written exclusively for the piano until 1840; he later composed works for piano and orchestra; many lieder (songs for voice and piano); four symphonies; an opera; and other orchestral, choral, and chamber works. His writings about music appeared mostly in the *Neue Zeitschrift für Musik* (*New Journal for Music*), a Leipzig-based publication which he jointly founded.

Schumann had considerable influence in the nineteenth century and beyond. He left an array of acclaimed music in virtually all the forms then known. Partly through his protégé Johannes Brahms, Schumann's ideals and musical vocabulary became widely disseminated. Composer Sir Edward Elgar called Schumann "my ideal."

Schumann's first known love was the 16-year-old Ernestine von Fricken—the adopted daughter of a rich Bohemian-born noble—to whom he became engaged in the summer of 1834. Schumann broke off that engagement the next year, partly due to learning that she was illegitimate, which meant that she would have no dowry, and partly due to his attraction to and budding romance with Clara Josephine Wieck (13 September, 1819–20 May, 1896). Robert and Clara first met in March, 1828, when at the age of eight, Clara, already a talented pianist, gave a private performance for friends. Schumann took lessons from her father, Friedrich, and by the time she was seventeen, Schumann was in love with her. The next year (1837), Schumann asked Friedrich for Clara's hand in marriage, but he refused. Friedrich did everything he could to prevent their marriage, forcing the lovers to take him to court. Despite the opposition, they continued a clandestine relationship which matured into a full-blown romance. They exchanged love letters and met in secret. Robert would often wait in a cafe for hours just to see Clara for a few minutes after one of her concerts. During this period Schumann, inspired by his love for Clara, wrote many of his most famous songs. They eventually married on 12 September, 1840, and had eight children: Marie (1841–1929), Elise (1843–1928), Julie (1845–1872), Emil (who died in infancy in 1847), Ludwig (1848–1899), Ferdinand (1849–1891), Eugenie (1851–1938) and Felix (1854–1879). Clara continued to perform and compose after the marriage, even as she raised their children. In the various tours on which she accompanied her husband, she extended her own reputation beyond Germany, and her efforts to promote his works gradually made Schumann accepted throughout Europe.

For the last two years of his life, after experiencing visions, Schumann attempted suicide and was confined to a mental institution, at his own request.

To Clara Wieck in Dresden.

Leipsic, July, 1834.

> *My dear honoured Clara,*
> *Some misanthropists maintain that the swan is only a larger kind of goose. With quite as much reason one might call distance merely an extended vicinity. But it really is so, for I talk to you every day (and in a gentler whisper even than usual), and feel that you understand me. At first I made all sorts of plans about our correspondence. For instance, I thought of making our letters public in the Zeitung, then of filling my balloon (did you know I had one?) with unwritten thoughts, and sending it off to you, properly addressed, and with a favourable wind. I longed to catch butterflies to be my messengers to you, I thought of getting my letters posted in Paris, so as to arouse your curiosity, and make you believe I was there. In short, a great many quaint notions came into my head, and have only just been dispersed by a postilion's horn. The fact is, dear Clara, that postilions have much the same sort of effect upon me as the most excellent champagne. One quite forgets that one has a head, it makes one feel so delightfully light-hearted to hear them blaring away to the world so merrily. Their merry strains seem to me like very dances of rapturous longing, and seem to remind one of something one does not possess. But as I said before, that postilion with his horn sent me out of my old dreams into new ones...*

Waiting for the Zwickau coach, 10 p.m.
13 February, 1836.

> *I was terribly sleepy. I have been waiting two hours for the express coach. The roads are so bad that perhaps we shall not get away till two o'clock... To-day I have been agitated by various things; the opening of my mother's will, hearing all about her death, etc, but your radiant image shines through the darkness and helps me to bear everything better...*
> *At Leipsic my first care shall be to put my worldly affairs in order. I am quite clear about my heart. Perhaps your father will not refuse if I ask him for his blessing. Of course there is much to be thought of and arranged. But I put great trust in our guardian angel. Fate always intended us for one another. I have known that a long time, but my hopes were never strong enough to tell you and get your answer before... The room is getting dark. Passengers near me are going*

to sleep. It is sleeting and snowing outside. But I will squeeze myself right into a corner, bury my face in the cushions, and think only of you.

    Your Robert.

You will get my next letter the day after your concert. Write to me often; every day.

On the morning of the 1st, 1838.

    What a heavenly morning! All the bells are ringing; the sky is so golden and blue and clear—and before me lies your letter. I send you my first kiss, beloved.

2 January, 1838.

    Clara,

    How happy your last letters have made me—those since Christmas Eve! I should like to call you by all the endearing epithets, and yet I can find no lovelier word than the simple word 'dear,' but there is a particular way of saying it. My dear one, then, I have wept for joy to think that you are mine, and often wonder if I deserve you. One would think that no one man's heart and brain could stand all the things that are crowded into one day. Where do these thousands of thoughts, wishes, sorrows, joys and hopes come from? Day in, day out, the procession goes on. But how light-hearted I was yesterday and the day before! There shone out of your letters so noble a spirit, such faith, such a wealth of love!

    What would I not do for love of you, my own Clara! The knights of old were better off; they could go through fire or slay dragons to win their ladies, but we of to-day have to content ourselves with more prosaic methods, such as smoking fewer cigars, and the like. After all, though, we can love, knights or no knights; and so, as ever, only the times change, not men's hearts...

    You cannot think how your letter has raised and strengthened me... You are splendid, and I have much more reason to be proud of you than you of me. I have made up my mind, though, to read all your wishes in your face. Then you will think, even though you don't say it, that your Robert is a really good sort, that he is entirely yours, and he loves you more than words can say.

    You shall indeed have cause to think so in the happy future. I still see you as you looked in your little cap that last evening. I still hear you call me du. Clara, I heard nothing of what you said but that du.

    Don't you remember?

    But I see you in many another unforgettable guise. Once you were in a black dress, going to the theatre with Emilia List; it was during our separation. I know you will not have forgotten; it is vivid with me. Another time you were walking in the Thomasgasschen with an umbrella up, and you avoided me in desperation. And yet another time, as you were putting on your hat after a concert, our eyes happened to meet, and yours were full of the old unchanging love.

I picture you in all sorts of ways, as I have seen you since. I did not look at you much, but you charmed me so immeasurably... Ah, I can never praise you enough for yourself or for your love of me, which I don't really deserve.

Leipzig, 15 April, 1838.
Sunday morning.

... I am half inclined to give up the idea of seeing you this summer. If I have survived without it two years, two more of the same penance will not kill me. What satisfaction is there in the few disjointed words we should steal at odd moments, in fear and trembling? I want you for always—days, years, eternities. I have done with quixotic notions. Of course I will come if you want it very much, but otherwise let us give it up as useless... I want you for my wife. This is my earnest, sacred wish; to all else I am indifferent.

Easter Tuesday, 17 April, 1838.

... It is very curious, but if I write much to you, as I am doing now, I cannot compose. The music all goes to you...

Percy Bysshe Shelley

Percy Bysshe Shelley (4 August, 1792–8 July, 1822) was one of the major English Romantic poets and is critically regarded among the finest lyric poets in the English language. Shelley was famous for his association with John Keats and Lord Byron. He is most famous for such classic anthology verse works as *Ozymandias*, *Ode to the West Wind*, *To a Skylark*, and *The Masque of Anarchy*, which are among the most popular and critically acclaimed poems in the English language. He wrote the Gothic novels *Zastrozzi* (1810) and *St. Irvyne* (1811) and the short prose works "The Assassins" (1814), "The Coliseum" (1817) and "Una Favola" (1819). His major works, however, are long visionary poems which included *Queen Mab*, *Alastor*, *The Revolt of Islam*, *Adonaïs*, and the unfinished work *The Triumph of Life*. *The Cenci* (1819) and *Prometheus Unbound* (1820) were dramatic plays in five and four acts respectively. Although he has typically been figured as a "reluctant dramatist" he was passionate about the theatre, and his plays continue to be performed today.

Aged 19, Shelley eloped to Scotland with the 16-year-old schoolgirl Harriet Westbrook (1 August, 1795–c.9 November, 1816) to get married. After their marriage on 28 August, 1811, Shelley brought her to Keswick in the Lake District, intending to write. She gave birth to their first child, Ianthe Eliza (June, 1813–16 June, 1876), in 1813 but even by then, Shelley was unhappy and often left his wife and child alone, first to study Italian with a certain Cornelia Turner, and eventually to visit William Godwin's home and bookshop in London. There he met and fell in love with Godwin's daughter, Mary Wollstonecraft Godwin (30 August, 1797–1 February, 1851). On 28 July, 1814, Shelley abandoned his pregnant wife and child and ran away with Mary, then 16, inviting her stepsister Claire Clairmont along for company. The three sailed to Europe, crossed France, and settled in Switzerland, an account of which was subsequently published by the Shelleys. After six weeks, homesick and destitute, the three young people returned to England. Harriet gave birth in November to a son, Charles Bysshe (30 November, 1814–1826) and Mary the next February to a daughter, Clara (22 February, 1815–6 March, 1815) but the baby died within a few weeks. Their son, William (24 January, 1816–7 June, 1819) was born in early 1816. In October, 1816, Mary's half-sister killed herself and in November, Shelley's estranged wife Harriet, heavily pregnant, drowned herself in the Serpentine in Hyde Park, London. Her body was found on 12 December. On 30 December, 1816, Shelley and Mary Godwin were married. The marriage was intended, in part, to help secure Shelley's custody of his children by Harriet, but the plan failed: the courts gave custody of the children to foster parents. In 1817 Mary completed the manuscript for her novel, *Frankenstein; or, The Modern Prometheus* (which was first published on 1 January, 1818), and gave birth to a daughter Clara Everina (2 September, 1817–24 September, 1818). By 1818 the Shelleys were based in Italy, travelling from city to city. A baby girl, Elena Adelaide, was born on 27 December, 1818, in Naples, Italy and registered there as the daughter of Shelley and a woman named "Marina Padurin". However, the identity of the mother is uncertain, scholars suggesting it was in fact Claire Clairmont. Elena was placed with foster parents a few days after her birth where she died 17 months later, on 10 June, 1820. Mary gave birth to another son, Percy Florence (12 November, 1819–5 December, 1889) but suffered a nervous breakdown the same year, following the deaths of Clara and then William. She suffered a miscarriage in June 1822, and Shelley was killed a month later while sailing. After his death Mary devoted herself to the upbringing of their son and a career as a professional author.

To Mary Godwin

27 October, 1814.[23]

 Oh my dearest love why are our pleasures so short and so interrupted? How long is this to last?... Know, my best Mary, that I feel myself, in your absence, almost degraded to the level of the vulgar and impure. I feel their vacant, stiff eyeballs fixed upon me, until I seem to have been infected with their loathsome meaning,—to inhale a sickness that subdues me to languor. Oh! those redeeming eyes of Mary, that they might beam upon me before I sleep! Praise my forbearance, O beloved one, that I do not rashly fly to you, and at least secure a moment's bliss. Wherefore should I delay? Do you not long to meet me? All that is exalted and buoyant in my nature urges me toward you, reproaches me with cold delay, laughs at all fear, and spurns to dream of prudence. Why am I not with you? Alas! we must not meet...

 I did not, for I could not, express to you my admiration of your letter to Fanny; the simple and impressive language in which you clothed your argument, the full weight you gave to every part, the complete picture you exhibited of what you intended to describe, was more than I expected. How hard and stubborn must be the spirit that does not confess you to be the subtlest and most exquisitely fashioned intelligence! that among women there is no equal mind to yours! And I possess this treasure! How beyond all estimate is my felicity! Yes; I am encouraged,—I care not what happens; I am most happy. Meet me to-morrow at three o'clock in St. Paul's, if you do not hear before. Adieu! remember, love, at vespers before sleep. I do not omit my prayers.

---

[23] Written while Shelley was in hiding from creditors, who threatened his arrest.

London, 15 December, 1816.[24]

    I have spent a day, my beloved, of somewhat agonizing sensations, such as the contemplation of vice and folly and hard-heartedness exceeding all conception must produce. Leigh Hunt has been with me all day, and his delicate and tender attentions to me, his kind speeches of you, have sustained me against the horror of this event. The children I have not got. I have seen Longdill, who recommends proceeding with the utmost caution and resoluteness; he seems interested. I told him I was under contract of marriage to you, and he said that in such an event all pretence to detain the children would cease. Hunt said, very delicately, that this would be soothing intelligence to you. Yes, my only hope, my darling love, this will be one among the innumerable benefits which you will have bestowed upon me, and which will still be inferior in value to the greatest of benefits,—yourself.

    How is Claire? I do not tell her, but I may tell you, how deeply I am interested in her safety. I need not recommend her to your care. Give her any kind message from me, and calm her spirits as well as you can. I do not ask you to calm your own.

    I am well in health, though somewhat faint and agitated; but the affectionate attentions shown me by Hunt have been sustainers and restoratives more than I can tell. Do you, dearest and best, seek happiness—where it ought to reside—in your own pure and perfect bosom; in the thoughts of how dear and how good you are to me; how wise and how extensively beneficial you are perhaps now destined to become. Remember my poor babes, Ianthe and Charles. How tender and dear a mother they will find in you!—darling William, too. My eyes overflow with tears. To-morrow I will write again.

Florence, Thursday, 11 o'clock.
20 August, 1818.

    ... Well, my dearest Mary, are you very lonely? Tell me truth, my sweetest, do you ever cry? I shall hear from you once at Venice, and once on my return here. If you love me you will keep up your spirits,—and, at all events, tell me truth about it; for, I assure you, I am not of a disposition to be flattered by your sorrow, though I should be by your cheerfulness; and, above all, by seeing such fruits of my absence as were produced when we were at Geneva.[25] What acquaintances have you made? I might have travelled to Padua with a German, who had just come from Rome, and had scarce recovered from a malarial fever, caught in the Pontine Marshes, a week or two since; and I conceded to C—'s[26] entreaties, and to your absent suggestions, and omitted the opportunity, although I have no great faith in such species of contagion. It is not very hot,—not at all too much so for my sensations; and the only thing that incommodes me are the

---

[24] Written during the progress of the suit for his children.
[25] Referring to the inspiration for her novel *Frankenstein*.
[26] Claire Clairmont.

gnats at night, who roar like so many humming-tops in one's ear,—and I do not always find zanzariere.[27] How is Willmouse and little Clara? They must be kissed for me,—and you must particularly remember to speak my name to William, and see that he does not quite forget me before I return. Adieu, my dearest girl, I think that we shall soon meet. I shall write again from Venice. Adieu, dear Mary!

---

[27] Insect repellant.

Sir Richard Steele

Sir Richard Steele (March, 1672–1 September, 1729) was an Irish writer and politician. A member of the Protestant gentry, he was educated at Charterhouse School, where he first met friend and literary collaborator, Joseph Addison. After starting at Oxford University, he joined the Life Guards of the Household Cavalry in order to support King William's wars against France. He was commissioned in 1697, and rose up in the ranks to captain of the 34th Foot in 2 years. Steele's first published work, *The Christian Hero*, appeared in 1701. He wrote a comedy the same year titled *The Funeral*. The play was met with wide success and was performed at Drury Lane, bringing him to the attention of the King and the Whig party. Next, Steele wrote *The Lying Lover* (1703), which was one of the first sentimental comedies, but was a failure on stage. In 1705, he wrote *The Tender Husband* with Addison's contributions, and left the army. In 1706 he was appointed to a position in the household of Prince George of Denmark, consort of Queen Anne. He also gained the favour of Robert Harley, Earl of Oxford.

The Tatler, Steele's first journal, came out on 12 April, 1709, and ran three times a week. Steele wrote under the pseudonym Isaac Bickerstaff and gave him an entire, fully-developed personality. Following the demise of *The Tatler*, the two men founded *The Spectator*, in 1711, for which they are both perhaps now best known. Steele became a Member of Parliament in 1713, but was soon expelled for issuing a pamphlet in favour of the Hanoverian succession. When George I came to the throne in the following year, Steele was knighted and given responsibility for the Theatre Royal. While at Drury Lane, Steele wrote and directed *The Conscious Lovers* (1722), which was an immediate hit. However, he fell out with Addison and with the administration over the Peerage Bill (1719).

In 1698, Steele had an illegitimate daughter with Elizabeth Tonson. She was the niece of Jacob Tonson, the publisher and founder of the Kit Cat Club. He did not acknowledge the fact at first, but later adopted the child, named Elizabeth Ousley, and brought her up. On 1 March, 1705, Steele married a widow, Margaret Stretch, who died in the following year. At her funeral he met his second wife, Mary Scurlock (4 November, 1678–26 December, 1718), whom he nicknamed "Prue" and they married on or around 9 September, 1707. In the course of their courtship and marriage, he wrote over 400 letters to her. They were a devoted couple, their correspondence still being regarded as one of the best illustrations of a happy marriage. However, the marriage was a stormy one, and for much of it, Steele lived in London and Mary in Wales. They had four children: Elizabeth (26 March, 1709–1782), Richard (25 May, 1710–1716), Eugene (4 March, 1712–1723) and Mary (1713–18 April, 1730). His wife, Mary, died in 1718, and in 1724 Steele retired to Wales, where he spent the remainder of his life.

To Mary Scurlock

11 August, 1707.

Madam,
I writ to you on Saturday by Mrs. Warren, and give you this trouble to urge the same request I made then; which was, that I may be admitted to wait upon you. I should be very far from desiring this, if it were a transgression of the most severe rules to allow it. I know you are very much above the little arts, which are frequent in your sex, of giving unnecessary torment to their admirers; therefore hope you will do so much justice to the generous passion I have for you, as to let me have an opportunity of acquainting you upon what motives I pretend to your good opinion. I shall not trouble you with my sentiments till I know how they will be received; and as I know no reason why difference of sex should make our language to each other differ from the ordinary rules of right reason, I shall affect plainness and sincerity in my discourse to you, as much as other lovers do perplexity and rapture. Instead of saying "I shall die for you," I profess I should be glad to lead my life with you. You are as beautiful, as witty, as prudent, and as good-humoured, as any woman breathing; but I must confess to you, I regard all these excellencies as you will please to direct them for my happiness or misery. With me, Madam, the only lasting motive to love, is the hope of its becoming mutual. I beg of you to let Mrs. Warren send me word when I may attend you. I promise you I will talk of nothing but indifferent things; though, at the same time, I know not how I shall approach you in the tender moment of first seeing you after this declaration which has been made by, Madam,
Your most obedient and most faithful humble servant,
Rich. Steele.

Smith Street, Westminster
August, 1707.

Madam,
I lay down last night with your image in my thoughts, and have awak'd this morning in the same contemplation. The pleasing transport with which I am delighted, has a sweetness in it attended with a train of ten thousand soft desires, anxieties, and cares. The day arises on my hopes with new brightness; youth, beauty, and innocence, are the charming objects that steal me from myself, and give me joys above the reach of ambition, pride, or glory. Believe me, fair one, to throw myself at your feet is giving myself the highest bliss I know on earth. Oh, hasten ye minutes! Bring on the happy morning wherein to be ever her's will make me look down on thrones!
Dear Molly I am tenderly, passionately, faithfully thine,
Rich. Steele.

St. James's Coffee House
1 September, 1707.

   Madam—It is the hardest thing in the world to be in love, and yet attend to business. As for me, all who speak to me do find out, and I must lock myself up, or other people will do it for me.

   A gentleman asked me this morning, "What news from Lisbon?" and I answered, "She is exquisitely handsome." Another desired to know "when I had been last at Hampton Court?" I replied, "It will be on Tuesday come se'nnight." Pr'ythee allow me at least to kiss your hand before that day, that my mind may be in some composure. Oh love!

   A thousand torments dwell about thee,

   Yet who would live, to live without thee?

   Methinks I could write a volume to you; but all the language on earth would fail in saying how much, and with what disinterested passion,

   I am ever yours,

   Rich. Steele.

Laurence Sterne

Laurence Sterne (24 November, 1713–18 March, 1768) was an Irish novelist and an Anglican clergyman. After receiving a Bachelor and Master of Arts degree from Jesus College, Cambridge, Sterne was ordained a deacon in March, 1737, and a priest in August, 1738. Shortly thereafter Sterne was awarded the vicarship living of Sutton-on-the-Forest in Yorkshire. His early writing life was unremarkable. He was involved in, and wrote about, local politics in 1742. He wrote letters, had two ordinary sermons published in 1747 and 1750, and tried his hand at satire with *A Political Romance* (1759), aimed at conflicts of interest within York Minster. But it was while living in the countryside, trying his hand at farming and struggling with tuberculosis, that Sterne began work on his most famous novel, *The Life and Opinions of Tristram Shandy, Gentleman*, the first volumes of which were published in 1759. The publication made Sterne famous in London and on the continent. He was delighted by the attention, and spent part of each year in London, being fêted as new volumes appeared.

Having discovered his talent at the age of 46, Sterne turned over his parishes to a curate, and gave himself up to the exercise and delight of humour writing for the rest of his life. Sterne continued to struggle with his illness, and departed England for France in 1762 in an effort to find a climate that would alleviate his suffering. Aspects of his trip were incorporated into his second novel, *A Sentimental Journey Through France and Italy* (1768), written during a period in which he was increasingly ill and weak.

Sterne married Elizabeth Lumley in 1741 at York Minster. Both were already ill with consumption. A daughter born in 1745 died within a day. In 1747, a second daughter, Lydia (1747–1780), was born. For almost twenty years Sterne resided with his family at Sutton, living the life of a rural parson, with the occasional flirtation or more. However, his marriage, which was becoming less and less happy, reached a crisis in 1758, when his wife, after learning of his affair with a maid-servant, had a nervous breakdown and threatened suicide. She was eventually placed under the care of a doctor in a private house in York. Her state of mind eventually began to improve, but Sterne continued to neglect her. His fame in London led to a social life he had never before experienced and to the advances of several young women. In the 1760s he fell in love with and had an affair with a young French singer called Catherine "Kitty" Fourmantelle. Lady Percy, a daughter of Lord Bute, was his mistress for some time. In December 1766, he met Mrs. Elizabeth "Eliza" Draper (1744–1778), the wife of an official from Bombay, and fell in love with her. Within two months she was summoned home to her husband, and Sterne never saw her again, but he was not willing to let the relationship go, publishing *Journal to Eliza* (1767), the next year.

To Elizabeth Lumley

1740.

   Yes! I will steal from the world, and not a babbling tongue shall tell where I am—Echo shall not so much as whisper my hiding-place—suffer thy imagination to paint it as a little sun-gilt cottage, on the side of a romantic hill—dost thou think I will leave love and friendship behind me? No! they shall be my companions in solitude, for they will sit down and rise up with me in the amiable form of my L. We will be as merry and as innocent as our first parents in Paradise, before the arch fiend entered that indescribable scene.

   The kindest affections will have room to shoot and expand in our retirement, and produce such fruit as madness, and envy, and ambition have always killed in the bud. Let the human tempest and hurricane rage at a distance, the desolation is beyond the horizon of peace. My L. has seen a polyanthus blow in December— some friendly wall has sheltered it from the biting wind.—No planetary influence shall reach us, but that which presides and cherishes the sweetest flowers. God preserve us! how delightful this prospect in idea! We will build, and we will plant, in our own way—simplicity shall not be tortured by art—we will learn of Nature how to live—she shall be our alchymist, to mingle all the good of life into one salubrious draught.—The gloomy family of Care and Distrust shall be banished from our dwelling, guarded by thy kind and tutelar deity—we will sing our choral songs of gratitude, and rejoice to the end of our pilgrimage.

   Adieu, my L.—Return to one who languishes for thy society.
   L. Sterne.

1740.

   You bid me tell you, my dear L., how I bore your departure for S—, and whether the valley where D'Estella stands, retains still its looks—or, if I think the roses or jessamines smell as sweet, as when you left it—Alas! everything has now lost its relish and look! The hour you left D'Estella, I took to my bed.—I was worn out by fevers of all kinds, but most by that fever of the heart with which thou knowest well I have been wasting these two years—and shall continue wasting till you quit S—. The good Miss S—, from the forebodings of the best of hearts, thinking I was ill, insisted upon my going to her.—What can be the cause, my dear L., that I never have been able to see the face of this mutual friend, but I feel myself rent to pieces? She made me stay an hour with her, and in that short space I burst into tears a dozen different times—and in such affectionate gusts of passion, that she was constrained to leave the room, and sympathise in her dressing-room—I have been weeping for you both, said she, in a tone of the sweetest pity—for poor L.'s heart, I have long known it—her anguish is as sharp as yours—her heart as tender—her constancy as great—her virtue as heroic— Heaven brought you not together to be tormented. I could only answer her with a kind look, and a heavy sigh—and returned home to your lodgings (which I have

hired till your return), to resign myself to misery—Fanny had prepared me a supper—she is all attention to me—but I sat over it with tears; a bitter sauce, my L., but I could eat it with no other—for the moment she began to spread my little table, my heart fainted within me.—One solitary plate, one knife, one fork, one glass!—I gave a thousand pensive, penetrating looks at the chair thou hadst so often graced, in those quiet and sentimental repasts—then laid down my knife and fork, and took out my handkerchief, and clapped it across my face, and wept like a child.—I do so this very moment, my L.; for, as I take up my pen, my poor pulse quickens, my pale face glows, and tears are trickling down upon the paper, as I trace the word L. O thou! blessed in thyself, and in thy virtues—blessed to all that know thee—to me most so, because more do I know of thee than all thy sex. This is the philtre, my L., by which thou hast charmed me, and by which thou wilt hold me thine, whilst virtue and faith hold this world together. This, my friend, is the plain and simple magic, by which I told Miss— I have won a place in that heart of thine, on which I depend so satisfied, that time, or distance, or change of everything which might alarm the hearts of little men, create no uneasy suspense in mine. Wast thou to stay in S— these seven years, thy friend, though he would grieve, scorns to doubt, or to be doubted— 'tis the only exception where security is not the parent of danger. I told you poor Fanny was all attention to me since your departure—contrives every day bringing in the name of L. She told me last night (upon giving me some hartshorn), she had observed my illness began the very day of your departure for S—; that I had never held up my head, had seldom, or scarce ever, smiled, had fled from all society—that she verily believed I was broken-hearted, for she had never entered the room, or passed by the door, but she heard me sigh heavily—that I neither ate, or slept or took pleasure in anything as before—judge then, my L., can the valley look so well—or the roses and jessamines smell so sweet as heretofore? Ah me!—But adieu!—the vesper bell calls me from thee to my God!
    L. Sterne.

To Catherine Fourmantelle

London, 8 March, 1760.

    My dear Kitty,
    I have arrived here safe & sound, except for the Hole in my Heart, which you have made like a dear enchanting Slut as you are. I shall take Lodgings this Morning in Picadilly or the Haymarket, & before I seal this letter, will let you know where to direct a Letter to me, which Letter I shall wait for by the return of the Post with great impatience; so write, my dear Love, without fail. I have the greatest honours paid & most civilities shewn me, that were ever known from the Great; and am engaged all ready to ten Noble Men & Men of fashion to dine. Mr. Garrick pays me all & more honour than I could look for. I dined with him to-day, & he has promised Numbers of great People to carry me to dine with 'em. He has given me an Order for the Liberty of his Boxes, and of every part of his

House for the whole Season; and indeed leaves nothing undone that can do me either Service or Credit; he has undertaken the management of the Booksellers, & will procure me a great price—but more of this in my next.

And now my dear, dear Girl! let me assure you of the truest friendship for you, that ever man bore towards a woman. Where ever I am, my heart is warm towards you, & ever shall be till it is cold for ever. I thank you for the kind proof you gave me of your Love, and of your desire to make my heart easy, in ordering yourself to be denied to you know who;—whilst I am so miserable to be separated from my dear, dear Kitty, it would have stabb'd my soul to have thought such a fellow could have the Liberty of comeing near you. I therefore take this proof of your Love & good principles most kindly, & have as much faith & dependence upon you in it, as if I was at your Elbow;—would to God I was at it this moment! but I am sitting solitary & alone in my bed Chamber (ten o'clock at night, after the Play), and would give a Guinea for a squeeze of your hand. I send my Soul perpetually out to see what you are adoing;—wish I could send my Body with it. Adieu, dear & kind girl! and believe me ever your kind friend & most affectionate Admirer. I go to the Oratorio this night.—Adieu! Adieu!

P. S.—My service to your Mama.

Direct to me in the Pell Mell, at ye 2nd House from St. Alban's Street.

To Lady Percy

Mount Coffee House, Tuesday, 3 o'clock. c.1765.

There is a strange mechanical effect produced in writing a billet-doux within a stonecast of the lady who engrosses the heart and soul of an inamorato—for this cause (but mostly because I am to dine in this neighbourhood) have I, Tristram Shandy, come forth from my lodgings to a coffee-house, the nearest I could find to my dear Lady's house, and have called for a sheet of gilt paper, to try the truth of this article of my creed. Now for it—

O my dear lady—what a dishclout of a soul hast thou made of me? I think, by the by, this is a little too familiar an introduction, for so unfamiliar a situation as I stand in with you—where heaven knows, I am kept at a distance—and despair of getting one inch nearer you, with all the steps and windings I can think of to recommend myself to you. Would not any man in his senses run diametrically from you—as far as his legs would carry him, rather than thus causelessly, foolishly, and foolhardily expose himself afresh, where his heart and reason tells him he shall be sure to come off loser, if not totally undone?

Why would you tell me you would be glad to see me? Does it give you pleasure to make me more unhappy—or does it add to your triumph, that your eyes and lips have turned a man into a fool, whom the rest of the town is courting as a wit? I am a fool—the weakest, the most ductile, the most tender fool that ever woman tried the weakness of—and the most unsettled in my purposes and resolutions of recovering my right mind.

It is but an hour ago, that I kneeled down and swore I never would come near you, and after saying my Lord's Prayer for the sake of the close, of not being led into temptation, out I sallied like any Christian hero, ready to take the field against the world, the flesh, and the devil; not doubting but I should finally trample them all down under my feet. And now I am got so near you—within this vile stone's cast of your house—I feel myself drawn into a vortex, that has turned my brain upside downwards; and though I had purchased a box ticket to carry me to Miss —'s benefit, yet I know very well, that was a single line directed to me to let me know Lady — would be alone at seven, and suffer me to spend the evening with her, she would infallibly see every thing verified I have told her. I dine at Mr C—r's in Wigmore Street, in this neighbourhood, where I shall stay till seven, in hopes you purpose to put me to this proof. If I hear nothing by that time, I shall conclude you are better disposed of—and shall take a sorry hack, and sorrily jog on to the play. Curse on the word. I know nothing but sorrow—except this one thing that I love you (perhaps foolishly, but) most sincerely,

L. Sterne

Jonathan Swift

Jonathan Swift (30 November, 1667–19 October, 1745) was an Anglo-Irish satirist, novelist, essayist, political pamphleteer (first for the Whigs, then for the Tories), poet and cleric. After spending many years as secretary and personal assistant of Sir William Temple, a politician, based in England, Swift was ordained a priest, and set up home in Kilroot in County Antrim in 1694. He returned to Temple during 1696–99 where he was employed in helping to prepare Temple's memoirs and correspondence for publication. After Temple's death Swift received his Doctor of Divinity degree from Trinity College, Dublin in 1702. With the publication of *A Tale of a Tub* and *The Battle of the Books* (1704), Swift began to gain a reputation as a writer, and became increasingly active politically. With the fall of the Tory government, he secured the Deanery of St. Patrick's Cathedral, Dublin and returned to Ireland in disappointment, a virtual exile. Once in Ireland, however, Swift began to turn his pamphleteering skills in support of Irish causes, producing some of his most memorable works: *Proposal for Universal Use of Irish Manufacture* (1720), *Drapier's Letters* (1724), and *A Modest Proposal* (1729), earning him the status of an Irish patriot. However his masterpiece was *Gulliver's Travels* (1726), which made him a success overnight. Both a satire on human nature and a parody of the "travellers' tales" literary sub-genre, it is Swift's best known full-length work, and a classic of English literature. He originally published all of his works under pseudonyms—such as Lemuel Gulliver, Isaac Bickerstaff, M.B. Drapier—or anonymously. He is also known for being a master of two styles of satire: the Horatian and Juvenalian styles.

In 1689 Swift met Esther Johnson (13 March, 1681–28 January, 1728), then 8 years old, the fatherless daughter of one of Temple's household servants. Swift acted as her tutor and mentor, giving her the nickname "Stella", and the two maintained a close but ambiguous relationship for the rest of her life. She often accompanied him, along with Rebecca Dingley, another member of Temple's household. In *The Journal to Stella* (1710–1713), written to both Stella and Rebecca, he collectively called them "MD". Though Rebecca is constantly associated with Stella in the affectionate greetings in the *Journal*, she seems to have been included merely as a cloak to enable him to express more freely his affection for her companion. While at Kilroot, Swift became romantically involved with Jane Waring, who he addressed as "Varina". He offered to marry her in 1696, promising to leave and never return to Ireland if she refused. She presumably refused, because Swift left his post and returned to England. Another lady with whom Swift had a close relationship was Anne Long (c.1681–22 December, 1711), a toast of the Kit-Cat Club. During his years in London, Swift became acquainted with the Vanhomrigh family and became involved with one of the daughters, Esther Vanhomrigh (c.14 February, 1690–2 June, 1723), yet another fatherless young woman and another ambiguous relationship to confuse

Swift's biographers. They met in 1707 at Dunstable, and it was here that their intense 16-year relationship began. 23 years younger than Swift, he served as her tutor, and furnished her with the nickname "Vanessa". She features as one of the main characters in his poem *Cadenus and Vanessa* (1713). The poem and their correspondence suggests that Esther was infatuated with Swift, and that he may have reciprocated her affections, only to regret this and then try to break off the relationship. She followed Swift to Ireland in 1714, where there appears to have been a confrontation, possibly involving Stella. Rumours abounded in 1716 that Swift and Stella had got married. In 1727 Swift received word that Stella was dying and rushed back home to be with her, she died in January, 1728; Swift had prayed at her bedside. After her death Swift suffered from fits of madness, and a debilitating stroke in 1742.

To Stella

London, 21 September, 1710.

Here must I begin another letter, on a whole sheet, for fear saucy little MD should be angry, and think MUCH that the paper is too LITTLE. I had your letter this night, as told you just and no more in my last; for this must be taken up in answering yours, saucebox. I believe I told you where I dined to-day; and to-morrow I go out of town for two days to dine with the same company on Sunday; Molesworth the Florence Envoy, Stratford, and some others. I heard to-day that a gentlewoman from Lady Giffard's house had been at the Coffee-house to inquire for me. It was Stella's mother, I suppose. I shall send her a penny-post letter to-morrow, and contrive to see her without hazarding seeing Lady Giffard, which I will not do until she begs my pardon.

5 February, 1711.

Morning. I am going this morning to see Prior, who dines with me at Mr. Harley's; so I can't stay fiddling and talking with dear little brats in a morning, and 'tis still terribly cold.—I wish my cold hand was in the warmest place about you, young women, I'd give ten guineas upon that account with all my heart, faith; oh, it starves my thigh; so I'll rise and bid you good-morrow, my ladies both, good-morrow. Come, stand away, let me rise: Patrick, take away the candle. Is there a good fire?—So—up-a-dazy.—At night. Mr. Harley did not sit down till six, and I stayed till eleven; henceforth I will choose to visit him in the evenings, and dine with him no more if I can help it. It breaks all my measures, and hurts my health; my head is disorderly, but not ill, and I hope it will mend.

To Vanessa.

c.1714.

I received your letter when some company was with me on Saturday night; and it put me in such confusion, that I could not tell what to do. I here send you the paper you left me. This morning a woman who does business for me told me she heard I was in...[28] with one, naming you, and twenty particulars, that little master and I visited you, and that the Archbishop did so; and that you had abundance of wit, etc. I ever feared the tattle of this nasty town, and told you so; and that was the reason why I said to you long ago that I would see you seldom when you were in Ireland. And I must beg you to be easy if for some time I visit you seldomer, and not in so particular a manner. I will see you at the latter end of the week if possible. These are accidents in life that are necessary and must be submitted to; and tattle, by the help of discretion, will wear off.

---

[28] John Hawkesworth (c. 1715–1773) was an English journalist and playwright who edited Swift's letters. He prints "in love" here.

Count Leo Tolstoy

Count Leo Tolstoy (born Lyev Nikolayevich Tolstoy, 9 September, 1828–20 November, 1910), was a Russian writer many consider to have been one of the world's greatest novelists. Tolstoy's earliest works, the autobiographical novels *Childhood*, *Boyhood*, and *Youth* (1852–1856), tell of a rich landowner's son and his slow realisation of the chasm between himself and his peasants. Though he later rejected them as sentimental, a great deal of Tolstoy's own life is revealed in them. He served as a second lieutenant in an artillery regiment during the Crimean War, recounted in his *Sevastapol Sketches* (1855). His experiences in battle helped stir his subsequent pacifism—as evinced in *A Letter to a Hindoo* (1908)—and gave him material for realistic depiction of the horrors of war in his later work. His literal interpretation of the ethical teachings of Jesus, centring on the Sermon on the Mount, caused him in later life to become a fervent Christian anarchist and anarcho-pacifist. His ideas on nonviolent resistance, expressed in such works as *The Kingdom of God is Within You* (1894) were to have a profound impact on such pivotal twentieth-century figures as Mahatma Gandhi and Martin Luther King, Jr. His literary masterpieces *War and Peace* (1865–9) and *Anna Karenina* (1875–7) represent, in their scope, breadth and vivid depiction of 19th-century Russian life and attitudes, the peak of realist fiction. Tolstoy's further talents as essayist, dramatist, and educational reformer made him the most influential member of the aristocratic Tolstoy family.

Tolstoy was briefly engaged to Valeria Arsenev, the daughter of a neighbouring nobleman, in 1856. When he left for St. Petersburg they entered into a correspondence, but the relationship did not survive the distance. On 23 September, 1862, aged 34, Tolstoy married Sofya Andreyevna Behrs (22 August, 1844–4 November, 1919), who was 16 years his junior and the daughter of a court physician. She was called Sonya, the Russian diminutive of Sofya, by her family and friends. They had thirteen children, five of whom died during childhood. The marriage was marked from the outset by sexual passion and emotional insensitivity when Tolstoy, on the eve of their marriage, gave her his diaries detailing his extensive sexual past and the fact that one of the servants on his estate had borne him a son. Even so, their early married life was ostensibly happy and allowed Tolstoy much freedom to write, with Sonya acting as his secretary, proof-reader and financial manager. However, Tolstoy's relationship with his wife deteriorated as his beliefs became increasingly radical. This saw him seeking to reject his inherited and earned wealth, including the renunciation of the copyrights on his earlier works. After many years of an increasingly troubled marriage, Tolstoy left Sonya abruptly in 1910, aged 82, with his doctor, and daughter Alexandra. He died 10 days later in a railway station.

To Valeria Arsenev

2 November, 1856.

I already love in you your beauty, but I am only beginning to love in you that which is eternal and ever precious—your heart, your soul.

Beauty one could get to know and fall in love with in one hour and cease to love it as speedily; but the soul one must learn to know.

Believe me, nothing on earth is given without labour, even love, the most beautiful and natural of feelings.

But the more difficult the labour and hardship, the higher the reward.

To Sofya Andreyevna Behrs

16 September, 1862.

Sofya Andreyevna, the situation has become intolerable to me. Every day for three weeks I have sworn to myself: today I shall speak; and every day I leave you with the same anguish, the same regret, the same terror, the same joy in my heart... I am bringing this letter with me, to give to you in case I lack the opportunity, or the courage to speak... Tell me, tell me truthfully, do you want to be my wife? But do not answer yes unless you can do so fearlessly, from the bottom of your heart. If you cannot, if you have the shadow of a doubt, then it is better to answer no. For the love of God, be certain! If you say no, it will be awful for me, but I am expecting it and shall find strength to bear it. For if I were your husband and were not loved as much as I love, it would be more awful still.

Moscow
1867.

I am sitting alone in my room upstairs, having just read your letter... For God's sake, don't stop writing daily to me... I am a dead man without you.

1910.

... As I loved you when I was young, so I never stopped loving you in spite of the many causes of estrangement between us, and so I love you now. Leaving aside the cessation of our conjugal relations (a fact that could but add to the sincerity of our expressions of true love), those causes were as follows: first, my increasing withdrawal from society, whereas you neither would nor could forgo it, because the principles which lead me to adopt my convictions were fundamentally opposed to yours: this is perfectly natural and I cannot hold it against you... In recent years, you have grown more and more irritable, despotic *and uncontrollable. This could not fail to inhibit any display of feeling on my part, if not the feelings themselves. That is the second point. And in the third place, the principal, fatal cause, was that of which we are both equally innocent: our totally opposite ideas of the meaning and purpose of existence. For me property is a sin, for you an essential condition of life. I forced myself to accept the painful circumstances of our life in order not to leave you, but you saw my acceptance as a concession to your views, and this only deepened the misunderstanding between us... Your life has been such that I can have absolutely nothing to reproach you with.*

Mark Twain

Samuel Langhorne Clemens (30 November, 1835–21 April, 1910), better known by his pen name Mark Twain, was a popular American author and humourist. Twain grew up in Hannibal, Missouri, apprenticed with a printer at age 12, worked as a typesetter and contributed articles to his older brother Orion's newspaper. After toiling as a printer in various cities, he became a master riverboat pilot on the Mississippi River, before heading west to join Orion. He was a failure at gold mining, so he next turned to journalism. While a reporter, he wrote a humourous story, *The Celebrated Jumping Frog of Calaveras County* (1867), which proved to be very popular and brought him nationwide attention. His travelogues were also well-received. Twain had found his calling. He achieved great success as a writer and public speaker. His wit and satire earned praise from critics and peers, and he was a friend to presidents, artists, industrialists, and European royalty. He is especially noted for his novels *The Adventures of Tom Sawyer* (1876) and *Adventures of Huckleberry Finn* (1885), called "the Great American Novel." He was lauded as the "greatest American humourist of his age", and William Faulkner called Twain "the father of American literature".

In 1867, Twain's friend, Charles Langdon showed him a picture of his sister, Olivia; Twain claimed to have fallen in love at first sight. The two met in 1868, and he courted her mainly by letter. She rejected his first proposal of marriage, but they became engaged in November, 1868. The engagement was announced in February, 1869, and in February, 1870, they were married, in Elmira, New York. Olivia Langdon (27 November, 1845–5 June, 1904) came from a wealthy but liberal family, and through her he met abolitionists, socialists and activists including Harriet Beecher Stowe, Frederick Douglass, and William Dean Howells, who became a longtime friend. The couple lived in Buffalo, New York from 1869 to 1871 when they moved to Hartford, Connecticut. Their first child and only son, Langdon (7 November, 1870–2 June, 1872), died of diphtheria at 19 months. While living in Connecticut, Olivia gave birth to three daughters: Olivia Susan "Susy" (19 March, 1872–18 August, 1896), Clara (8 June, 1874–19 November, 1962) and Jane "Jean" (26 July, 1880–24 December, 1909). The family left for Europe in 1891, and in 1895, Olivia and their daughter, Clara, accompanied Twain on his around-the-world lecture tour. The next year, their daughter Susy died of spinal meningitis at age 24, a devastating blow. The family lived in Europe until 1902. They then returned to the United States, but by the end of 1903, the doctor's advice led the family to move to Italy, for the warm climate. They resided in a villa outside of Florence. The couple's marriage lasted 34 years, until Olivia's death in 1904.

To Olivia Langdon

New York, 28 November, 1868.

> *My Dear, Dear Livy:*
> *When I found myself comfortably on board the cars last night (I see Dan has just come in from breakfast, and he will be back here, within five minutes and interrupt me,)—when I found myself comfortably on board the cars, I said to myself: "Now whatever others may think, it is my opinion that I am blessed above all other men that live; I have known supreme happiness for two whole days, and now I ought to be ready and willing to pay a little attention to necessary duties, and do it cheerfully." Therefore I resolved to go deliberately through that lecture, without notes, and so impress it upon my memory and my understanding as to secure myself against any such lame delivery of it in future as I thought characterized it in Elmira. But I had little calculated the cost of such a resolution. Never was a lecture so full of parentheses before. It was Livy, Livy, Livy, Livy, all the way through! It was one sentence of Vandal to ten sentences about you. The insignificant lecture was hidden, lost, overwhelmed and buried under a boundless universe of Livy! I was sorry I had ever made so reckless a resolve, for its accomplishment seemed entirely hopeless. Still, having made it, I would stick to it till it was finished, and I did—but it was rather late at night. Then, having a clear conscience, I prayed, and with good heart—but it was only when I prayed for you that my tongue was touched with inspiration. You will smile at the idea of my praying for you—I, who so need the prayers of all good friends, praying for you who surely need the prayers of none. But never mind, Livy, the prayer was honest and sincere—it was that, at least—and I know it was heard.*
> *I slept well—and when I woke my first thought was of you, of course, and I was so sorry I was not going to see you at breakfast. I hope and believe you slept well, also, for you were restful and at peace, darling, when I saw you last. You needed rest, and you still need it, for you have been so harassed, and so persecuted with conflicting thoughts of late—I could see it, dear, though I tried so hard to think my anxiety might be misleading my eyes. Do put all perplexing reflections, all doubts and fears, far from you for a little while, Livy, for I dread, dread, dread to hear you are sick. No mere ordinary tax upon your powers is likely to make you ill, but you must remember that even the most robust nature could hardly hold against the siege of foodless, sleepless days and nights which you have just sustained. I am not talking to you as if you were a feeble little child, for on the contrary you are a brave, strong-willed woman, with no nonsense and no childishness about you—but what I am providing against is your liability to indulge in troubled thoughts and forebodings. Such thoughts must come, for they are natural to people who have brains and feelings and a just appreciation of the responsibilities which God places before them, and so you must have them,—but as I said before, my dearest Livy, temper them, temper them, and be you the mistress and not they. Be cheerful—always cheerful—you can think more coolly, and calmly, and justly for it. I leave my fate, my weal, my woe, my life, in your hands and at your mercy, with a trust, and a confidence and an abiding sense of*

security which nothing can shake. I have no fears—none. I believe in you, even as I believe in the Savior in whose hands our destinies are. I have faith in you—a faith which is as simple and unquestioning as the faith of a devotee in the idol he worships. For I know that in their own good time your doubts and troubles will pass away, and then you will give to me your whole heart and I shall have nothing more to wish for on earth. This day I prize above every earthly gift so much of your precious love as I do possess, and so am satisfied and happy. I feel no exacting spirit—I am grateful, grateful, unspeakably grateful for the love you have already given me. I am crowned—I am throned—I am sceptred. I sit with the Kings.

I do love, love, love you, Livy! My whole being is permeated, is renewed, is leavened with this love, and with every breath I draw its noble influence makes of me a better man. And I shall yet be worthy of your priceless love, Livy. It is the glad task of my life—it is the purest ambition and the most exalted, that ever I have known, and I shall never, never swerve from the path it has marked out for me, while the goal and you are before me. Livy, I could not tell your honored father and mother how deeply I felt for them, and how heartless it seemed in me to come, under cover of their trusting, generous hospitality, and try to steal away the sun out of their domestic firmament and rob their fireside heaven of its angel. I could not tell them in what large degree (and yet feebly in comparison with the reality,) I appreciated and do still appreciate the tremendous boon I was asking at their hands. I could not tell them how grateful I was, and how I loved them for pausing to listen to my appeals when they could have upbraided me for my treachery and turned me out of doors in deserved disgrace. I call these things by their right names, Livy, because I know I ought to have spoken to them long before I spoke to you—and yet there was nothing criminal in my intent, Livy— nothing wilfully and deliberately dishonorable—I could say it in the high court of Heaven. You know I would scorn to do a shameful act, my darling—you know it and will maintain it.—for never yet had any friend a stauncher, braver defender than you—you—you Perfection! Ah, how "deluded" I am, and how I do love to be so "deluded!" I could not tell them those things, Livy, but if it shall seem necessary, I know that you can. And moreover you can always say, with every confidence, that I have been through the world's "mill"—I have traversed its ramifications from end to end—I have searched it, and probed it, and put it under the microscope, and I know it, through and through, and from back to back; its follies, its frauds and its vanities—all by personal experience and not through dainty theories culled from nice moral books in luxurious parlors where temptation never comes and it is easy to be good and keep the heart warm and one's generous best impulses fresh and strong and uncontaminated—and now I know how to be a better man, and the value of so being, and when I say that I shall be, it is just the same as if I swore it! Now!

Good-bye, Livy. You are so pure, so great, so good, so beautiful. How can I help loving you? Say, rather, how can I keep from worshipping you, you dear little paragon? If I could only see you! I do wish I could. Write me immediately. Don't wait a minute. You are never out of my waking thoughts for a single fraction of a second, and I do so want to hear from you. Ah, well, I suppose I shall lecture to those Rondout pirates about you, and yet, poor confiding creatures, they think I am going to talk about the Vandal. But such is life. And mind you just keep on, writing until you begin to feel tired.—but not a moment afterward, my peerless Livy, for I love you too dearly to have you do irksome things, even to gratify me.

Tell me the name of that book you were going to lend me, Livy, so that I can get it. I shall send those books by Ed, if I can find him...

Good-bye, Livy. All this time I have felt just as if you were here with me, almost—as if I could see you standing by me. But you are vanished! I miss a gracious presence—a glory is gone from about me. I listen for a dear voice, I look for a darling face, I caress the empty air! God bless you, my idol. Good-bye—and I send a thousand kisses—pray send me some.

Most lovingly, Yours

Forever—Samuel.

P.S.—I do LOVE you, Livy!

P.P.S.—I enclose a ferrotype—don't you see how soft, rich, expressive, the lights and shades are, and how human the whole picture is? If you can't get me the porcelain picture, Livy, do please have a ferrotype taken for me. This pretty little sixteen-year-old school-girl is Gov. Fuller's daughter—Fuller gave it to me this morning. I never saw the young lady but once—at a party in Brooklyn a short time ago—and then I petrified her by proposing with frozen gravity, (just after introduction,) to kiss her because I was acquainted with her father. He enjoyed the joke immensely (because he has known me so long and intimately,) but she didn't.

P.P.P.S.—I do love, love, LOVE you, Livy, darling. Write immediately—do.

Livy, shan't you come to New York this winter?

I love, love, love you, Livy!

P.P.P.P.P.S.—I do love you, Livy!

Hartford, Conn., 6 March, 1869.
9 PM.

Livy dear,

I have already mailed to-day's letter, but I am so proud of my privilege of writing the dearest girl in the world whenever I please, that I must add a few lines if only to say I love you, Livy. For I do love you, Livy—as the dew loves the flowers; as the birds love the sunshine; as the wavelets love the breeze; as mothers love their first-born; as memory loves old faces; as the yearning tides love the moon; as the angels love the pure in heart. I so love you that if you were taken from me it seems as if all my love would follow after you and leave my heart a dull and vacant ruin forever and forever. And so loving you I do also honor you, as never vassal, leal and true, honored sceptred king since this good world of ours began. And now that is honest, and I think you ought to reach up and give me a kiss, Livy.

Goodnight and God bless you, my darling. Take my kiss and my benediction, and try to be reconciled to the fact that I am

Yours forever and always,

Sam

P.S.— I have read this letter over and it is flippant and foolish and puppyish. I wish I had gone to bed when I got back, without writing. You said I must never tear up a letter after writing it to you and so I send it. Burn it, Livy, I did not think I was writing so clownishly and shabbily. I was in much too good a humor for sensible letter writing.

Hartford, 12 May, 1869.
Wednesday Eve.

Was there ever such a darling as Livy? I know there never was. She fills my ideal of what a woman should be in order to be enchantingly lovable. And so, what wonder is it that I love her so? And what wonder is it that I am deeply grateful for permission to love her? Oh you are such an exquisite little concentration of loveliness, Livy! I am not saying these things because I am stricken in a new place, dearie—no, they are simply the things that are always in my mind—only they are demanding expression more imperiously than usual, maybe, because (9:30 P. M.) I am just in from one of those prodigious walks I am so fond of taking in these solemn and silent streets by night, and these pilgrimages are pretty thoroughly devoted to thinking of you, my dainty little idol.

How could I walk these sombre avenues at night without thinking of you? For their very associations would invoke you—every flagstone for many a mile is overlaid thick with an invisible fabric of thoughts of you—longings and yearnings and vain caressings of the empty air for you when you were sleeping peacefully and dreaming of other things than me, darling. And so now, and always hereafter, when I tread these stones, these sad phantoms of a time that is gone, (thank God!) will rise about me to claim kinship with these new living thoughts of you that are all radiant with hope, and requited love, and happiness. God bless and keep you always, my Livy!

I am in the same house (but not in the same room—thanks!) where I spent three awful weeks last fall, worshipping you, and writing letters to you, some of which I mailed in the waste-paper basket and the others never passed from brain to paper. But I don't like to think of those days, or speak of them.

Now that I am well again, dearie, I am not afraid to tell you that I have been sick for a day or two. It was of no particular consequence (I worked nearly all the time) and it was useless to make you uneasy. This morning I felt almost persuaded that I was going to have a severe attack—but it is all gone, now, and I am well and cheery, and am enjoying the warm night and writing you in my night-clothes for comfort—and smoking. The good God that is above us all is merciful to me.— from Whom came your precious love—from Whom cometh all good gifts—and I am grateful. ...

I guess I'll have to have a letter every day, dearie. Except, of course, when it would be too much of a hardship. I did not hear from you to-day, and do assure you I wanted to. However, this is all pure selfishness and I will not be guilty of it. Write every other day—that is work enough for such a dear little body as you.

I expect to scribble very meagre letters to you, because I confess that I use you as a sort of prize for good behavior—that is, when I transact all my duties, my abundant and ample reward is the luxury of writing to you—and when I fail to finish up my duties, Jack must go without his supper which is to say, I must lose the luxury of writing you. But the other night I did a vast deal of work, keeping myself to it with the encouraging assurance that I might talk to Livy when it was all done—and so at last I worried through—but alas for my reward, I could hardly sit up, and so I had to go to bed and lose all I had worked for so well. Now I have reached my goal for to-day, for I finished my work before supper.

(The picture of you with Hattie strikes me a little better, now, but it still looks a little thin, and I am haunted with the fear that you are not as well as usual. Am I right? Excuse this solicitude—for you are very dear to me, Livy—dearer than all things else on earth combined.)...

Oh you darling little speller!—you spell "terrible" right, this time. And I won't have it—it is un-Livy-ish. Spell it wrong, next time, for I love everything that is like Livy. Maybe it is wrong for me to put a premium on bad spelling, but I can't help it if it is. Somehow I love it in you—I have grown used to it, accustomed to expect it, and I honestly believe that if, all of a sudden, you fell to spelling every word right, I should feel pain, as if something very dear to me had been mysteriously spirited away and lost to me. I am not poking fun at you, little sweetheart...

From the stillness that reigns in the house, I fancy that I must be the only person up, though I know it is not late. However, the very dearest girl in the wide world has given me strict orders to go to bed early and take care of myself, and I will obey, though I had rather write to her than sleep—for, writing to her, it is as if I were talking to her—and to talk to her so, is in fancy to hold her tiny hand, and look into her dear eyes, and hear her voice that is sweet as an answered prayer to me, and clasp her pigmy foot, and hold her dainty form in my arms, and kiss her lips, and cheeks, and hair, and eyes, for love, and her sacred forehead in honor, in reverent respect, in gratitude and blessing. Out of the depths of my happy heart wells a great tide of love and prayer for this priceless treasure that is confided to my life-long keeping. You cannot see its intangible waves as they flow toward you, darling, but in these lines you will hear, as it were, the distant beating of its surf.

I leave you with the ministering spirits that are in the air about you always. Good-night, with a kiss and a blessing, Livy darling.

Sam

Hartford, 27 November, 1875.[29]

Livy darling,

Six years have gone by since I made my first great success in life and won you, and thirty years have passed since Providence made preparation for that happy success by sending you into the world. Every day we live together adds to the security of my confidence, that we can never any more wish to be separated than that we can ever imagine a regret that we were ever joined. You are dearer to me today, my child, than you were upon the last anniversary of this birthday; you were dearer then than you were a year before—you have grown more dear from the first of those anniversaries, and I do not doubt that this precious progression will continue on to the end.

Let us look forward to the coming anniversaries, with their age and gray hairs without fear and without depression, trusting and believing that the love we bear each other will be sufficient to make them blessed.

So, with abounding affection for you and our babies, I hail this day that brings you the matronly grace and dignity of three decades.

Always Yours,

S. L. C.

---

[29] On her thirtieth birthday.

Voltaire

François-Marie Arouet (21 November, 1694–30 May, 1778), better known by the pen name Voltaire, was a French Enlightenment writer, historian and philosopher, famous for his wit and for his advocacy of civil liberties, including freedom of religion and free trade. Most of Voltaire's early life revolved around Paris. He became secretary to the French ambassador in the Netherlands but left after a scandal. His actions over the years were to result in numerous imprisonments and exiles. In 1717 and 1725 he was imprisoned in the Bastille. Fearing an indefinite prison sentence the second time, Voltaire suggested his own exile to England as an alternative punishment, an idea the French authorities accepted. His exile lasted nearly three years, and his experiences there greatly influenced many of his ideas. He spent the majority of the rest of his life in France until he joined Frederick the Great, a close friend and admirer of his, in Germany in 1750. After he annoyed Frederick, and found that he was banned from Paris, he turned to Geneva, and then to Ferney in France.

Voltaire was known as a prolific writer and produced works in almost every literary form including plays, poetry, novels, essays, historical and scientific works, more than 20,000 letters and more than 2,000 books and pamphlets. He was an outspoken supporter of social reform, despite strict censorship laws and harsh penalties for those who broke them. As a satirical polemicist, he frequently made use of his works to criticise intolerance, religious dogma and the French institutions of his day. His most famous work is the novel, *Candide; ou, l'Optimisme* (*Candide; or, The Optimist*, 1762), a satire written in 1759. Voltaire was one of several Enlightenment figures (along with Montesquieu, John Locke, Jean-Jacques Rousseau and Émilie du Châtelet) whose works and ideas influenced important thinkers of both the American and French Revolutions.

A notorious womaniser, Voltaire never married and as far as we know, did not father any children. In the Netherlands around 1712, he fell in love with a French Protestant refugee named Catherine Olympe Dunoyer. Their scandalous elopement led to Voltaire being imprisoned, and he was forced by his father to return to France. Around 1729 he met the Marquise du Châtelet, Gabrielle Émilie le Tonnelier de Breteuil (17 December, 1706–10 September 1749), and moved into her husband's Château de Cirey. Their relationship, which lasted for fifteen years, had a significant intellectual element. Voltaire and the Marquise collected over 21,000 books, an enormous number for the time. Though deeply committed to her, Voltaire by 1744 found life at the château confining. On a visit to Paris that year, he found a new love: his niece. Marie Louise Mignot (1712–1790) was the daughter of Voltaire's sister. After her husband's premature death in 1744, she was taken in by Voltaire and became his housekeeper, hostess and companion. She refused to follow Voltaire to the court of Frederick the Great and only re-joined him at Ferney, where they lived until Voltaire's death in 1778, on which she inherited the majority of his estate. However, preferring Paris society, she sold off his château to move back to Paris.

To Catherine Olympe Dunoyer

The Hague, 1713.

I am a prisoner here in the name of the King; they can take my life, but not the love that I feel for you. Yes, my adorable mistress, to-night I shall see you, even if I had to put my head on the block to do it.

For heaven's sake, do not speak to me in such disastrous terms as you write; you must live and be cautious; beware of madame your mother as of your worst enemy. What do I say? Beware of everybody; trust no one; keep yourself in readiness, as soon as the moon is visible; I shall leave the hotel incognito, take a carriage or a chaise, we shall drive like the wind to Sheveningen; I shall take paper and ink with me; we shall write our letters.

If you love me, reassure yourself; and call all your strength and presence of mind to your aid; do not let your mother notice anything, try to have your pictures, and be assured that the menace of the greatest tortures will not prevent me to serve you. No, nothing has the power to part me from you; our love is based upon virtue, and will last as long as our lives. Adieu, there is nothing that I will not brave for your sake; you deserve much more than that. Adieu, my dear heart!

Arouet

Richard Wagner

Wilhelm Richard Wagner (22 May, 1813–13 February, 1883) was a German composer, conductor, theatre director and essayist, primarily known for his operas. Initially establishing his reputation as a composer of works such as *The Flying Dutchman* (*Der Fliegende Holländer*, 1843) and *Tannhäuser* (1843), Wagner transformed operatic thought through his concept of the *Gesamtkunstwerk* ("total work of art"). This would achieve the synthesis of all the poetic, visual, musical and dramatic arts, and was announced in a series of essays between 1849 and 1852. Wagner realised this concept most fully in the first half of the monumental four-opera *The Ring Cycle* (*Der Ring des Nibelungen*, 1848–1874). His compositions, particularly those of his later period, are notable for their complex texture, rich harmonies and orchestration, and the elaborate use of leitmotifs: musical themes associated with individual characters, places, ideas or plot elements. Unlike most other opera composers, Wagner wrote both the music and libretto for every one of his stage works. His *Tristan and Isolde* (1865) is sometimes described as marking the start of modern music. Wagner's influence spread beyond music into philosophy, literature, the visual arts and theatre. He had his own opera house built, the Bayreuth Festspielhaus, which contained many novel design features. It was here that *The Ring* and *Parsifal* (1882) received their premieres and where his most important stage works continue to be performed today. Wagner's views on conducting were also highly influential. Wagner achieved all of this despite a life characterised, until his last decades, by political exile, turbulent love affairs, poverty and repeated flight from his creditors. His pugnacious personality and often outspoken views on music, politics and society made him a controversial figure during his life and to this day.

In 1834 Wagner fell for the actress Christine Wilhelmine "Minna" Planer (5 September, 1809–25 January, 1866), already the mother of an illegitimate daughter. The two married in Königsberg on 24 November, 1836. Their relationship was stormy, allegedly there were several infidelities during the courtship, and they even argued in front of the minister who was to marry them. In May, 1837, Minna left Wagner for another man, but he took her back; this was but the first debacle of a troubled marriage. In Zürich in 1852 Wagner found inspiration in Mathilde Wesendonck (23 December, 1828–31 August, 1902), the wife of Otto Wesendonck, a fan of Wagner's music, who placed a cottage on his estate at Wagner's disposal. During the course of the next five years, the composer was became infatuated with his patron's wife. In 1858, Wagner's wife intercepted one of his love letters to Mathilde. After the resulting confrontation, Wagner left for Venice, alone. In a letter to a friend on 5 June, 1863, Wagner wrote of Mathilde "She is and stays my first and only love... the summit of my life... Repeated attempts have convinced myself and friends that a continued dwelling with my wife is clean impossible, and thoroughly injurious to us both."

In 1865 Wagner's daughter Isolde (10 April, 1865–7 February, 1919), was born. The mother was Cosima von Bülow (born Cosima Francesca Gaetana de Flavigny, 24 December, 1837–1 April, 1930), the wife of the conductor Hans von Bülow. She was 24 years younger than Wagner, and the illegitimate daughter of composer Franz Liszt. He disapproved of his daughter seeing Wagner, though the two men were friends. The indiscreet affair scandalised Munich. Wagner's wife Minna died in early 1866 and he moved to Switzerland, with Cosima. She had two more children with Wagner; another daughter, named Eva (17 February, 1867–26 May, 1942), and a son Siegfried (6 June, 1869–4 August, 1930). Eventually, Cosima convinced Hans von Bülow to grant her a divorce, and she and Wagner were married on 25 August, 1870. The marriage to Cosima lasted to the end of Wagner's life.

To Mathilde Wesendonck

April, 1858.

And my dear Muse still stays afar? In silence I awaited her visit; with pleadings I would not disquiet her. For the Muse, like Love, beatifies but freely; woe to the fool, woe to the loveless, who fain would constrain what will not yield itself of its free will. They cannot be constrained; is it not so? Not so? How could Love be Muse withal, did it let itself be forced?
And my dear Muse stays far from me?

22 May, 1858.

Ah, the lovely pillow! Too dainty, though!
Tired and heavy as often is my head, I should never dare to lay it on it, not even in sickness; at most, in death! Then I may couch my head for once as easily as if I had a right to! Then you shall spread the pillow under me. There you have my testament!

6 July, 1858.
Tuesday morning.

Surely thou didst not expect me to leave thy marvellously beautiful letter unanswered? Or was I to forgo the privilege of replying to the noblest word? And how could I reply to thee, but in a manner worthy of thee?—
The stupendous conflicts we have passed, how could they end but with the victory over every wish and longing?

In the most fervent moments of approximation, did we not know that this was our goal?—Assuredly! Only because its difficulty was so untold, was it only to be reached after the hardest of combats; but have we not fought out all our battles now? What others could there still remain ahead?—Of a truth, I feel it deep within: they are at end!—

When a month gone by I told thy husband my resolve to break off personal commune with you, I had given thee up, albeit I was not yet altogether whole in that. For I merely felt that nothing save a total separation, or a total union, could secure our love against the terrible collisions to which we had seen it exposed in these latter times. Thus the sense of the necessity of our parting was haunted by the possibility present to the mind, if not to the will of union. In that still lay a racking suspense which neither of us could bear. I approached thee, and clear as day it stood before us, that that other possibility involved a crime which could not be so much as thought of.

But hereby the necessity of our renunciation of itself acquired another character: the strain resolved into a gentle reconcilement. The last taint of egoism vanished from my heart; and now my decision to revisit you was the triumph of purest humanity over the last stirring of selfish desire. I wished naught any longer but to reconcile, assuage, console—cheer up; and thus procure myself withal the only happiness that still can come to me.—

So deeply and terribly as in these last few months, have I never been affected in my life. All earlier impressions were void of meaning 'gainst these last. Shocks such as I endured in that catastrophe were bound to plough deep furrows in me; and if aught could add to the great seriousness of my reflections, it was my wife's condition. For two whole months I was threatened each day with the possible news of her sudden death; for the doctor had felt obliged to warn me of that possibility. Everything round me breathed the scent of death; all my prospects and retrospects became images of death, and life—as such—lost its last lure for me. Admonished to the utmost sparing of the unhappy soul, nevertheless I had to make up my mind to raze our last hearth and home, so lately founded, and at last to tell her so, to her deepest dismay.

With what feelings dost thou think in this sweet summertide I viewed this charming Asyl,[30] the sole and perfect counterpart of my former aims and wishes, when I wandered through the tiny garden of a morning, watched the flowers springing into bloom, and listened to the white-throat that had built her nest within the rosebush? And what this tearing loose from my last anchor meant for me, that tell thyself, who know'st my inmost thought as none!

If I have fled from the world once before, dost dream I could return into it now? Now, when each nerve of me has grown so sensitive and tender with the lengthier weaning from all contact with it? Even my recent interview with the Grand Duke of Weimar shewed me plainer than ever that I can thrive in nothing but most absolute independence, so that I earnestly had to decline every possible kind of obligation to be entered, even towards this really not unamiable prince. I cannot—cannot face towards the world again; to settle down in a big city, is

---

[30] German for sanctuary, refuge, or haven of rest. The name of his home.

inconceivable to me. And if not that—how could I think again of founding a new refuge, a new hearth, after having to break up this, scarce tasted, which friendship and the noblest love had founded for me in this charming paradise? No, no! To go forth hence, for me is tantamount to going under!

With wounds like these in my heart, I can try to found me no new home again! My child, there's only one salvation for me I can think of; and that can only arise from the innermost depth of the heart, not from any sort of outer dispensation. Its name is Asyl! A truce to yearning! Allaying of every desire! Worthy, noble overcoming! Life for others, for others—in relief to ourselves!

Thou know'st the whole solemn resolve of my soul now; it relates to all my views of life, to my whole future, to all that stand near me, and so to thee, too, who art dearest to me! Upon the ruins of this world of longing, let me—bless thee! See, never in my life, in any manner of relation, have I ever been importunate, but always of an almost exaggerated sensibility; so for the first time will I seem to be importunate, and implore thee to be profoundly tranquil as regards me. I shall not often visit you, for in future you must only see me when I'm sure of shewing you a calm and cheerful countenance.—Of old, maybe, I have sought thy house in suffering and longing: thither, whence I wanted solace, have I brought unrest and suffering. That shall be no more. Wherefore if thou dost not see me for a length of time, then—pray for me in silence! For, then be sure that I am suffering! But when I come, be sure I'm bringing to your house a gracious gift of my being, a boon such as lent perhaps to me alone to shed, who have endured so much and willingly.—

Probably, nay, certainly, the time is at hand—I conjecture the beginning of next winter—when I shall depart from Zurich altogether for a spell; my amnesty, expected soon (in vain!), will reopen to me Germany, whither I shall periodically return for the only thing I could not make good to myself here. Then I often shall not see you for long. But then to return again to the Asyl so endeared to me, to recover from worry and unavoidable vexation, to breathe pure air, and gain new zest for the old work for which Nature has chosen me, this, if you grant it me, will ever be the point of mellow light that buoys me up there, the sweet relief that becks me here.

And wouldst thou then have shewn my life no highest benefaction? Should I not owe to thee the only thing that yet can seem worth thanks to me upon this earth? And ought not I to seek to requite what thou has won for me with suffering and sacrifices so indicible?

My child, these last months have perceptibly blanched the hair on my temples; there is a voice in me that cries with yearning after rest, that rest which long, long years ago I made my Flying Dutchman yearn for. It was the yearning after "home," not after the seductive joys of love: only a grandly faithful woman could gain for him that homeland. Let us vow ourselves to this fair death, which stills and buries all our hankerings and cravings! Let us fade away, with peacefully transfigured gaze, and the holy smile of beautiful self-victory! And—no one then shall lose, when we—are victors!

Farewell, my dear hallowed angel!

August, 1858.

It must be so!

17 August, 1858.

Farewell! Farewell, dear love!
I'm leaving tranquilly. Where'er I be, I shall be wholly thine now. Try to keep the Asyl for me, goodbye! Goodbye! Dear soul of my soul, farewell, goodbye!

George Washington

George Washington (22 February, 1732–14 December, 1799) was the dominant military and political leader of the new United States of America from 1775 to 1799. Strong, brave, eager for combat and a natural leader, young Washington quickly became a senior officer of the colonial forces, 1754–58, during the first stages of the French and Indian War. He led the American victory over Britain in the American Revolutionary War as commander in chief of the Continental Army in 1775–1783. He forced the British out of Boston in 1776, but was defeated and nearly captured later that year when he lost New York City. Negotiating with Congress, governors, and French allies, he held together a tenuous army and a fragile nation amid the threats of disintegration and invasion. Washington is given full credit for the strategies that forced the British evacuation of Boston in 1776 and the surrender at Yorktown in 1781. After victory had been finalised in 1783, Washington resigned rather than seize power, and returned to his plantation at Mount Vernon. His retirement was short-lived. He made an exploratory trip to the western frontier in 1784, was persuaded to attend the Constitutional Convention in Philadelphia in the summer of 1787, and was unanimously elected President of the Convention. Washington presided over the Constitutional Convention that drafted the United States Constitution in 1787 because of his dissatisfaction with the weaknesses of Articles of Confederation that had time and again impeded the war effort.

In 1789 the Electoral College elected Washington unanimously as the first President of the newly formed United States of America, and again in the 1792 election; he remains the only President to have received 100 percent of the electoral votes. John Adams, who received the next highest vote total, was elected Vice President. At his inauguration, Washington took the oath of office as the first President of the United States of America on 30 April, 1789, at Federal Hall in New York City. As President he developed the forms and rituals of government that have been used ever since, such as using a cabinet system and delivering an inaugural address. He avoided war with Britain and guaranteed a decade of peace and profitable trade. He built a strong, well-financed national government that avoided war, suppressed rebellion and won acceptance among Americans of all types, and Washington is now known as the "Father of his country".

Sometime in the 1750s, Washington met Sally *née* Cary Fairfax (c.1730–1811), the wife of a friend. Surviving letters suggest that he may have been in love with her, at the least they prove that a strong relationship between the two certainly existed. Sally had been well-educated, and as a young man with limited education and a low rung on the social ladder, Washington was impressed with this attractive, popular, and intelligent woman. He wrote her a now infamous letter, in September, 1758, whilst already engaged to the wealthy widow Martha *née* Dandridge Custis (2 June, 1731–22 May, 1802). On 6 January, 1759,

Washington and Martha were married. They made a compatible marriage, because Martha was intelligent, gracious, and experienced in managing a slave plantation. Together the two raised her two children from her previous marriage, John Parke Custis (1754–1781) and Martha Parke Custis (1756–1773). John later served as an aide to Washington and died during his military service. After his death, the Washingtons raised John's children, Eleanor and George. Washington never had any of his own children—his earlier bout with smallpox in 1751 may have made him sterile.

The newly wed couple moved to Mount Vernon, near Alexandria, where he took up the life of a farmer and political figure for several years. Each year of the revolution, General Washington wrote for his wife to join him at military camp, which she did. They were separated often, when Washington was either fighting the war or leading the country. During the Revolutionary War, the British intercepted one of their letters and used it as a kind of blackmail against him. Having felt the sting of this offense, Martha burned many of his letters after his death.

To Martha Custis

Fort Cumberland
20 July, 1758.

We have begun our march to the Ohio. A courier is starting for Williamsburg, and I embrace the opportunity to send a few words to one whose life is now inseparable from mine. Since that happy hour when we made our pledges to each other, my thoughts have been continually going to you as to another Self. That All-powerful Providence may keep us both in safety is the prayer of your faithful and ever affectionate friend, G. Washington.

To Sally Fairfax

12 September, 1758.

'Tis true I profess myself a votary of love. I acknowledge that a lady is in the case and further I confess that this lady is known to you. Yes, Madame, as well as she is to one who is too sensible to her charms to deny the power whose influence he feels and must ever submit to. I feel the force of her amiable beauties and the recollection of a thousand tender passages that I could wish to obliterate till I am bid to revive them. But experience, alas! sadly reminds me how impossible this is and evinces an opinion which I have long entertained that there is a Destiny which has the control of our actions, not to be resisted by the strongest efforts of Human Nature. You have drawn me, dear Madame, or rather have I drawn

myself into an honest confession of a simple fact. Misconstrue not my meaning; doubt it not nor expose it. The world has no business to know the object of my love, declared in this manner to you, when I want to conceal it. One thing above all things in this world I wish to know, and only one person of your acquaintance can solve me that, or guess my meaning. But adieu to this till happier times, if I shall ever see them.

To Martha *née* Custis Washington

23 June, 1775.

My Dearest,

I am now set down to write you on a subject which fills me with inexpressible concern—and this concern is greatly aggravated and increased when I reflect on the uneasiness I know it will give you—It has been determined in Congress that the whole army raised for the defence of the American cause shall be put under my care and that it is necessary for me to proceed immediately to Boston to take upon me the command of it.

You may believe, my dear Patsy, when I assure you, in the most solemn manner, that, so far from seeking this appointment I have used every endeavour in my power to avoid it, not only from my unwillingness to part with you and the family, but from a consciousness of its being a trust too great for my capacity, and that I should enjoy more real happiness and felicity in one month with you, at home, than I have my most distant prospect of reaping abroad, if my stay was to be seven times seven years.

It was utterly out of my power to refuse this appointment, without exposing my character to such censure as would have reflected dishonor upon myself, and have given pain to my friends... I shall feel no pain from the toil or danger of the campaign; my unhappiness will flow from the uneasiness I know you will feel from being left alone.

I shall rely, therefore, confidently on that Providence which has heretofore preserved and been bountiful to me, not doubting but that I shall return safe to you in the fall.

24 June, 1776.

My dearest life and love,

You have hurt me, I know not how much, by the insinuation in your last, that my letters to you have lately been less frequent, because I have less concern for you. The suspicion is most unjust—may I not add, it is most unkind! Have we lived, now almost a score of years, in the closest and dearest conjugal intimacy to so little purpose, that, on appearance only of inattention to you, and which you might have accounted for in a thousand ways more natural and more probable, you should pitch upon that single motive which alone is injurious to me?

I have not, I own, wrote so often to you as I wished, and as I ought. But think of my situation, and then ask your heart, if I be without excuse.

We are not, my dearest, in circumstances the most favorable to our happiness, but let us not, I beseech thee, idly make them worse, by indulging suspicions and apprehensions which minds in distress are too apt to give way to.

I never was, as you have often told me, even in my better and more disengaged days, so attentive to the little punctillios of friendship, as, it maybe, became me, but my heart tells me, there was never a moment in my life, since I first knew you, in which I did not cleave and cling to you with the warmest affections; and it must cease to beat ere it can cease to wish for your happiness, above anything on earth.

Your faithful and tender husband, G. W.

Oscar Wilde

Oscar Fingal O'Flahertie Wills Wilde (16 October, 1854–30 November, 1900) was an Irish writer and poet. At university Wilde proved himself to be an outstanding classicist, first at Dublin, then at Oxford. However, he became known for his involvement in the rising philosophy of aestheticism (led by two of his tutors, Walter Pater and John Ruskin) though he also profoundly explored Roman Catholicism (and later converted on his deathbed). Wilde then moved to London, into fashionable cultural and social circles. As a spokesman for aestheticism, he tried his hand at various literary activities; he published a book of poems, lectured America and Canada on the new "English Renaissance in Art" and then returned to London where he worked prolifically as a journalist. Known for his biting wit, flamboyant dress, and glittering conversation, Wilde had become one of the major personalities of his day. After writing in different forms throughout the 1880s, he became one of London's most popular playwrights in the early 1890s. He refined his ideas about the supremacy of art in a series of dialogues and essays; and incorporated themes of decadence, duplicity and beauty into his only novel, *The Picture of Dorian Gray* (1890). The opportunity to construct aesthetic details precisely, combined with larger social themes, drew Wilde to writing drama. He wrote *Salomé* (1891) in French in Paris, but it was refused a licence. Unperturbed, Wilde produced four society comedies in the early 1890s, which made him one of the most successful playwrights of late Victorian London: *Lady Windermere's Fan* (1892), *A Woman of No Importance* (1893), *An Ideal Husband* (1895) and *The Importance of Being Earnest* (1895).

In 1881 in London, Wilde had been introduced to Constance Lloyd (2 January, 1859–7 April, 1898), daughter of Horace Lloyd, a wealthy Queen's Counsel. She happened to be visiting Dublin in 1884, when Wilde was lecturing at the Gaiety Theatre. He proposed to her, and they married on the 29 May, 1884, at the Anglican St. James' Church, Paddington, London. The couple had two sons, Cyril (5 June, 1885–9 May, 1915) and Vyvyan (3 November, 1886–10 October, 1967). In the 1880s Wilde also had numerous now infamous, homosexual relationships. Robert Baldwin Ross (25 May, 1869–5 October, 1918) was a alleged to be his first. In mid-1891 Wilde was introduced to Alfred Bruce Douglas (22 October, 1870–20 March, 1945), an undergraduate at Oxford at the time. Known to his family and friends as "Bosie", he was a handsome and spoilt young man. An intimate friendship sprang up between Wilde and Douglas and by 1893 Wilde was infatuated with him and they consorted together regularly in a tempestuous affair. If Wilde was relatively indiscreet, even flamboyant, in the way he acted, Douglas was reckless in public. Wilde indulged Douglas's every whim. At the height of his fame and success, whilst his masterpiece, *The Importance of Being Earnest*, was still on stage in London, Wilde sued his lover's father for libel after he called Wilde a "sodomite". After a series of trials, Wilde was convicted of gross indecency and imprisoned for two years hard labour. In prison he wrote *De Profundis*, a 50,000-word letter to Douglas. Upon his release he left immediately for France, never to return to Ireland or Britain. There he wrote his last work, *The Ballad of Reading Gaol* (1898) a long poem commemorating the harsh rhythms of prison life. He died destitute in Paris at the age of 46.

To Alfred Douglas

Savoy Hotel, Victoria Embankment, London
March, 1893.

Dearest of All Boys,
Your letter was delightful, red and yellow wine to me; but I am sad and out of sorts. Bosie, you must not make scenes with me. They kill me, they wreck the loveliness of life. I cannot see you, so Greek and gracious, distorted with passion. I cannot listen to your curved lips saying hideous things to me. I would sooner be blackmailed by every renter in London than to have you bitter, unjust, hating. You are the divine thing I want, the thing of grace and beauty; but I don't know how to do it. Shall I come to Salisbury? My bill here is 49 pounds for a week. I have also got a new sitting-room over the Thames. Why are you not here, my dear, my wonderful boy? I fear I must leave—no money, no credit, and a heart of lead.
Your own, Oscar

5 Esplanade, Worthing
August, 1894.

Dear, dear boy, you are more to me than any one of them has any idea; you are the atmosphere of beauty through which I see life; you are the incarnation of all lovely things. When we are out of tune, all colour goes from things for me, but we are never really out of tune. I think of you day and night.
Write to me soon, you honey-haired boy!
I am always devotedly yours
Oscar

2 Courtfield Gardens
20 May, 1895.

My child,
Today it was asked to have the verdicts rendered separately. Taylor is probably being judged at this moment, so that I have been able to come back here.

My sweet rose, my delicate flower, my lily of lilies, it is perhaps in prison that I am going to test the power of love. I am going to see if I cannot make the bitter waters sweet by the intensity of the love I bear you.

I have had moments when I thought it would be wiser to separate. Ah! moments of weakness and madness! Now I see that that would have mutilated my life, ruined my art, broken the musical chords which make a perfect soul. Even covered with mud I shall praise you, from the deepest abysses I shall cry to you. In my solitude you will be with me. I am determined not to revolt but to accept every outrage through devotion to love, to let my body be dishonoured so long as my soul may always keep the image of you. From your silken hair to your delicate feet you are perfection to me.

Pleasure hides love from us but pain reveals it in its essence. O dearest of created things, if someone wounded by silence and solitude comes to you, dishonoured, a laughing-stock to men, Oh! you can close his wounds by touching them and restore his soul which unhappiness had for a moment smothered. Nothing will be difficult for you then, and remember, it is that hope which makes me live, and that hope alone.

What wisdom is to the philosopher, what God is to his saint, you are to me. To keep you in my soul, such is the goal of this pain which men call life.

O my love, you whom I cherish above all things, white narcissus in an unmown field, think of the burden which falls to you, a burden which love alone can make light. But be not saddened by that, rather be happy to have filled with an immortal love the soul of a man who now weeps in hell, and yet carries heaven in his heart.

I love you, I love you, my heart is a rose which your love has brought to bloom, my life is a desert fanned by the delicious breeze of your breath, and whose cool springs are your eyes; the imprint of your little feet makes valleys of shade for me, the odour of your hair is like myrrh, and wherever you go you exhale the perfumes of the cassia tree.

Love me always, love me always. You have been the supreme, the perfect love of my life; there can be no other.

I decided that it was nobler and more beautiful to stay. We could not have been together. I did not want to be called a coward or a deserter. A false name, a disguise, a hunted life, all that is not for me, to whom you have been revealed on that high hill where beautiful things are transfigured.

O sweetest of all boys, most loved of all loves, my soul clings to your soul, my life is your life, and in all the worlds of pain and pleasure you are my ideal of admiration and joy.

Oscar

Woodrow Wilson

Thomas Woodrow Wilson (28 December, 1856–3 February, 1924) was an American politician and the 28th President of the United States. Beginning his career as a lawyer in Atlanta, he studied for a doctorate in history and political science and became a lecturer. He published *Congressional Government* in 1885. A leader of the Progressive Movement, he served as President of Princeton University from 1902 to 1910, and then as the Governor of New Jersey from 1911 to 1913. Wilson's popularity as governor and his status in the national media gave impetus to his presidential campaign in 1912. With Theodore Roosevelt and William Howard Taft dividing the Republican Party vote, Wilson was elected President as a Democrat in 1912 (serving 4 March, 1913–4 March, 1921). He is the only U.S. President to hold a Ph.D. degree.

Narrowly re-elected in 1916, Wilson's second term centred on World War I, and in April, 1917, Wilson asked Congress to declare war on Germany. In the late stages of the war, Wilson took personal control of negotiations with Germany, including the armistice. He went to Paris in 1919 to create the League of Nations and shape the Treaty of Versailles, with special attention on creating new nations out of defunct empires. Largely for his efforts to form the League, he was awarded the Nobel Peace Prize. He ended up fighting with the Republican-controlled Senate over the U.S. joining the League of Nations. He refused to compromise, effectively destroying any chance for ratification. The League of Nations was established anyway, but the United States never joined.

On 24 June, 1885, Wilson married Ellen Louise Axson (15 May, 1860–6 August, 1914), the daughter of a minister from Rome, Georgia. That same year, Bryn Mawr College offered Wilson a teaching position and he and his bride lived near the campus, keeping her little brother with them. They had three daughters: Margaret (16 April, 1886–12 February, 1944), Jessie (28 August, 1887–15 January, 1933) and Eleanor Randolph (16 October, 1889–5 April, 1967). Ellen died in 1914. Wilson is one of only three presidents to be widowed while in office. In 1915, Wilson met Edith *née* Bolling Galt (15 October, 1872–28 December, 1961), a widow. They were engaged within the year, but gossip and rumours quickly abounded in the press due to the speed of the relationship. Wilson offered her the opportunity to back out of their engagement. She spurned the offer, replying that she would stand by him not for duty, pity or honour, but for love. They married later that year, on 18 December. He was 58, she 43. As First Lady during World War I, Edith Wilson led by example during rationing. She submerged her own life in her husband's, trying to keep him fit under tremendous strain. In September, 1919, Wilson had a series of debilitating strokes and on 2 October, 1919, he suffered a serious stroke that almost totally incapacitated him, leaving him paralyzed on his left side and blind in his left eye. He was confined to bed for weeks, sequestered from nearly everyone but his wife and his physician. For at least a few months, he used a wheelchair. Later, he could walk only with the assistance of a cane. With few exceptions, Wilson was kept out of the presence of his cabinet for the remainder of his term. His wife, Edith, served as his steward, selecting issues for his attention and delegating other issues to his cabinet heads. Eventually, Wilson did resume his attendance at cabinet meetings, but his input there was perfunctory at best. In 1921, Wilson and his wife retired from the White House to a home in the Embassy Row section of Washington, D.C, where Wilson died 3 years later.

To Edith Galt

The White House
19 September, 1915.

> *My noble, incomparable Edith,*
> *I do not know how to express or analyze the conflicting emotions that have surged like a storm through my heart all night long. I only know that first and foremost in all my thoughts has been the glorious confirmation you gave me last night—without effort, unconsciously, as of course—of all I have ever thought of your mind and heart.*
> *You have the greatest soul, the noblest nature, the sweetest, most loving heart I have ever known, and my love, my reverence, my admiration for you, you have increased in one evening as I should have thought only a lifetime of intimate, loving association could have increased them.*
> *You are more wonderful and lovely in my eyes than you ever were before; and my pride and joy and gratitude that you should love me with such a perfect love are beyond all expression, except in some great poem which I cannot write.*
> *Your own,*
> *Woodrow*

English Rose Publishing®

Eclectic titles, unique design, quality editions

At English Rose we believe that every book is special. So, whether it be a novel, romance, children's book or collection, an old classic revived or a brand new commission, we guarantee that every English Rose book will be professional *and* distinctive.

Some of our other titles include:

| The Broken Wings by Kahlil Gibran | The Nursery Alice by Lewis Carroll | How to Tell a Story and Other Essays by Mark Twain | John Carter of Mars by Edgar Rice Burroughs |

You can find out more about English Rose, view our catalogue, and find out about our newest releases at: www.englishrosebooks.co.uk

Our email address is: publishing@englishrosebooks.co.uk we would be happy to hear from you with any feedback, comments, suggestions or requests!

Lightning Source UK Ltd.
Milton Keynes UK

171889UK00002B/10/P